LEADING AMERIC⬦⬦⬦ W9-AHW-482
WINNING MOVES!

"A great 'how to' book for many skills, techniques and approaches normally only learned after many years of trial and error. The chapter dealing with specific suggestions on how women selling in a male buyers' world should dress, act and react is alone worth the price of the book!"
—Ray L. Girouard, Sales Training Manager, Grocery Products Sales Division, General Mills, Inc.

"Valuable . . . certain to enhance any individual's reactions with others in the business and social worlds."
—Jack C. Pope, Manager of Human Resources Development, Bethlehem Steel Corporation

" 'Winning' can mean either charming or successful. Winning Moves is both. Ken Delmar provides witty and wise advice on how to always be yourself at your very best, as well as how to leverage 'little things' that will turn prospects into customers."
—Douglas C. Floren, Vice President, Sales Division, Smith Barney, Harris Upham & Co. Incorporated

"A systematic and scientific approach to good salesmanship . . . teaches the reader all the necessary techniques for selling anything . . . by simple methods that enable you to actually read the signals of a prospective client and use them to your best advantage."
—Marvin H. Green, Jr., Chairman of the Board, Reeves Communications Corporation

"Outlines in a lively anecdotal manner the ploys and plays you need to command and maintain the power to conduct your business . . . shows you how to improve your own nonverbal signals and read those given by others so all your moves are winning ones."
—Susan Strecker, editor, Executive Female Magazine

more . . .

"An important book for anyone in business, not just selling, because understanding how to sell oneself and relate to other people is the major task for everyone."

—**Dudley E. Lyons, Managing Director,**
Marketing Corporation of America

"I'm only surprised that Ken has waited so long to teach his survival techniques to his fellow men. . . . He cuts through the difficult language used by most 'how to' authors and brings his point home with color, humor, and everyman's prose."

—**Patrick C. Parsons, President,**
Far East Molasses Corp., Philippines

ATTENTION: SCHOOLS AND CORPORATIONS

WARNER books are available at quantity discounts with bulk purchase for educational, business, or sales promotional use. For information, please write to: SPECIAL SALES DEPARTMENT, WARNER BOOKS, 666 FIFTH AVENUE, NEW YORK, N.Y. 10103.

ARE THERE WARNER BOOKS
YOU WANT BUT CANNOT FIND IN YOUR LOCAL STORES?

You can get any WARNER BOOKS title in print. Simply send title and retail price, plus 50¢ per order and 50¢ per copy to cover mailing and handling costs for each book desired. New York State and California residents add applicable sales tax. Enclose check or money order only, no cash please, to: WARNER BOOKS, P.O. BOX 690, NEW YORK, N.Y. 10019.

Winning Moves

The Body Language of Selling

Ken Delmar

WARNER BOOKS

A Warner Communications Company

WARNER BOOKS EDITION

Copyright © 1984 by Ken Delmar
All rights reserved.

Book design: *H. Roberts Design*

Warner Books, Inc.
666 Fifth Avenue
New York, N.Y. 10103

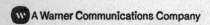 A Warner Communications Company

Printed in the United States of America

This book was originally published in hardcover by Warner Books

First Printed in Paperback: February, 1986

10 9 8 7 6 5 4 3 2 1

To Ulli, who makes all the right moves.

CONTENTS

INTRODUCTION

You have something to sell. An idea, a product, a service, a promise, yourself. You work hard to secure an opportunity to make the sale. It is important to you and those who depend on you that you succeed.

The moment of truth arrives. You feel yourself being overwhelmed by doubt, fear, self-consciousness. You worry about your clothes, your hair. You hesitate in your entrance; your walk is indecisive, tentative. Your palms perspire. Your voice is high and thin and catches in your throat. Your posture is weak. Your hands or legs start to quiver. Your gestures are jerky and uncertain. Your facial expressions feel and look contrived. Your muscles are tensing, making your moves stiff and awkward. Your mouth feels cotton-dry. Your nervous tic starts up. You feel yourself sweating, and worry that it shows on your brow and temples. There is the glint of terror in your eyes.

You lost the sale without uttering a word.

Anyone who has had to sell something to someone else has had to come to grips with nonverbal impression management. Head-on front-line selling, with its routine rejection, disappointment, and conflict of wills, is something almost all of us dread.

Winning Moves is a practical blend of applied observation, behavioral psychology, acting technique, and common sense. Its goal is to show salespeople, or anyone selling anything face-to-face, how to use and interpret nonverbal signals to sell more effectively, and how to overcome fear, doubt, self-consciousness, and the debilitating effect of disappointment and depression.

Part One, "Preparation," explains the necessity for a deep-seated emotional/philosophical base or subscript for you to draw from. Techniques used by actors to "get into" a character and make him believable (sell him to the audience) are adapted for the salesperson. Part Two, "Presentation," examines in depth the nonverbal aspects of a typical one-on-one sales presentation, including typical prospect responses. Part Three, "Particulars," is devoted to specific situations; it both augments and draws from Parts One and Two.

The masculine pronouns *he* and *his* are to be understood as applying to both sexes, unless otherwise specified. "Salesperson" is used to embrace both sexes, while "salesman" and "saleswoman" will be used to refer to men and women respectively.

This is not a scientific text. There are too many generalizations, subjective assumptions, and unprovable hypotheses in the realm of human nonverbal communications to call it a science. Behavioral science is a contradiction in terms. I feel it is part of our charm that every human being is a potential exception to a rule. I am sure we wouldn't want it any other way.

This is a practical compendium of observations, patterns, suggestions, and techniques you can use and develop to improve your selling ability. It is a reconstruction of the basic grammar of a silent language that was lost long ago in the roar of verbalization, the whisper of the telephone, and the more recent stridency of broadcast media.

The level of fluency you achieve will depend on your sensitivity, application, and your desire to understand and communicate more effectively.

TRUE LIFE STORY: *The Importance of Luck*

It was cold and raining hard. I was calling on a buyer who could, in one stroke and under his own authority, put over a quarter of a million dollars' worth of business in my pocket. The parking lot was a block away from the building. I was glad I had my umbrella in the car. I took the last vacant space in the lot. It was a numbered spot, but I was late, and it was any port in a storm.

On my way to his building, I stepped into a shallow-looking puddle that filled my left shoe with oily slime. A few yards farther on, I ran into a strip where the sidewalk had been torn up, and I tiptoed as best I could across moguls of claylike muck. In the reception area, I did my best to clean my shoes on a mat that looked like a pit for tiny mud wrestlers. I checked to make sure I wasn't leaving any tracks. The marble floor behind me was clean. I announced myself and was ushered promptly into the prospect's office, which was decorated tastefully in a Colonial motif.

When I entered his office, the prospect suggested I hang my coat behind the door. There was only one hook, and his coat was on it. Since my coat was soaking wet and I didn't want to squish and soak his collar, I tried to move his coat, a heavy camel-hair thing, onto the lower prong of the hook. I tried to hang it by the little strip of fabric garment manufacturers put there as a sort of little joke. It instantly ripped off on one side, of course. I moved the coat back to the upper prong and settled my coat gingerly down on top of it. Something moved; something didn't feel right. I lifted my coat up again and saw that the prong had penetrated through the prospect's coat at the seam. It looked like a dead camel on a meat hook. I knew the prospect was wondering what was taking so long. He looked up from his desk with growing interest. I hung his coat by threading the prong up toward one shoulder. I flung my own coat across a chair, keeping the wet side up, and leaned my umbrella against the side of the coat, so it wouldn't get anything wet. The carpet was thick beige wool, so I knew the tip of the umbrella wouldn't slip out from under it in the middle of my presentation.

At this point, my palms were moist with nervous perspiration, so I stuck my right hand into my pants pocket and rubbed it dry on the fabric. My briefcase in my left hand, I crossed directly to the prospect's desk for the handshake. I pulled my right hand out of the pocket and stuck it forward enthusiastically to shake. Unfortunately, a ball of lint, about the size of a pea, had stuck to the tip of my fingers and was now drifting slowly down onto the document he had been reading. We both watched it descend, as compelling as the ball on New Year's Eve. We shook hands, anyway. I said, "Excuse me," and bent forward to blow the ball of lint off the document. As I did so, I put a dent in the front edge of his desk with my briefcase. Naturally, I blew the document off the desk along with the lint. The piece of paper zigzagged down and landed at my feet. The prospect had stubbed his middle finger on the desk as he grabbed for the falling document. He was cradling his benumbed hand in agony as I bent over to retrieve the paper. As I did, I stepped back and noticed that one of my shoes had left a giant print of black, oozy slime on the carpet. I glanced back, retracing my steps, and saw that I had been trailing this muck off my left foot ever since I entered the carpeted office. There were sizable little clumps sticking up, like buttes in the badlands. I also noticed a puddle of water forming around the tip of my umbrella.

I tried to position my body as I returned the document to his uninjured hand, to block his vision of Parasol Pond and the Tracks of Bigfoot. I gesticulated broadly to keep his eyes on me. Still moving with exaggeration, I crossed to an armchair I intended to sit in. I tried to put as little weight as possible on my left shoe and walked sort of on the heel. I grabbed the armchair, a handsome Colonial antique, by the arms, and tried to lift and pull it closer to his desk. Naturally, one of the arms pulled up out of the post on which it rested.

There was a sickening crack and a crunching sound, like an old person getting a compound spiral fracture of the tibia in a revolving door. The arm didn't actually break off in my hand; there were one or two stubborn splinters left at the joint. I was mortified, of course. I started to apologize and was flashing on the bill for restoring an original Morris chair, or whatever it was, when the prospect assured me it already had been broken, and he should have had it repaired weeks ago.

I sat down and, by crossing my legs, tried to show I was still calm and in control. Smooth, collected, and confident—with a hole in my sock, right over that bone in your ankle that sticks out like a jockey's elbow. A hole the size of a maraschino cherry, and just as obvious. I glanced at the prospect's eyes. He was looking right at the hole. I crossed my legs the other way and forged on.

I couldn't quite focus on it, but I had the feeling there was a mote of black soot or a cinder on the side of my nose. I must have looked like a Siamese cat the couple of times I tried to sight down the side of my nose. I knew I didn't have a freckle there. I decided whatever it was had to go. I casually brushed it off with my thumb. No, it wasn't brushed off, it was smeared into a black streak. Now I *really* could see it. It was at least an inch long and had blended with the natural oils of my skin to form indelible India ink. I turned the unblemished side of my face toward the prospect while I dug in my jacket pocket for my emergency tissue. I pretended to blow my nose, and as I did so, I scrubbed the black streak off my nose. The prospect pulled his wastebasket out and held it where I could toss the used tissue easily into it. It was an easy shot, like a slam-dunk when you're seven foot three. But I was too smart to risk missing, so I leaned forward and deposited the tissue into the basket. Unfortunately, I leaned too far over a bronze golf trophy, an inkwell that was obviously one of the prospect's prize possessions. I bent the little figure's gold club about forty degrees off-center. I felt the head of the club punch into my torso and put a nasty bruise on one of my ribs. It was so unexpected, it knocked the wind out of me. I found myself sputtering and wheezing and examining the front of my shirt for bullet holes. The prospect was diverted from watching my amusing dance when he spotted the bent little club. I watched with a sinking heart as he tried to straighten up the shaft of the club and it snapped off in his hand.

Nothing I said after that seemed to register. I started talking faster. My voice cracked. I was perspiring so badly it looked like my underarms were trying to talk to one another with smoke signals. My forehead and upper lip were sweating like a glass of iced tea in July. The frog in my throat was turning into a Gila monster. My gestures were starting to make Frankenstein's monster look smooth. My face couldn't seem to eradicate the hysterical rictus of an impressionable person trapped in a horror-film festival.

I tried to "mask" with my hand. I scratched the side of my jaw. I had to keep reminding myself to breathe. I could feel the quarter of a million dollars' worth of business slipping through my fingers. But no, what was actually slipping through my fingers was blood. I had scratched open a shaving cut. And now a neat rivulet of fresh bright-red blood was running down the side of my jaw and had already found its way over two fingers. My emergency tissue! Gone, of course! It was the side of my face turned away from the prospect. Perhaps he hadn't noticed. But, of course, he had. He had just seen me suddenly hold my bloody fingers up in front of myself. Maybe I could somehow sort of pretend that it was just something that happened to me occasionally, like stigmata. I then realized that I was losing my mind, as well as the sale. I couldn't go on. Why fight such odds? I knew then that some poltergeist or Fury from the past was operating here. Some karmic debit from an evil ancestor's unforgivable deed was being collected. I bolted for the door; I couldn't even shake hands as a parting gesture—my right hand was the one with the type O positive. I mumbled something unintelligible, kicked a couple of my mud mountains into smaller foothills, and disappeared down the hall, a broken man.

I reached the parking lot just in time to see my car being towed away. I had parked in some executive's reserved spot. It merely corroborated my suspicion that I was being punished for some ancestral misdeed. Maybe I am related to Torquemada, or Attila the Hun?

Moral of the story:

This salesman got everything he deserved. He was responsible for every terrible thing that he feels "happened" to him because of fate or bad luck. If he hadn't been late, he wouldn't have taken the reserved parking slot. If he had gone into the bathroom before the meeting, he could have cleaned all the muck out of the arch of his left shoe. Shoes that don't leave tracks on marble or linoleum may well do so on thick carpet. He would have seen and washed off the mote of black soot and noticed the shaving cut and made a mental note not to touch it. He should have gotten rid of his coat and umbrella in the reception area, or in any case, never messed with the prospect's coat. One *never* brings a wet umbrella into a prospect's office, never picks up an antique armchair by the arms. If he had dried his hands off in the bathroom or hallway, he would not have picked up the piece of lint and unloaded it onto the prospect's desk. You carry more than one tissue, and you never lean over a prospect's desk or move in any way that might jeopardize his personal possessions.

PART ONE
Preparation

1

The Secret of Winning Moves

Going into an important sales confrontation, you are likely to be tense and apprehensive. You may worry that your product or services aren't all they're supposed to be, that you or your products have other impediments, that the competition has an edge on you one way or the other.

You know that if the prospect picks up on any of your doubts or fears, through involuntary expressions of body or face, you will probably lose the sale. You also recognize, in the same moment, that worrying about transmitting such signals increases the likelihood of sending them.

You want to know what you can do so you won't reveal your doubts, fears, and insecurities. You want to learn the physical moves and expressions you can effect to mask or camouflage these problems.

Can you learn moves and expressions that will reliably hide all your signals of doubt and fear?

No.

The secret of effective nonverbal signals is *not* to acquire a set of automatic, puppetlike moves to hide or camouflage your doubts and fears, but to attack and destroy, or bypass and overcome your very doubts and fears. You replace them with deep-seated confidence in yourself.

Once you have removed the malady (doubt or fear), it is easy to remove the symptoms (negative signals).

Before we tell you how to do it, let's make sure we understand why it has to be done this way. Why can't you learn to fake it?

Look at a picture of yourself when someone caught you *really* laughing. Now look at one in which you posed, and *effected* a nice phony smile for the camera. Maybe you said "cheese" to help yourself. Catch yourself in a mirror *really* smiling, laughing, glowing with enthusiasm, overcome by grief and sorrow, anger, loneliness, lust. Now look at your best attempt to recreate that totality of posture: expression, gesture, and aura.

We concede that some percentage of your prospects will not recognize or sense the difference between fake, effected signals and real ones. They are not, however, in the majority, as is easily demonstrated by comparing the sales revenues of salespeople who fake it with those who are believers—who believe in what they are selling, saying, and doing.

This is the common denominator in outstanding political leaders, brilliant actors, top trial lawyers, famous religious leaders, rich con-artists, and supersalesmen. They are all convincing. We believe them. We believe them because they believe in themselves, in what they are communicating. They may have had to convince themselves to believe. They may even be able to turn it on and off at will, but when they are communicating (selling), they are believing.

Your posture, gestures, and expressions must flow freely and naturally from your deep-seated faith and conviction in what you are selling, and in the very act of selling it. You simply can't use the external pieces of physical business without having a genuine conviction wholly established in yourself as the source and generator of those pieces of action. That is:

YOU MUST BUY BEFORE YOU CAN SELL

This makes it pretty easy for the person who is selling something everyone believes in: an established line with a reputation or first-class, state-of-the-art merchandise, service, or expertise.

What do you do when you're selling Brand X when you'd really rather be selling A#1? Unless you quit and go to work for A#1, you *have* to believe in Brand X. But you know, let's say you have every reason to believe that the competition's widget is better. How can you believe something that you know is not true or is probably not true?

You sell *yourself* on the idea that your product or service is the best. You inflate its assets and minimize its shortcomings. You convince yourself, and you *allow yourself to be convinced*, that your product is everything you are going to say it is because you are in business to succeed. You are engaged in the operation of selling something to someone. You must make a conscious effort to believe subconsciously, through every fiber of your mind, body, and spirit, in what you are selling.

What do you think all those pep talks and rah-rah sales meetings and positive books and manuals are trying to do? They are trying to help you make a believer out of yourself. To fire up your faith. Not only to give you the courage and energy to make some tough calls but also to give you the ammunition of deep-seated conviction so your message will transmit, ungarbled by negative or mixed nonverbal signals.

Sales training managers and sales directors have been doing it for years—regularly turning the salespeople on with programs designed to make believers out of them. Believers in the product, believers in themselves. But it wasn't until recently that we were able to understand why it works so well to improve the entire array of nonverbal communication.

Your "true," involuntary expressions come mainly from the right hemisphere of your brain, while the forced, phony expressions are consciously generated by the left hemisphere. The right side of your brain doesn't have to construct a display of legitimate-looking expressions; whatever signals spring from it *are* sincere and legitimate. The left, or rational, side designs a reasonable facsimile of the legitimate display and mounts this secondhand reconstruction in lieu of the real thing. Your "say cheese" smile is a brass clinker. That's why you have to really believe in your product and yourself. Then all your expressions flow sincerely, naturally, and without conscious effort.

To cause yourself to believe in something . . . this calls for imagination, inspiration, faith, things that you may find hard to conjure up in a lean time when the mortgage is due and letters keep coming from the IRS. You must accomplish it, however, or you can never be an outstanding political leader, brilliant actor, top trial attorney, famous religious leader, rich con-artist, or supersalesperson—or anyone who has to make his living convincing someone of something.

You may worry that your product is so flawed that you just couldn't sustain a solid, heartfelt belief in it for very long. And you go through phases, biorhythmical ups and downs, when your belief in your own abilities may wane. How can you still give a believable performance when you temporarily lose the faith?

Through an acting technique. Let's look at the process most outstanding actors go through, at one level or another, to play a role and sustain freshness and believability over many repetitions.

Unless an actor is playing himself, or something very close to his natural type, he frequently has to work backward. That is, instead of discovering the emotional subtext in a scene, and letting his postures, gestures, and expressions flow from the emotional source, he has to discover and learn the external gestures of the character—which are different from the ones he would make naturally himself—and then build the emotional sincerity into the external signals. In other words, he erects the siding and the windows and roof shingles, and then he builds the frame and foundation.

This is the most effective way to build a believable character whose nonverbal communication is essentially different from what your natural one would be in an identical situation. Once the actor finds the emotional framework to give substance to the external bits of business, then those pieces of business assume the dimension of credibility. They seem sincere. For the great actor, they *are* sincere, because he is so good at making himself believe in the substance and pith of that character—his desires, needs, and emotions—that he *becomes* the character.

This sounds like a lot of work to have to go through every night before the curtain goes up or the cameras start rolling.

Fortunately, once you have discovered and learned the nonverbal externals and infused them with life and depth by finding the appropriate emotional subtext, you can record the process and file it for use whenever you need it. And you can use it again and again.

Really believing in yourself makes you feel better about yourself; it gives you a positive emotional surge. You feel successful. You have experienced the essence of the sensation after closing an important deal. There's nothing quite like it. You are floating. You are filled with new power, new energy. What you feel in the middle of a critical sale—when you are on a roll, all cylinders firing smoothly and you know you are going to win—is an effective emotional framework or source to help you generate the sincere, believable nonverbal skills of a winning supersalesperson.

THE COURAGE KEY

You rightfully worry that you can't always rely on being able to conjure up that emotional rush of confidence and power. Even a great actor cannot simply cough up a given emotion on command. There is a process. He finds a key, a memory of a similar experience, mood, or frame of mind, which triggers and supports the emotional subtext and its concurrent nonverbal display. He finds the key rationally, consciously, just as you search your memory for something funny if you want to create a genuine smile.

You consciously recall the earlier scene, the picture of it or the sounds of it, and you allow yourself to reexperience it. Your smile then comes naturally, as an involuntary reaction, subconsciously—but only because you are using a conscious key to stimulate and govern the flow of subconscious nonverbal displays.

In a sales situation, you must come prepared with the conscious key or keys that will work for you to stimulate the subconscious, emotional source that will generate and legitimize your nonverbal signals. Sounds complex, but it's simple in practice. Example: You go in front of the camera armed with some personal memory of something that always tickled you—the time Grandpa fell down the stairs without spilling his drink—and up comes your wonderfully genuine smile, just as the shutter clicks.

We have all heard Abe Lincoln's dictum "It is true that you may fool all the people some of the time; you can even fool some of the people all the time; but you can't fool all of the people all the time."

Add to that "Unless you've fooled yourself first." Now replace the verb "fool" with "convince." Effective selling, in all its permutations, begins with the salesman selling himself. Not selling himself to the prospect but selling himself and his line *to himself*.

Unlike the actor called upon to create and play an alien character, you will be assuming a role much closer to your natural self. We are going to tell you, in Parts Two and Three, the external signals you'll encounter in a typical sales confrontation. We will try to explain the motivation or psychology behind each posture, gesture, and expression.

It is your responsibility to build the emotional sincerity into the external signals. We will give you the facade, but you must erect the frame and foundation.

Let's assume that you understand the process we have been discussing. Now, how do you find the key or keys to the emotional base that will add sincerity and depth to your nonverbal signals?

Let's first define exactly what we are looking for. The key, once again, is a consciously invoked image or word that will stimulate the subconscious to generate sincere nonverbal displays for specific effect. In other words, we want to come up with something to think about that will make us move and gesture convincingly when we sell.

Let's look first for an image. An obvious one would be a role model. It could be a person you know or a character you saw in a movie, play, sales course, or on TV. Or it can be a composite character that is the sum of several effective salespersons you know and have seen at work. It may not necessarily be a professional salesperson. Your role model may be Winston Churchill, Joan of Arc, your uncle Sid, or Billy Graham. Your role model should be forceful, pertinacious, and courageous—he could even be you, at a time when you were at peak performance. It could be nothing more than a flash of memory, an image of you when you made an important touchdown, achieved a goal, won an award. It is not necessary for your role model to be, or even resemble, the traditional role model who is a superior performer in your exact line of work. The key must work much faster. There is no time for conjuring up a memory of what a role model would do in X situation, then emulating it. Your key must work on a subconscious level. It must trigger involuntary reactions, drives, and power you may not even be consciously aware you possess. Instantaneously.

Since the ultimate goal of the key is to sustain and fuel your flinty fearlessness and staunch pertinacity, let's call it, for convenience's sake, a *courage key*.

If you cannot find a courage key that gets your juices flowing, look for a word. It could be a single word, such as "Granite," "Winner," "Charge," "Go-getter," or "Popeye." It could be a short phrase, such as "Can't stop me," "Salesman of the Year," "Doesn't bother me," or "I have just begun to fight." You want it short, so you can run it through your mind quickly without having to concentrate on the recitation. No one can tell you what courage key will work best for you. You know your weaknesses and fears—you are the most qualified to create a key that will work for you. You may have more than one key, and your key may change as your circumstances and needs change. Since your key is sacred in a way (it's personal and it's going to help make you a success), don't tell it to anyone else. It's your personal property. Cherish it and keep it to yourself.

Your courage key, whether it is a word or an image, or both, should *not* be based on your tangible desires or needs. Say, for example, that you really want to buy your own home. That's mainly what you're working for, right? (Many sales programs encourage salespeople to build their courage and enthusiasm by picturing the worldly object of their desire, the house, the yacht, the desirable person.) Shouldn't you go into a sales presentation with a key derived from your tangible goal?

Absolutely not. Your tangible goals are less than secondary. *To the prospect*, they are totally irrelevant. Your tangible goals are not strong enough to save your presentation when the prospect is making a forceful attack on your product's weakest feature. A courage key based on how you're as imperturbable as Mt. Rushmore, as stubborn as granite, as tough as Patton, or as honest as Abe, will provide you much better sustenance. The base for your key is not need or greed. It must be positive and of limitless dimensions of character, such as conviction, enthusiasm, faith, guts, spirit—even righteous indignation for some recalcitrant prospects.

Your key may change slightly with different prospects, just as your personality differs slightly in various circumstances. You do not need your General Patton courage key when you are going into a meeting with one of your best customers. But if you are going to try to persuade him to give you additional opportunities, you might well engage your F. Lee Bailey key.

It is practical and safer, however, to create and sustain one image, based in one courage key. This is the character that you will learn, assume, and project so well, so sincerely, that you will eventually become the character.

The character you are already playing, the one you call "you," is no less a creation of outside, random, and negative forces. The character you create will be a better character, because he will be made up of the stuff of positive forces: belief; faith; enthusiasm. He certainly will function better as a salesperson. And since he is already "in" you, we are committing no act of fraud or counterfeit in bringing him out.

In addition to increasing your sales and advancing your career, the creation of your supersalesperson character has another important benefit. It enables you to overcome your fear of rejection. For, though the supersalesperson *is* you, it is also *outside* you. As something outside you, it can function as a kind of shield or buffer zone, like the force fields of science fiction.

In a front-line situation where you are taking heavy hits, and it's clear that you are going to go down in flames, let your supersalesperson character take the rejection, indifference, or antipathy. "You" stay safe and sound inside, untouchable by any sense of personal affront. You are not discouraged or disappointed because you are sheltered by your projection, your super-you.

This is one effective way actors protect themselves from the slings and arrows of looking for acting work—selling themselves. They must be able to sustain a positive attitude in the face of a flurry of rejection, insult, disappointment, and embarrassment. Their mechanism for survival is to put on the block not their own head but the head of a character who is, at the same time, them, but is also someone else, a projection or extension of them. A less sensitive character, naturally, with a thicker hide, who *doesn't take it personally*. Because this character is not a person. Otherwise, they'd be dehydrated at the end of the day from spent tears.

You can use your character, your supersalesperson, in the same way. Project it from within, in a 360-degree force field, and watch rejection and invective bounce off like BBs on a Sherman tank.

DEPERSONIFICATION

This additional dimension of your character allows you to create a new and more effective version of the age-old trick of depersonification. Almost all sales training programs, even ones that are no more than verbal advice from one salesperson to another, recommend some form of prospect depersonification. In essence, a difficult or very important prospect is reduced by imagining him as something less or other than he is, or cutting down his intimidating stature by imagining him engaged in some embarrassing or belittling act, such as sitting on the toilet. So, we have been advised to imagine the assertive prospect as a child or as if he were naked. We have been told that if it is difficult to sustain eye contact with a forceful prospect, look at a point on the tip of his nose or at the middle of his forehead.

All these processes are forms of depersonification of the prospect—*and they are dangerous and frequently counterproductive*. For example, people will sense that you are not looking in their eyes. When someone looks in your eyes, they tend to check one eye, then the other. When you stare at the middle of someone's forehead or the tip of their nose, your eyes lock on one point, and the prospect senses something is wrong. If you are sitting face-to-face, closer than five feet in a well-lit office, chances are a prospect with normal vision will actually be able to see that you are not looking in his eyes. At this range, looking at the prospect's forehead or nose makes your eyes look "crooked" or "funny." You sort of look like a Siamese cat. Have someone try it on you at close range, and you'll see what we mean.

As for the belittling forms of depersonification, how can you sell sincerely and communicate with a naked prospect, or one sitting on a toilet? Even if this ploy does succeed in taking the threat out of the threatening prospect, is it worth it? You can't help looking a bit strangely at the prospect as you force yourself to imagine him or her naked, or in a compromising or embarrassing act. Does your little game make a tough question any easier to answer? Did you think for a moment that you can't be rejected by someone who happens to be naked?

Don't depersonify the prospect. Depersonify yourself.

Learn the external signals, find your courage key, and let it stimulate those deeper levels that produce sincere, real gestures; assume your role of supersalesperson, and put that character to work for you. Let that "you" withstand the impact of the difficult or intimidating prospect or prospects.

EXERCISE: Selling Something to Yourself

Consider some common expressions: "I convinced myself that..."; "He believes his own lies"; "She persuaded herself not to..."; "He's totally sold himself on...." We are all conscious of two entities within ourselves, which evaluate and argue and then try to "sell" us their opinions, perspectives, or conclusions. It is usually a question of pro and con, yes and no, why and why not. If you go into a presentation with only one of these internal voices on your side, you're only half a salesperson. Before you attempt to sell someone else, the least you can do is sell the negative, reluctant, or skeptical side of you. Here's one technique:

Alone, at home or in your office, or alone with your product or demo mode, *sell it to yourself.* Let your positive, "up," enthusiastic, ambitious, persuasive self sell your product, service, or idea to your negative, skeptical, indecisive, defeatist side. Don't pull any punches. Let the negative voice have full rein. This will probably be the toughest prospect you will go up against. It knows all the faults and weaknesses of your product, and of you, too. Keep working at it until it gives in and yields up to the positive you. Do it aloud, and go through all the demonstrations and sales aids you would use on a tough prospect. When you've won over this side of yourself, you are ready to tackle other prospects. *Totally* ready.

THE URY BASE

I have devised a basic key that anyone can use to conjure up and sustain the proper subtext for effective winning moves. It is an acronym, or word formed by the first letters of several words. Spoken as a word, "URY," it means nothing in English (which makes it a handy mantra, if you're into meditation), but read out, letter for letter, we hear, "You are why." "You are why" is always there to remind us of who is the beneficiary of more effective nonverbal signals and who is responsible for making sure that this critical aspect of your presentation works for you and not against you. *You* are why.

But the URY base key generates most of its power in the three words for which the letters stand:

Up

Relax

Yes

Up. In the early sixties, *up* was a hot fad word used in the press (Senate Ups Taxes), as a book title (*Up the Corporation*), and conversationally ("I'm up for that"). Teenagers today are recirculating the word in a positive response to an invitation to participate in some activity ("I'm up!"). For us, the word will define an attitude and the physical embodiment of that attitude.

Up is more than a direction; it is a mental attitude and a state of being; well-informed (up on); capable (up to); and enterprising, alert, and promising (up and coming). *Up* is where you are, but it's also where you're heading. *Up* describes how you look; it's a visible aspect of your physical presence. You are not bent and crushed by your disappointments and problems, your doubts and fears, because you will not be beaten by them. You are stronger than the inevitable obstacles and opponents you will meet. Your upness will take you over most hurdles, and when you are unable to leap over a particular pitfall, your upness of character will make it easier for you to climb out of the hole and continue in pursuit of your goal.

Up shows in your face. Your features are not drooping, your crest has not fallen, your cast is not down. You are not down in the mouth but up. Your posture and carriage are up, held high, away from the ground. Your head isn't bent or tilted with failure, rejection, confusion, or submission. Your head is up, ready for any adversary, full of confidence, power, and enthusiasm. Your gestures are not heavy, burdened, downhearted; they are characterized by lightness, action, success. Thumbs up, not thumbs down. In your mind's eye, grab yourself by the hair on top of your head (or ears, if you're bald) and pull steadily upward. You feel your spine straightening; your shoulders can't slump or cave forward. You breathe easier. You look taller, more important, more confident; and that's how you feel.

Relax. Easy to say, not so easy to do. Most of us have had the image of the successful overachiever drummed into us; we feel we are not working hard if we are not frantic, frenzied, and frenetic. We are assured by books, articles, and training programs that winners are energetic, dynamic whirlwinds. When was the last time you bought something from a whirlwind?

You can be terribly effective without whizzing through the territory like a dust devil on the brink of a breakdown. Most prospects would really rather not be swept off their feet by a whiz-bang, high-strung, fast-talking, tornadolike bolt of energy. If you are a bundle of energy, a veritable whirlwind, keep most of it in your internal engine room, letting just a little bubble to the surface as even-keeled energy, enthusiasm, and drive.

Henry Kissinger and George Shultz have whirled about as

much wind as anyone else in this century, but in person they are confident and relaxed. You may start at dawn, cover a hundred miles, and see twenty prospects before lunch, but you must appear relaxed before each and every one of them. Not tired, not phlegmatic, not complacent, not weak—relaxed.

How do you relax? Thinking about it is a good start. Wanting to be relaxed, agreeing with yourself that it is a desirable thing to do, experience, and project. Look into some of the programs that exist to help you relax. They all work to some degree or another. You might be quite capable of doing it yourself. Your sense of humor is a built-in catalyst for relaxation. A philosophical or objective point of view is helpful. You must appreciate that it isn't the end of the world if you lose a sale, have a bad week, or even a bad year. That was all yesterday. You can profit from your mistakes in any case. Thomas A. Edison said, "I did not fail a thousand times; I learned a thousand ways that it wouldn't work." You can't go into a meeting or make a presentation thinking, "I've *got* to make this sale or I'll kill myself or starve to death or ruin my career forever." That's what you'll project. You might as well carry a sign.

Yes is your answer to "can you?" It is your attitude, your philosophy, and your commitment. It's your key to the power of positive thinking. Where you feel *nos* and *maybes* cropping up in your path, hack them out of your way with a sharp, unyielding *yes*. *Yes* doesn't mean you are a yes-man, or a sycophant who doesn't know when to say no. When you embrace the positive energy of *yes*, you'll know when to say no, and people will take you far more seriously.

Yes is the contagious power of enthusiasm. It's a turn-on you experience, and one you can impart to others. *Yes* is a statement that you can and you will. Your product can and will. *Yes* means you are excited about possibilities. You are a starter and a finisher, and you deliver. You don't get bogged down on negativism, regret, guilt, and pessimism. You fly over it all on the wings of a commitment to *yes*, which springs from deep within your character. You trust in the power of the wonders that can be worked with *yes*. And you know that your yes will still be bravely and pertinaciously sustaining a positive note, even in the midst of a sea of strident negatives.

Up, *Relax*, *Yes*. You are why. Conjure up the URY on your way to a presentation. Personalize the terms for yourself so they work fast to get you Up, Relaxed, and Yes. Concentrate on them just before you walk through the door. Use them in conjunction with your courage key—explained in this chapter and the next—to stimulate in you in very short order a confident, positive attitude and a persuasive, winning, irresistible personality.

2

Creating a Character

In Chapter One, "The Secret of Winning Moves," we gave you the reasoning behind the necessity for believing in your character and in your product. We explained why deep-seated conviction is more effective than superficial artifice. We hope we communicated to you that you must not underestimate your prospect's ability to see through effected nonverbal covering and camouflage. We translated some of the techniques used by actors; finding a memory or role model "source" or subtext that will give emotional depth and provide parameters for the character you build, basing that source on a character trait and reducing it all to a short "key" that can conjure up the essence of the source instantly. We also indicated the necessity, when the role you want to create is quite different from your own natural one, to learn the physical externals and then "put the cake inside the icing."

But what role should you create? Isn't the most effective role just a refined and polished "you"? And if it isn't, won't you always feel like you're acting? If you are going to play a role, a supersalesperson, is there only one ideal character? We seem to have opened several cans of worms.

Yes, the most effective salesperson is a refined and polished "you"—providing you're already close to perfecting the role on your own. On the question of feeling like you're acting, consider that when you are selling you *are* acting, and when you are acting you are selling. The snake in Eden was selling and he was acting. Eve, the first salesperson, "acted" for Adam. Any actor can tell you about selling his character to the audience, and selling himself at an audition. Strong salespeople understand that they are strong actors. Brilliant actors know they are brilliant salespeople.

There is more than one ideal supersalesperson character. The dimension that makes the realm of character so fascinating is its kaleidoscopic variation. It is not desirable to have a conveyor-belt salesperson-making machine, churning out cookie-molded salespersons, because: 1) as various people are forced into a role, too many of them may be forced to stifle and twist too much of their innate personality, thereby losing spontaneity and natural charisma; 2) your company gets the reputation for creating identical sales-Frankensteins, types that prospects tend to dislike and distrust; and 3) there is a substantial loss of the sense of individual accomplishment for salespeople forced into a rigid mold; salespeople, like actors, like to have a strong hand in interpreting their own role. Sales directors, like theatrical directors, must learn to walk a fine line between governing and encouraging independent creativity.

What role should you develop? The one you're closest to. The one you've been working on for years. Maybe all you have to do is take out a few minor wrinkles, polish here and there, and *believe* in it. Here are a few examples of sales characters, all of them as "super" as they want to be.

> The Upper-middle-class Belonger
> The Irrepressible Optimist
> The Relentless Bulldog
> The Enthusiastic Sport
> The Solid, Reliable One
> The Good Old Boy
> The Daring Young Person

Any one of these types, or a number of others, can be a very effective salesperson. To suggest that you must force yourself to be only one or the other is simplistic and purely unsupportable elitist drivel. Clearly, a Southern Good Old Boy is going to encounter plenty of resistance in Boston. Obviously, an Upper-middle WASP is going to have a rough time selling chicken feed in the back country. An effete Ivy League intellectual shouldn't be selling tools to auto mechanics. Presumably, you have some grasp of the obvious; you try to avoid a situation where you're the only white insurance salesperson in Harlem or where you are using your college English on a gang of characters that thinks a deterrent is something you wash laundry with.

Ideally, you fit your customers—socially and in education, taste, and background—as closely as possible. You are, ideally, a bird of their feather. You can even be a notch higher or two on the social or educational ladder than your prospect, but it's not wise to rub it in. If you continually find yourself facing prospects who are totally alien to you (unless you're selling in another country, of course), you must: 1) tailor your character to lean more toward your prospects'; 2) ask for a different region or territory; 3) change jobs; or 4) move.

Don't try to open on Broadway. Try out your super-you character and polish and perfect it on less important prospects. You are likely to make a few mistakes at first; that's standard procedure. Let them occur in front of someone who doesn't matter to you that much. Then work your way up. This is good practice, incidentally, no matter what your approach or technique: Get yourself in shape for an important performance by trying out your stuff on a less crucial audience.

You will know your super-you character is working when you don't feel you are playing it. Of course, you are always consciously aware of the fact that you created and shaped it. But a moment comes when it somehow escapes your parameters and flies on its own, and from then on you have possession of an instrument with which you can exceed your own limitation.

Finally, of course, you will know your super-you character is working by your rave reviews, your commissions, your profits, constituents, buyers, disciples, converts, unanimous juries, deals, and conquests.

PART TWO

Presentation One-on-one, in the Office

> You show up to learn that the prospect forgot the meeting, can't see you, or is out of town.
>
> Since you are there, try to see his boss or another buyer. Reschedule immediately, in any case. To augment guilt, tell them you flew in or canceled your wedding just for this meeting.

3

The Entrance

Do not knock on the prospect's door. Walk in without hesitation. You have, after all, already been green-lighted by the prospect's secretary or a receptionist. Your entrance is announced and expected; knocking will signal timidity or lack of status. There is no reason why you should hesitate in the doorway like a school kid entering the principal's office. Yet salespeople everywhere frequently make this mistake. It is vitally important that you do not hesitate or pause in your entrance.

Even if the prospect is on the phone, drinking out of a flask, or tying his shoe, walk in confidently and directly. Put down your briefcase. Shake the prospect's hand. And sit down. A smooth, confident entrance, unimpeded by self-conscious vacillation, instantly augments your stature in the prospect's eye. He sees that you do not *expect* to be asked to wait. You are accustomed to walking into offices directly, without fear and hesitation. As in most areas concerning the sales confrontation, the salesperson will be viewed and treated largely according to *how he expects to be treated.* And these expectations are communicated entirely in nonverbal signals.

You enter a familiar prospect's office, and he or she has been replaced with someone you don't know.

Don't panic. Don't react with horror. Congratulate the new person on their new job. Don't keep bringing up the previous occupant of the office. Take nothing for granted. Treat this prospect like a totally new venture; don't try to pressure the new person to buy from you because of previous understandings developed between you and the previous buyer. If the former buyer was fired or transferred suddenly, there's probably good reason to suspect some prejudice or ill will on the part of the ex-buyer's superiors. Start from scratch; don't be patronizing or make the new buyer feel like "the new kid on the block."

You gain confidence and seem at ease by imagining that you are in a familiar place, like the office of your best friend. Do not gawk around at things like a tourist. You want the prospect to be comfortable and at ease. The prospect spends interminable hours in his office; it is utterly familiar to him—this is his world. If you walk in and start looking around and reacting to things as if they were strange (maybe even accidentally revealing in your expression that you don't favor the decor), the prospect then sees you more as an uncomfortable intruder into his environment, rather than as a guest or fellow inhabitant of his world. Relax. Feel comfortable and at home. You belong here.

Obviously, if the prospect has a ten-foot marlin mounted over his head, it won't hurt to comment on it the first time you see it. If the walls are covered with antique firearms, and you are interested or know something about the subject, by all means, express your mutual interest or enthuse awhile on his rare British fowling piece. If his desk is littered with tennis or sailing trophies and you play or race, you won't lose any points letting him know you appreciate and understand the magnitude of his accomplishments.

You enter the prospect's office for your appointment, and he's nowhere in sight.

Do not wait around near the door. Enter and sit. Do not try to read anything on the prospect's desk. Take something out of your own briefcase and go over it. Or, sit in the casual area and read a magazine or paper until he comes. Do not use his phone to call your sister in Dublin.

POSTURE

Your walk should be brisk and businesslike but not rushed. Your posture is almost military but not stiff and uncomfortable-looking. Your shoulders are not stooped with the weight of the world, because you are not bent and broken by your burdens. Whatever your burdens are, you don't let them get you down. You are a winner, and you are confident you will prevail. Your carriage tells observers that this is your character. Your face is on a vertical plane, direct and open; the chin is not pulled back into the neck. In fact, there is a definite link, a two-way street between your posture and your attitude or mood. People who sustain good posture, who carry themselves erect and proudly with their shoulders comfortably back, their stomachs under control, pelvis tipped slightly up and forward (by flexing the gluteus maximus muscles), and their lungs full of air, *feel* better. That happens within seconds of assuming proper posture, and in the long term, their entire attitude improves generally.

Just before you enter, you psych yourself for the meeting by running over the URY and your personal courage key. When you have the peak burst of confidence, you walk through the door.

With a little practice, you can think through the URY and courage key in about five seconds. It becomes like throwing a switch, and the effect of the whole sequence hits you all at once with a pervasive surge of energy and self-confidence.

Obviously, it is convenient if you have a couple of minutes to concentrate in the reception area or your car to clear your mind and let the calming effect of URY and your courage key gradually take effect on a deeper level. But eventually, it will come easier and faster. You will start to have better posture and be more relaxed and more positive and confident everywhere, in everything you do. It won't be such a big jump to go from the everyday you to the supersalesman you, because the two will gradually merge.

APPURTENANCES

If possible, leave your coat and other outerwear in the reception area. If you must bring overcoats, scarves, gloves, hats, and umbrellas into the prospect's office, try to have them off and over your arm before you enter. Then your goal is to get rid of them as quickly as possible and with the least amount of hassle. The prospect is a busy person. He isn't particularly diverted by having to watch you struggle out of your soggy overcoat. Even more annoying is the chore of having to get up and show you where to hang your coat, etc. If you don't instantly see a free hanger or an easily used closet, lay your outer garments on an extra chair or anywhere they won't bend, fold, or mutilate anything else. *Do not hang your coat over his*, on either a hook or a hanger, especially if your coat is damp from rain, snow, or perspiration.

Under no circumstances should you take a wet umbrella into the prospect's office. There is simply no inoffensive place to put it. You can't stand it up or hang it, because it's going to make a cute little puddle for him to remember you by. And you don't want to lay it down, because then you have to bend over or squat, postures you're better off not displaying to someone you are trying to impress. Laying down an umbrella looks dumb, anyway. Leave it in the hall. Beware of recently waxed or marble floors; no matter how carefully you lean it, the umbrella will crash to the floor right in the middle of your closing. Try laying it on the floor. (All right, this will seem unnecessary advice to many of you—who would be *that* dumb? The fact is, all of us have our blind spots or moments when the cogs slip, and it's better to belabor the obvious than let yourself in for a needless loss of yardage.)

There is another good reason for getting rid of your outerwear and related paraphernalia. When you enter the prospect's domain, you do not want to accentuate your image as invading outsider. The prospect's fellow workers appear in interior office clothes. They belong; they fit in this environment. If you enter bundled up in outerwear, you underline the fact that you are out of your element here, that you are different. This is undesirable, because anything that helps make you look different or like an outsider makes it easier for the prospect to think of you and treat you like one.

Smart saleswomen who sell door-to-door have learned this, or intuited it, and try to appear on a prospect's doorstep dressed as if they were the woman next door just popping by to drop off a piece of misdelivered mail or return a borrowed book. They forgo heavy winter gear as much as possible. One imagines this would result in a greater tendency to catch colds, but perhaps the few moments of chill are offset by the warm glow of increased commissions.

EXERCISE: Getting from the Door to the Prospect

You can do this alone, but it's really much more fun with a second party or parties. The exercise requires a room with a door. Inside the room is a "prospect," a desk, and several other pieces of furniture. You go out of the room and wait in the hall. Your associate or associates rearrange the furniture in various ways, designed primarily to make it hard for you to make a smooth entrance. When they are ready, they signal you to come in. You are carrying a raincoat and a briefcase. You enter, get rid of your coat as quickly as possible, decide where you will sit, get rid of your briefcase, and smoothly try to get to a good position for the handshake (i.e., not across the desk) and then sit, which may require moving a chair. This is good practice to help you cope with the many layouts prospects are likely to come up with. As the salesperson gets more proficient, his associates can have fun making it really difficult for him to enter smoothly. They may hide the "prospect" behind a rubber tree plant and rig the coat rack to tip over if you breathe on it. To play alone, you arrange the furniture yourself and then negotiate your entrance through it. The surprise value is, of course, removed, but engineering the moves and practicing them is still of value.

THE PROSPECT'S SIGNALS

Let's examine our prospect at this point. Let us assume that this is no easy sale. The prospect is signaling that he has no intention of buying your products or services. The only reason he has given you this chance was because of your persistence in calling. The prospect wants you to know how he feels. He wants to project hostility or indifference so you won't be encouraged. He wants to break you right up front, convince you by his signals that he will never give in and that you are wasting his time. You read the signals—there is no denying them; the prospect makes them quite obvious, *even though his words are relatively polite*, as if he is really going to give you a fair chance. You ignore the perfunctory verbiage and read the prospect's nonverbal signals for his true position.

The prospect leaves you waiting in the reception area for twenty minutes or more, after your appointment time.

Have the receptionist call in and ask if the prospect would like to reschedule. Or, take out your papers or books and start catching up on some of your homework. When the prospect's secretary or he, himself, comes to get you, don't pack up in a harried panic.

The prospect sits behind his fortress-desk, close to it, his legs further protected by its sides. He is trying to make himself as inaccessible as possible. His feet are flat on the floor, part of his utterly businesslike posture. He uses his hands and arms like shields to block you and fend you off. His hands are closed, or laced into one another, or down on the desktop. He is avoiding eye contact with you. He is sitting stiffly, uncomfortably. He wants you to know that he is uncomfortable.

The prospect's face shows his displeasure and dread. The eyes are narrow, the brows knit, and the forehead furrowed, especially between and above the eyes. His jaw and mouth are set and tensed. His lips are dry and thin. You take it all in, but you are not rattled. You refuse to reflect or even acknowledge all the negative signals being mounted for you.

THE HANDSHAKE

On the way to the handshake, you drop your briefcase or samples on the chair you will sit in. It is more effective to have everything out of your hands when you go for the handshake. For salesmen, if you are a warm, physical type, or have one of those sweep-'em-off-their-feet personalities, you can apply the two-handed handshake. As you shake hands right, you put your left hand on his right arm or forearm. This gives you tremendous psychological control if you can bring it off fearlessly. *Don't* use it on a female prospect. Think twice before using it on a man who is well above you in status, because he will probably be doing it to you.

Move in fairly close for the handshake, a bit closer than you normally do. If you can, come at the prospect from the side of his desk—this means an easier, more comfortable reach for you both. Your body faces the prospect directly; do not turn to the side. Another little trick to gain control quickly: *pull the prospect toward you a little as you shake.* Just a bit. Men can do this with a female prospect also. It shows your lack of fear of the prospect, and your warmth. Don't be surprised if you feel the prospect pulling back slightly. Now he knows you are not afraid. Here you are in the lion's den, and you're pulling the lion right up into your face. But don't try this if the prospect is much taller than you; the closer you get to him, the smaller you will seem.

Let the prospect decide when to end the handshake. If he attempts to terminate it with undue haste, hold on a beat longer. Don't let him get away from you so soon. If you are male and the prospect is female, however, you must end the handshake *immediately* when she signals she wants it to end.

You get to the prospect's reception area, already late for your meeting, but you are dying to use the bathroom first.

By all means, use the bathroom first. It's better to be three minutes later than go through a thirty-minute meeting with your legs crossed in two places, your teeth grinding, and your hair standing on end.

The handshake is how you and the prospect measure one another's strength and purpose. If you have a weak, sweaty, fragile, trembling grip, the prospect immediately assumes you are a pushover, and he'll feel confident that he can turn you down and send you on your way. If your grip is weak, build it up. Get one of those hand/forearm exercisers at a sporting goods store, or just squeeze an old tennis ball to death. To combat sweaty palms, wash your hands or dry them on a tissue just before the meeting. Keep your hands out of your pockets; let them desoggify in the air. Remove warm gloves at least ten minutes before a meeting, unless you are riding a motorcycle or horse through a blizzard. Don't let the client see you wiping your hands on your clothes—an instant loss of many points.

One of the worst mistakes you can make is to defuse the prospect's grip by tightening down prematurely on the tips of his fingers, before his hand can gain a complete and normal grip on yours. The origin of this annoying stunt is unclear, but I'm sure everyone who uses it thinks he is very clever indeed.

> *You enter a prospect's office for your meeting, and the competition's representative is still there. He or she is in the middle of a final story.*
>
> It will definitely cut your stature to wait in the hall until the story ends. You want to interrupt without it looking like you interrupted. You go directly up to the other salesperson, grab their hand in a warm, friendly way, and introduce yourself (or greet them if you know them already). Now, of course, you have to shake the prospect's hand—so he or she doesn't feel slighted. When you've finished all these introductions or greetings, throw the ball back to the other rep to finish his story. By then, the story will have lost its momentum, and it leaves him with a weak exit.

VOICE

Deeper voices carry more authority for men and women. Everything you say somehow seems truer or more important. If you don't already have one, you can develop one.

When you first wake up in the morning, you have a deeper voice; you have heard it, and it surprised you. What happens? Five or ten minutes later it's all gone, and you're left with your squeaky, insignificant voice again.

After a night's sleep, your throat, larynx, and pharynx are totally relaxed, loose. You speak and there is this wonderful Orson Welles or Patricia Neal rumble. Once you're up and worrying about this and that, your vocal cords tighten up, and when you speak, they tense into the range that they've been accustomed to all these years.

You can develop a deeper, more authoritative voice. There are two ways: go to a voice coach and tell him you want to develop a deeper and more authoritative voice; or do it yourself.

If you elect to take the second route, hum a lot. Low. Up and down the scales. Hum and then open your mouth and let out a vowel. Like *mmmmmMaaa*. And *mmmmmmmMMeeeee*, *mmmmmMMiiiii*, *mmmmMMooooo*, *mmmmMMuuuu*. Lower. As low as you can. Now try it without the *m*. Just *A, E, I, O, U*. Lower. One string of AEIOUs after another. Until you're out of breath. Louder. Lower. Let your spouse laugh. Wait'll they hear you after a few weeks. Run through these exercises a couple of times a day at least. In the car. In the shower. In the garage. In the woods. And then start speaking lower. Consciously. And slower. If you just slow down your speech a bit, you'll automatically start speaking in a lower register.

If you are wondering why we are discussing the pitch of your voice in a book on nonverbal communication, think about it for a moment. What you say is verbal. How you say it is nonverbal. And how you say it—the volume and the pitch—is easily as important as the definition of the words.

You are presenting, and you feel a "frog" growing in your throat.

Create pressure in your throat by holding your breath and trying to exhale at the same time. (Do this when you are not speaking, of course.) Then swallow once or twice. Speak louder and in a register different from your normal voice.

FIRST MOVES

Let's backtrack a bit and see where we are.

You have crossed confidently and directly to the *side* of the prospect's desk, so he won't have to reach clumsily across the desk to shake hands. You have neatly flanked the prospect's Maginot Line. You can see the prospect full-length, and the prospect can see you. The prospect may be slightly rattled at having you move so easily and quickly past his massive, defensive bulwark. Good.

With good eye contact and a firm grip, draw the prospect's hand a bit toward you and hit him with your deep, confident voice. What is the prospect's response? He tries to conclude the handshake prematurely, and you hold on for a second longer to establish some psychological control.

The prospect rises only perfunctorily, doesn't even really straighten up, signals that are an attempt to cut your status. You are not perturbed at all, you merely feel sorry for the prospect for being ill-bred. You conclude that this prospect may have some deep animosity toward your company, products, or services, or toward a former sales rep. Perhaps the prospect is misinformed or not yet apprised of updates, design alterations, procedural changes, or pricing that will affect his attitude toward your products or company. You resolve to find out what is on his mind.

The salesman maintains solid eye contact and sustains a friendly but businesslike smile. The saleswoman avoids smiling and uses eye contact only for emphasis. The prospect watches you very closely now, to see if all of the negative signals are starting to take their toll. You do not allow the prospect to put even a hairline crack into your confidence. You return no reflected negative signals. You refuse to mirror the prospect's mood or mind-set. You don't even acknowledge it.

In the middle of an important presentation that's going very well, you suddenly realize your face is exhausted from forcing a smile.

Stop smiling. Your prospect can spot a forced smile, and although he may enjoy and reflect the spirit of it for a while, he may suddenly decide he doesn't like it or wish you'd stop it. With any luck, you realize you're forcing the smile and stop just before the prospect notices it. You don't have to smile constantly to show you are enjoying yourself. Smile at the peaks. For the rest of the time, just look really interested in what the prospect is saying.

At the conclusion of the handshake, do not *drop* your hand and arm to your side like a dead eel. This is a gesture of a tired old man. You *move* your arm purposefully to your side. Keep your eyes on the prospect until your arm is at your side. He will be retreating back into his chair. Let him sit first.

SEATING STRATEGY

The prospect is supposed to ask you to sit at this point, if he hasn't already. You do not turn your back to find the chair you are going to use; rather, you back away and may turn your side to the prospect for a moment to move a chair closer to the side of the desk, if one isn't there already.

Although we caution in general against moving anything in the prospect's domain, the advantages of having a seat at the side of the prospect's desk are so great as to outweigh the liabilities. If the guest chair is too heavy or cumbersome to move easily, leave it where it is and sit in it without further ado. If you have a choice, take the chair closest to the "open" side of the desk (almost always the side closest to the door). This is the access and egress side, and is clearly more in the action center of the office. There is one disadvantage: If a secretary or co-worker enters during your meeting, they are directly behind you, and it is clumsy to twist around and acknowledge them or throw them one of your winning smiles.

Do not wait to be asked to be seated. If your prospect is a stickler for formality, he will ask you to sit before you will have a chance to wait for him to ask. That makes more sense the second time you read it. In other words, if someone is informal enough to neglect to ask you to have a seat, you can be informal enough to take one on your own initiative.

Remember your briefcase? You stood it up in this chair on your way to shake hands. Now you will move the briefcase to the floor next to you. Lean it against the chair legs if it doesn't stand up by itself. Put it on the side *where it will be most easily seen* by the prospect. Don't slide it into the crack between your chair and the prospect's desk. Whenever you reach into the briefcase, the prospect can't see what you are looking at, and from his point of view you are staring down into nothingness and rooting through a space which, as far as he can see, contains nothing. People like to see what you're looking at. Example: In a movie, the leading player reacts to something offscreen. You want to see what he/she is looking at immediately. The next cut had better be the object of the actor's gaze.

Not only should you keep your briefcase where the prospect can see it, you should, if it looks natural, position and open it so he can see what's inside. You may have noticed that prospects, like cats, are curious. Some prospects may feel they have the right to be downright nosy. Do not try to hide the contents of your briefcase, because it wouldn't support your role of the aboveboard, no-tricks-up-my-sleeves, ingenuous salesperson. If you have a chicken salad sandwich and an apple stuck in there with your sales aids, do not try to hide such things from the prospect. It may augment your humanity to him. Also, he may offer to trade a half a turkey breast for your chicken salad, which makes you a winner whether he buys or not.

You do not plop or crash into the chair. You lower yourself into it in a controlled physical move, like a panther stopping for a moment to scan the horizon. Tired old losers plop into chairs. Don't do it, even if you are tired and old.

One of the central tenets of behavioral psychology is the theory that you can change thought or attitude if you change behavior. You can, for example, alleviate a mood of depression by pasting a smile on your face and dancing around the room. It sounds absurd, but it holds some germ of truth. There is something about smiling and dancing madly around the room that makes your depression seem self-indulgent. Another example is drawn from posture; if you carry yourself with tall, courageous confidence, you *feel* more courageous and confident— and you start to think more courageously and confidently.

When your prospect looks like he was cut out of Mt. Rushmore, immobile, cold, and intransigent, your immediate task is to break his monolithic pose. If you can put a crack in his stony facade, you will be also causing a crack in his adamant resolve to resist you and your presentation. You may not succeed in inducing him to dance around the room, but you may well get him to smile, to sit back a bit, relax somewhat, cross his legs, put his foot up on something, move around—anything that serves to turn that block of marble into clay.

Your nonverbal strategy to effect such a change is not to mirror the prospect's stiff, closed posture but to lead him into more relaxed, open postures by your example. This is a gradual process; you don't directly assume a very relaxed, open posture and expect a hostile or indifferent prospect to instantly follow suit. You lead the prospect by starting closer to his posture and expression, and then gradually becoming more relaxed. You give the prospect opportunities to alter his posture and relax his physical rigidity by creating opportunities for him to move. You shake hands; you hand the prospect your card; you hand him brochures, pictures, samples, things that have to be unfolded, unrolled, opened.

EXERCISE: Sustaining Enthusiasm with Indifferent Prospects

You want to be able to maintain a high level of energy and enthusiasm while presenting to a prospect who is one degree away from snoring. To enable yourself to bypass the indifferent prospect's debilitating signals, you should practice presenting to extreme cases that won't matter. Try this:

Do a full, positive, enthusiastic presentation to your dog or cat, preferably when it is snoozing in front of the fireplace or radiator. Your pet will look up occasionally to see if you've broken out the treats yet, so it won't be a totally indifferent prospect. When you stay "up, relaxed, and yes" in front of your pet, you are ready to tackle a philodendron, mop, or party doll. For advanced professionals, try selling to a rock, file cabinet, or tuna fish sandwich. When you can sustain an even level of energy and undampened enthusiasm with an inanimate object, you can handle and overcome any indifference a mere mortal could conjure up.

As a salesperson, you understand that you cannot sell a prospect who is armed with the drawn and sharpened sword of sales resistance until you induce him to drop his guard or resheath the sword. Thus, the focus of the first moments of the meeting is to demonstrate to the prospect that you are an inoffensive, likable person, and this is not going to be an uncomfortable hard sell. You project your warmest, friendliest, most charming self. You are, in a word, disarming. By showing that you are not going to wade in, swinging the weapons of the hard sell, you cause your prospect to relax his rigid, armored defenses.

Let us say that this particularly tough prospect reacts to your opening by moving things or papers around on his desk. He is erecting an obstacle course between you and him. You cracked the marble, you got him moving, he is shifting out of his Mt. Rushmore pose—but you can see that you have a long way to go before he buys.

He pushes up the middle of his forehead with his fingers, a signal of boredom. He rubs his eyes like someone waking up from a nap, another boredom signal. He flicks imaginary lint off his clothes. This signal, which no doubt started out as a subconscious gesture, has become an official slight in some Mediterranean cultures. One "cuts" the object of the gesture by flicking imaginary lint off one's lapel. The gesture is displayed to a third party or parties, and the translation is, "I wish this character would flake off." Used involuntarily in our culture today, the gesture signals irritability with the speaker or the subject at hand.

A skeptical prospect signals his skepticism in a number of ways aside from verbal interjections. It is important to be watching for signals of skepticism, as the prospect may not want you to know he doubts your veracity on a particular point. He may figure that he can get rid of you sooner if you don't stop to prove each claim he doubts. The clearest signals will be sent just at the end of your statement or claim. Some of the signals of prospect skepticism are:

A sudden shift in posture.

Forced cough or clearing the throat.

The index finger is raised slightly for a second, then lowered.

The fingers of one or both hands are lifted, then dropped back to the surface upon which they were resting.

Looking suddenly up and to the side.

Touching the mouth, or masking the mouth with fingers or hand.

The prospect's finger to the side of his nose is a fairly sure sign of doubt. Look at yourself making this gesture in the mirror. That reflected person doesn't believe a word you just said.

If that finger is placed an inch and a half lower, between the upper lip and the nose, and is pressed into the flesh there, right after something you just said, the sender of that signal not only doubts you, he or she is convinced you are exaggerating, or just plain lying. I believe the gesture springs from the sudden urge to blurt out a blunt exclamation, such as "Bull!" or "You're full of it," and the signaler is just catching himself with a reminder to button his lip for a few moments and see where or how far the speaker goes.

It is interesting that salespeople who are in fact exaggerating wildly, or just plain lying, frequently punctuate their remarks by putting their fingers to the spot just above their upper lip. The signal seems to be universal in speaker and listener. Make a note: *Do not touch the area between your nose and upper lip when you are lying to a prospect.*

The tendency in the opening moments of a critical call is to draw one's shoulders about oneself, like a protective mantle, to shrink down in a sort of concave surrender. It is important, especially in the first several seconds of getting seated, to sustain the feeling and impression of confidence and courage you established in your entrance. Sit up, as if someone had a handful of your hair and was pulling up. Keep your shoulders back and carry them high. Don't lean hard against the back of the chair. A good-seated posture gives you a higher eye level, makes you look more substantial, telegraphs your pertinacity, and even makes it easier to speak—you are speaking from fuller lungs and a larger, more resonant chest cavity, which also makes it easier for you to speak deeper.

If your chair is at an angle to the prospect, turn it slightly more toward him. If this is not possible, turn your torso so your head and shoulders are facing the prospect head-on. Do not turn your upper body away from the prospect. It doesn't make you look casual; it makes you look afraid, uninterested, or even unfriendly. If it is very difficult for one reason or another to move your torso and shoulders to confront him directly, make absolutely certain that your face is at least facing the prospect's. If he can't see both your ears, you're out of position. A face turned to the side almost always transmits signals you don't want to send, like dishonesty, insult, humor, or flirting. A face turned down turns people off; it says defeat, exhaustion, guilt, or fear.

Do not cross your legs immediately. You want to be ready for sudden developments, like the prospect moving away from you or suggesting you both move somewhere else. Also, you don't want to look *too* casual yet. You and the prospect are still sizing each other up. Legs crossed too soon may be misread by the prospect as a lack of respect. In addition, you have items to take out of your briefcase, and it will be easier to lean forward to take them out with uncrossed legs.

GESTURES

Most salespeople move too fast, which conjures up the proverbial "fast-talker" and puts prospects on guard. Slow down. Your walk, entering and exiting, should be brisk and businesslike, yes. But once you are in position, slow your arms and legs down.

Rehearse the speed at which you gesture, either in a mirror or on videotape. Quick, jerky movement belies a calm interior or voice. If you are to appear cool and collected, in command of yourself, *your movements must be clear, deliberate, and uncomplicated*. Not fast but not painfully slow. To define which is which, pretend your eye is a motion-picture camera. Watch your hands move when you talk or gesture. Do your moves blur or "strobe"? If so, they are too fast, and you must slow them down. Slower moves are less likely to get you in trouble, especially if you tend to clumsiness under pressure, and impart an air of calm, self-assurance, strength, and deliberateness.

A move can be too slow, of course. If a movement is so slow that it conflicts with your speech rhythm, it will be distracting. Find that "blur" speed we discovered a moment ago, and slow it down just a notch, so that your hands are steadily visible and "trackable" throughout the gesture. Naturally, if you are making a point that calls for a rapid movement, such as describing how prompt service or deliveries will be, then you may blur for effect.

TRUE LIFE STORY: Slowing Down Your Moves, But Not Too Much

I put a meeting together at a prestigious yacht club. There was a young entrepreneur who needed something that an established venture capitalist could give him. I was introducing the young man to the financier. I thought it was a good fit; they could have created a profitable symbiosis.

Before the meeting, I gave the young guy a bit of friendly advice. I told him to stop clearing his throat all the time and to slow his movements down. "Sure," he said, "no problem."

I was proud of him for the first two-thirds of the meeting. He didn't clear his throat once. And his movements were clear and slow. Then they got slower. And slower. And slower. It was fascinating—the financier and I were sitting there watching a living person achieve a state of suspended animation. The end came when he went to spread some cheese on a cracker, which he then intended to eat, I suppose. It took him about two minutes just to sit forward (we were around a small round table off the bar). It took at least three minutes for him to select a cracker and load up the knife with cheese. Another minute to spread the cheese on the cracker. By now everyone in the area, including the bartender, was staring in rapt fascination. Would he ever get the cracker to his mouth? I watched the financier's brows knit. He was a busy man. I sensed that he wasn't likely to tune in next week for the concluding episode of *The Petrified Cracker*. The young man couldn't handle the pressure; he put the cracker down on the side of his dish and slumped back into his chair. About thirty people let out a sigh of relief. No one was looking forward to living through the month or so it would have taken for the young man to chew and swallow the cracker.

A minute later, the financier spread some cheese on another cracker and ate it, just to show how it's done. He left right after that.

The young man told me he got into a rut of moving slower the more nervous he became, and getting more and more nervous because he was so worried about his moves. I ran into the financier a few days later at a party and he asked me why I would introduce him to someone who was obviously addicted to tranquilizers.

You must also consider the speed and size of gestures relative to the distance from the observer. The closer something is to the eye, the larger it appears. The closer you are to the prospect, therefore, the slower and smaller your gestures should be.

We observed above that different cultures are comfortable at different working distances. Cultural patterns are also evident in the size, scope, and incidence of gestures. Generally, people of Nordic, Germanic, and Anglo-Saxon backgrounds tend to use minimal hand and arm gestures. The gestures they do use are primarily hand and forearm. This group also prefers greater distance, and shies from touching.

Eastern Europeans gesture with greater frequency and do most of it from the elbow down, although shrugging is a regular accompaniment to raised eyebrows. They stay within tactile range when possible, and start touching sooner than the group above. In this environment, touching is used to underline, punctuate, break down barriers, intimidate, censure, or signal status levels.

Southern Europeans gesture with their entire arms and shoulders. Facial expressions are broad and unmistakable. The scope of gestures is broad and often likely to penetrate the personal space of non-Southern Europeans. The incidence of gesture reference is very high, and friendly touching is a standard procedure.

American Blacks exercise a double standard. Among whites, they use very limited and careful gestures. With other Blacks they gesture with greater incidence and scope. They share an almost immediate synchronicity and "mirroring," and touching is quite natural. The same patterns hold, but to a lesser extent, with American Hispanics, who have the additional effect of the language factor. Hispanic cultural roots are in Southern Europe, but other influences pull in many directions. As with most examples of mixed cultural input, the overriding influence is a reflection of status rather than inculcated cultural patterns. In other words, your position on the social scale may have more to do with how you move and gesture than your inherited cultural or national influences.

Generally speaking, the higher you are on the social scale, the less you gesture and the smaller, slower, and more controlled your gestures will be. Watch a good actor play an upper-class ("up-scale" is the theatrical term) role in a film. Not on the stage where gestures must be broadened for a distant audience, but in a film. The person with status moves and gestures only minimally. The implication is simple, and it is as old as recorded history: People with status don't *have* to move. When there is no need to work, there is no need to move.

That still applies today. Watch a corporate board meeting. Those who are most secure in their positions seem to be the most immobile. They are more imperturbable, less easily shaken by minor tremors. Social status effects or generates (and to some extent is established by) reserve in movement, gestures, and expression.

What does all this mean to you? Your important prospects are going to be up-scale people. Now you won't be surprised or discouraged when they seem so stingy with gestures and expressions. Or when they recoil from your friendly Southern European touch. Or when their personal perimeter seems so far-flung. Or when they are put off by your broad arm-and-shoulder gesturing.

However, and this is important, *don't be afraid to gesture*. You might wisely gesture less violently with an up-scale WASP, but definitely do not try to stifle your natural instinct to gesture.

Gesturing, especially natural gesturing, sends solid signals of enthusiasm and energy. Gesturing also shows lack of fear. If you stand or sit there like a wooden Indian, you look scared, "frozen stiff" with fear, even if you're not. Watch your gesturing in a mirror or videotape. Try gesturing more broadly than you normally do, then less broadly. You want your gestures to support and augment your verbal communications, not to overrule or replace them. If you are searching for a word and it just won't come, and you end up "mugging" and gesticulating wildly to express the thrust of the word you are after, you look like an absentminded buffoon. Do not get into the habit of trying to communicate with your nonverbal systems only; your prospect cannot help but think you have a terribly limited vocabulary.

In addition to the speed and scope of a gesture, we must also consider muscular tension and "carriage" of the limb or digit. Your fingers are not limp streamers attached to your hand for decoration. Your hand is not a limp flag attached to your wrist for effect. Your wrist is not limp, period. There should be some sense of muscular tension in every part and participant of a gesture. The part that moves comes to life. All of it. When you shake hands, for example, you do not offer a powerful grip and a limp forearm, or a powerful forearm and a limp grip. There must be a sense of flow, or coordination. The entire gesture, whether it is standing up or raising a finger, must be purposeful, complete, controlled, and coordinated. Such a gesture is guided and charged with a muscular tension that signals you are fit, strong, and resolute.

Your repertoire and execution of gestures are a substantial part of your personal charisma. If you stifle natural gestures, you stifle personality. Your goal is to control and train your gestures to work harder for you. Let them come naturally as you speak, but modulate them to fit your prospect and the factors of familiarity, distance, personal space perimeters, and status.

DISTANCE AND TERRITORY

In the beginning, you work farther back. You don't want to impinge on the prospect's personal space, which is largest in the opening minutes of the presentation. Personal territory, we should observe in passing, is not a fixed quantity. There is obviously a substantial difference in the personal territory one projects in the company of an angry sumo wrestler and when with close friends. A prospect who is indifferent or antagonistic will have a larger personal space than will one who is a likely customer.

You will have no difficulty finding where the limits of a prospect's personal space lie. The moment you approach, the prospect will exhibit one of the you-are-trespassing signals: hunching; rocking; turning or looking away; drumming fingers; masking; and, most frequently, moving or leaning away to reestablish distance.

Ideally, you want to find a prospect's space limit and work just beyond it. By "work" I mean your body and face stay just outside the invisible shell. Occasionally, to stimulate attention and underline a point, you may approach and penetrate the personal space with your hands. Very carefully. And with slow, clear gestures. If you move gradually, unthreateningly, you effect a gradual shrinkage of the territorial border and a relaxation of the prohibition against trespassing on what is left.

The advantages of working close are:

1. You're better able to see and read the prospect's signals.
2. He is better able to read all the strong, confident, and believable signals you are sending.
3. Distance suggests fear. You go in as close as is appropriate and then push a bit farther to show you're not afraid.
4. You can speak at a lower volume. Lower inevitably leads to deeper, and deeper sounds are more authoritative.
5. Your proximity forces the prospect to pay closer attention; he picks up on more of your crucial sales points.
6. You don't have to gesture broadly. Smaller gestures have greater mileage.

The size and sensitivity of the personal space perimeter provide you with a very effective barometer of how the prospect is reacting to you overall. If he likes your style (even in spite of himself), his sense of personal space will diminish and the borders become blurry. If he doesn't like you, you'll feel that hard and far-flung border every time you try to move or gesture closer. Remembering that it is still possible to sell to someone who doesn't like you, the salesman continues to make the best possible presentation, at the distances established and maintained by the resistant prospect. You can still be very convincing at fifteen feet.

Some tips to jot in your notebook on variations in territory and distance:

1. Work farther back with a new prospect, closer with a familiar one. Men, work closer to women, generally. Women, work farther back with men, generally.
2. Work closer to those near to you in age, farther back with prospects substantially older or younger.
3. When you move a bit too close for a prospect, and stay there a bit too long, he may start sending those you-are-trespassing signals mentioned earlier. Here are some more: he masks his face with his hands or with some

papers or object; his eye blinks are overly long, and he actually closes his eyes for short periods of time; his eyes squint, pupils pinpointed.

The prospect will attempt to move away casually, in an effort to reestablish distance, without you noticing that it is a retreat on his part. Curiously, even though he has no fear of you (or antipathy toward you), the prospect will still move away or feel compelled to try to move away from a salesperson who is impinging on, or gesturing into, his personal territory; people become a little irritated and off-balance when you step over their imaginary lines.

There are times when it's worth it. Mild irritation is better than total indifference or apathy. It is also probably better for your prospect to be a bit off-balance once in a while than to think you are afraid and move on the offensive. You can use proximity to raise your prospect's level of concentration on what you are saying, to underline fearlessness and sincerity. Also, if you initiate a repositioning or closer gesturing, and the prospect reacts, you are establishing a subtle psychological edge: You act, he reacts. This is obviously a neat turning of the tables, and if it is done subtly, the prospect will never be conscious of it.

PERSISTENCE

You are halfway through your presentation, and the prospect shows no positive response. His signals translate clearly into indifference. You can't seem to break through. Maybe you simply can't break through to this particular prospect this week. Maybe he really is in bed with supplier X, and there's no way of sliding in between the covers. But then again, there's always next week. Or next year, when the other supplier lets him down or makes a costly mistake or sells him inferior merchandise, whatever. And then again, maybe this prospect is misinformed, or uninformed, and some piece of information you offer may turn him around. Or you may just stumble on his "hot button." Or tomorrow he may be moved to another department where he'll be more likely to buy or use whatever it is you're selling. The point is, *you never quit.*

You never even show that you feel like quitting. The instant you allow an "I quit" signal to creep into your performance, all the rest of your song and dance is wheel-spinning. But you don't worry about transmitting such a signal because on a deeper level you have determined, before going in, that you are *not* going to give up.

Of course, you will lose some sales. No doubt about it. But it won't be because of anything you did. You give it your best possible performance straight through, even if the prospect is throwing rotten fruit and vegetables at you.

This way, you always leave the door open for a return match. You can lose the sale because the prospect is happy with his present supplier or because you can't beat the price, delivery, or terms. But you can always try again later. The prospect never thinks of you as a loser, because you never lose. You are patient. You are stubborn. You never throw in the towel. He wishes, in fact, that you were selling for his company!

TRUE LIFE STORY: Never Quitting

My offices were in a prestigious New York skyscraper. We were targets for the wiliest, most pertinacious salespeople in the world. The poor, outnumbered guards in the lobby tried to run interference but couldn't really dampen the constant flow of salespeople. Most of them were selling office equipment. The most persistent was a copier salesman. He was offering a small, light desktop copier, and his first point was that it must be truly small and light, because he just carried it into your office and parked it on your desk. He breezed past receptionists with a line such as "This is for your boss."

I had just made two films for a life insurance company that wouldn't take "no" for an answer, so I fancied myself the World's Toughest Prospect. I told the salesman to remove himself from the premises or I would call building security. It didn't even break his stride. He had plugged in and was copying everything in sight. It was a pretty nifty copier, I noticed—but that wasn't the point. You can't have just anyone barging into your office unannounced. I called security. Two and a half minutes later, two security men came in and escorted our undauntable salesperson out of my office. He went without showing the least bit of fear or anger. The copies he had made were still on my desk. Not bad. I wondered if maybe I hadn't passed up a good thing. My secretary gave me a look, as if to say that I had been too hard on the guy.

A week later my secretary and I dropped into the security office to report a team of purse-snatching kids who where pretending to sell cookies for charity. There was the nifty little copier. The security office had prevailed upon building management to buy them one. Yes, they bought it from the salesman they had ejected from my offices. "I was sold before I hit the first floor," confessed one of the security personnel. They raved about how versatile and fast and easy to operate the copier was. I really did need one, anyway. My secretary suggested we get the salesman's name and number (I had made a great show of throwing his card away), and give him a call. I told her I didn't think that would be necessary. I was sure he'd be back.

Within two weeks, he reappeared and I became just another customer. I offered him a job selling for me. He was nice about declining; he explained how he had it all mapped out to become the president of his copier firm. And I was sure he would do it, too. One way or another.

THE HOSTILE PROSPECT

The antagonistic prospect seems to present a more serious obstacle. He is out to stick it to you, to get you to agree with him that something about you, your product, company, or services is bad. He's got some old problem or a prejudice or a misunderstanding stuck in his craw, and he intends to take it out on you. Unfortunately, it may take awhile to draw out the problem, to get the prospect to let you know what's on his mind. Indeed, he may never reveal to you why he is antagonistic toward you or your product. It may even be illegal, if it's because of your color, religion, sex, or nationality.

You must work to unearth the reason for his antagonism—it may be, and usually is, something you can overcome eventually. If you can't elicit a response through direct questioning, you might find your clue through observation of his nonverbal signals. As you touch on various points, watch the prospect for signals that will help reveal his problem. He will send them in spite of his conscious desire not to do so. The fact is, his subconscious *really wants you to know* what's bugging him, and his subconscious will use the subtle vocabulary of nonverbal signals to communicate the source of his antagonism, even while his conscious mind will not allow him to do so verbally.

For example, you say, "I understand that we were late on several deliveries to Canada, is that what's bothering you?" He denies, verbally, that he is still holding that against your company. But, in fact, he lost a promotion because your shipping department was late with the goods for Canada—and he'll *never* forgive you for it!

Subconsciously, he really wants you to know how bad it was, that he did lose the promotion, and that's why he will inevitably throw some signals for you to dig deeper in this area: He will look quickly down and to the side. His eyes will dart furtively, away from you and then hard at you. He will sit back right after denying that that's what's on his mind. He will shoot exaggerated facial expressions of denial at you. He may rub his eye. He may look hard at something on his desk. He is likely to lean, turn, or move away. He is likely to touch or press the first joint of his index finger to the space between his upper lip and his nose. In any case, he will become fidgety and nervous quite suddenly, and he will fight to stifle this, which will result in more nervous signals.

Remember the children's game of "Hot or Cold" to find a hidden object? You kept looking back at the hider to verify if he or she was telling the truth, and to help measure just how hot or cold you were. It still works; you just haven't trusted the signals enough. Ask the prospect questions and *watch* while he answers. Smell while he answers. Feel the vibrations while he answers. His mouth is talking to you, but his entire body is, too. Tune in to the unspoken signals, and you will find out what he's really communicating.

> *You enter on a first call, expecting a tough customer,
> but the prospect is a puling, cowardly little wimp, not
> intimidating at all. Now what do you do with all your
> courage keys, confidence, and undauntable character?*
>
> Your confidence and undauntability are constants in
> your character. However, you must adjust the degree of
> your forcefulness and ebullience with this Milquetoast
> prospect. Do not crush his weak little hand or pull him
> toward you a bit or use a two-handed shake. Work farther
> back. Speak softly. Do not drill him with your best Power
> Stare. Be especially polite; take special care never to
> interrupt. Move slowly; you can't rush this personality.
> Be persistent, not pushy. You may still use the subtle
> push technique, but don't go in so far. Generally, soft-
> pedal all the stronger moves in your arsenal.

THE PROSPECT TAKES A CALL

What do you do when, in the middle of your presentation,
the prospect suddenly takes or makes a phone call? Clearly, if
he *makes* the call, it is particularly intended to put a dent in
your stature and shake your confidence, unless it is to call in
another buyer to hear your wonderful offer. Whether a call is
made or taken with no ulterior motive, it still leaves you
suddenly in the clumsy role of odd man out.

Contrary to popular misconception, man cannot concentrate on two disparate things at once. At best, the mind may
give the impression of doing this by switching rapidly between two or three or more subjects. Like one-handed juggling,
only one ball is actually in the hand at a time. So the prospect
on the phone is going to have to tune you out at some point
and address himself to the party on the line. The antagonistic
or indifferent prospect will not try to hide the fact and will let
you know, by turning and looking away, that he is no longer
tuned to your frequency. The "open" prospect will signal you
that he is not purposely tuning you out by offering you eye
contact, weak smiles, and expressions conveying his reactions

to the communications of the party on the phone. And customarily, you, the salesperson, smile and reflect his expressions back—without, of course, having any idea whence they arise. This little ritual is silly and unnecessary. It accomplishes nothing. When the prospect is focused on you, he sees a grinning fool who has no reason to grin, and when he focuses on the voice on the phone, he's really looking right through you, and all his pleasant expressions are empty, automatic masks.

Rather than follow the standard procedure, try this: The minute a prospect makes or takes a call, signal him that you are going to let him concentrate on it fully. Put your presentation on hold for the duration of the call, like Johnny Carson does with a guest for a commercial interruption. Withdraw into your own personal space but with a sense of mission. You have something to do; you don't waste time. Sit back. Cross your legs. Take something out of your briefcase and read it or makes entries in it. Like the Japanese when a shoji screen is closed, you do not hear the prospect's conversation; you grant him the impression of respecting his privacy by tuning out his phone conversation. At the end of the call, you put away whatever you took out and resume your presentation. If the call was long, it is wise to recap crucial sales points briefly.

TRUE LIFE STORY: Dealing with a Prospect Who Won't Get Off the Phone

A saleswoman we know had been trying to sell computer consulting services to the director of information services for a large corporation. She had secured two appointments with the man, but both presentations had been destroyed by the prospect's penchant for taking and making lots of calls—right through the meeting. She decided to give him one more shot, except this time she had a surprise in her briefcase. Every time he took or placed a call, she flipped open her case, pulled out a phone handpiece, and made a call herself. By her second call, the prospect understood how rude he had been, was impressed with the stature of the saleswoman, and fascinated by the radiophone itself. He told his secretary to hold all calls for a while, and our saleswoman friend was able to complete her presentation uninterrupted.

The radiophone-in-a-case rents for a pretty penny, but this saleswoman had gotten it for free (less her calls), on a one-day trial basis. She got the prospect's business for her firm, and he ended up leasing radiophones for five top executives in his company. It was a win-win-win presentation.

TRUE LIFE STORY: First Line of Defense

I discovered a very effective nonverbal technique when I was in a meeting with a prospect who started out indifferent and, in response to some accurate probing, began to shift into a hostile mode. I could see him building up steam for his attack. I wished for a moment I could slip into a suit of armor or dig a wide moat between us until he ran out of arrows.

Without any conscious thought, I placed my pen down on the desk between us, perpendicular to the axis formed by our lines of vision to one another. It was a special pen; it was gold and had my initials engraved on it. That pen somehow took on a crucial new identity, and I'm sure the prospect felt it as well as I. The pen became my first line of defense: a border, a line in the sand the other hombre wouldn't dare cross. I resolved that no matter how forceful his assault was, it would not penetrate the perimeter defined by my pen, and it never did.

Whether this first line of defense works to blunt some of the prospect's attack, I am unable to ascertain, but it always helps you, the salesperson, in holding your ground convincingly. You can establish your first line of defense with a pen, a pair of glasses, a calculator, or some other prop, as long as it's yours. Remember to remove it or move it to a less obstructive position when the prospect starts to pull in his horns, or after you have successfully dealt with his objection or hostility, and you feel him backing off.

DEALING WITH A SECONDARY PROSPECT

An unexpected second party, presumably someone who will have some say in the decision process, suddenly joins the meeting. You make rapid judgments on the new man's stature and power by his dress, grooming, carriage, and handshake. You rise, of course, to meet the second man. You conclude, for example, that the new man is a subordinate to the prospect, because he hesitates at the door, he waits for the prospect to assign him a seat, and because you and your prospect did not move to the second man's office, but he came to you. Still, this second entity may have the power to approve or veto purchases or to influence the decision-maker. Try your best to jockey seating positions around so that you don't end up playing "monkey in the middle." Ideally, from your position, you should be able to see both parties at once, without moving your head.

The second party will have a specific question or line of questions. You must direct your response to his probes, or attack in a measure corresponding to his level of intensity. That is, if he comes on like gangbusters with a tough question about your company's weird bookkeeping techniques, do not hope to defuse the attack by directing your response to the primary prospect. You must meet the new, flanking movement head-on, and for this performance, your primary prospect functions as audience. This circumstance places an extra burden on the salesman, as he is now not only playing directly to one party, but also being carefully observed by another. And the observer is not hampered in any way by having to deal with your moves or expressions, or show of confidence, because your performance, your power, is directed to the second party.

The Devil's Advocate

Frequently, the new person or persons called in to the meeting are brought in specifically to be Devil's Advocate. They are likely to be rather direct about attacking that aspect of your product or services that was, or is, lacking, and their special expertise in that area lends special weight to their questions or assertions. On the negative side, the position taken or questions raised by the Devil's Advocate may be essentially unanswerable by you—or worse, his suppositions may be undeniably true. On the positive, the prospect has evidenced some weaknesses or softening by having had to call in the reserves. In any case, if you can survive this new assault, you probably stand a good chance of turning the prospect around.

One of the most interesting things one learns in hand-to-hand combat training is the psychology of one-against-two. The odds are against you; your opponents are double your strength, can come at you from opposite sides and attack in your blind sector. You learn not to await your fate defensively, but to attack! First one opponent, head-on, driving him back, then, the moment the first opponent is off-balance, you attack the second, also with your full energy and concentration, driving him back or putting him out of commission, which allows you to turn your attention to the first opponent again.

The psychological states of the two opponents initially will work in your favor. They will be overconfident and consequently less intense and alert. They think they have an easy victory. Each man in a team is likely to fall prey to the misconception that each individual member of the team magnifies the group's strength by one power. So each member is likely to slacken off a bit, relying on the team effort to somehow cover the shortfall. When the object of a two-against-one assault suddenly launches a fearless attack, he is frequently victorious simply because his assailants are expecting him to act in an entirely different way.

The thousands of years of experience of martial-arts masters will not be lost on us. The salesperson or negotiator who finds himself in a one-against-two confrontation can handle it with similar techniques. Show no fear or hesitation. Meet the immediate assault with an undaunted confidence, evidenced by your posture, unruffled expression, your controlled and deliberate movements. Turn and face the new person directly. Offer steady, unflinching eye contact. You do not retreat during the probing and verbal attack mounted by the Devil's Advocate. You do not look to the primary prospect for sympathy or support. Even if he does sympathize with your plight at the hands of a brutal inquisitor, he feels you have lost and he is reassured in not buying from you.

You must meet and vanquish, or at least come to an impasse with, the Devil's Advocate before you can go any further with your pitch to the primary prospect. Your best possible resolution to a substantial objection is, of course, to promise to straighten things out: solve the problem or see that it's done the way they want it in the future. In the moment of making this commitment, you address it directly to the Devil's Advocate. You "push" imperceptibly closer and turn your face to face his directly, if it doesn't already. At the conclusion of your response or promise, you turn to the primary prospect, reorienting your entire physical concentration on him, "pin" him with your eyes, and repeat your personal assurance to him.

He is momentarily caught off-guard, because he has slid into the role of audience, and suddenly you are putting him onstage again as one of the performers. You have his full attention immediately. You turn back to the Devil's Advocate and ask him if he doesn't agree that if you solve the problem as indicated, he should have no further objections. Whatever technique you use to elicit a response from a Devil's Advocate, watch for his positive signal to the decision-maker. Regardless of what he says to you, if he does not send a positive signal to the primary prospect, he will feel he is corroborated in continuing to resist your sales efforts. The Devil's Advocate will respond to you verbally, and if he really means it he will turn to the decision-maker and throw him positive raised eyebrows combined with two quick, small nods of the head. Or a scrunched-up sounds-okay-to-me mouth.

He will sit back, assume a more relaxed position (the conflict being satisfactorily resolved), and look at the primary prospect—in a way, he throws the meeting back to the decision-maker. The specialist Devil's Advocate will often ask the decision-maker, with words and/or signals, if he can leave the meeting at this point, or the decision-maker will thank him and signal him to leave. In either case, the reinforcements are retiring from the field, and that's fine with you. Now you can return your undivided attention to the primary prospect.

The prospect's secretary keeps barging in with inter-ruptions.

Don't continue until the prospect has the new problem resolved, or at least put on hold. If the interruptions are simply too much, use it as an excuse to reschedule.

Other types of supporting players who may appear or may be invited to express an opinion to the decision-maker during your presentation are the Doubting Thomas, the Man Kicked Upstairs, and the Consultant or Expert.

Generally, as with the entrance of all new players, it is best to create the impression that you welcome, and/or agreed to invite, these people. You rise immediately, move to meet them, and welcome them into the office as if it were your own. You have the advantage at first, because they are intruding on your meeting, invading territory you have already staked out. But you disarm them by being warm and friendly and welcoming them into the room. If you feel especially confident, try indicating to them where they should sit, with your eyes and a hand gesture. It's amazing, perhaps even amusing, but people will usually sit where you direct them, even though they are in a familiar office and you are on a first call.

Normally, the decision-maker will make some introduction and opening remarks to establish who you are and what the problem is, and he will give the second party a clear clue as to what area he is to probe or comment on.

Briefly, the Doubting Thomas wants to be reassured, the Man Kicked Upstairs wants to be shown respect, and the Consultant or Expert wants you to verify or remark upon his expertise.

The Doubting Thomas

It's disheartening when you've worked up a sincere flow of enthusiasm to have some inveterate nay-sayer walk in and start deflating all your balloons. Be assured that these types generally lack courage. They always take the negative position because it's safer; they can never be accused of saying thumbs-up to something that didn't pan out. Because they lack courage, they can be intimidated by your display of strong and confident nonverbal signals. Stand up to these characters. Chances are the decision-maker doesn't like the Doubting Thomas himself. Tough it out and show that you are not bothered in the least by this intractable character. Let his lack of spirit act as a foil for your spirit.

TRUE LIFE STORY: One Way to Get Around a Nay-sayer:

I was presenting a rather complex package to a firm that was headed up by two brothers. Evidently the father, who had built the firm in the first place, thought it would be constructive to leave one rein to each brother. In any case, it was never clear who was really in charge. One thing became clear after the first three meetings: One of the brothers was active, progressive, and positive while the other was intransigent, stubborn, and opposed to any change in the status quo. You could never be sure whether both, or one or the other, would attend a scheduled meeting. When I presented to the first brother, I always came away with an answer, information, a direction to go, areas to develop. When I got stuck with the Doubting Thomas, everything I presented was shot down with no hope and no constructive alternatives.

I found a solution. I would prepare two different presentations. I would give new ideas and offer new products or techniques to the positive brother. And I would present progress reports to the negative brother.

When they both showed up at the same meeting, I would present the progress report first, playing almost entirely to the negative brother, and then present the new options or ideas to the positive brother. This tactic worked very well. They seemed to have a sort of understanding as to areas of responsibility, one venturing and forging ahead and the other criticizing and holding back. I don't think they are aware that outsiders may perceive them this way. Indeed, they may not be consciously aware of it themselves. But the salesperson who was not sensitive to this distinction, and who did not develop a technique to deal with it, could easily spend many fruitless hours barking up the wrong brother.

The Man Kicked Upstairs

The Man Kicked Upstairs is usually a pussycat. No one around there really listens to him anymore. He liked it better when he had real executive power. They're keeping him around for a number of reasons that may have little do to with real need. But he has worked hard to achieve a high level of success. He has stature and expects respect. If you give it to him with both barrels, he'll be rooting for you in a matter of moments. You move deferentially with the Chairman figure. You jump up a little quicker when he enters. Tip your head a fraction of an inch forward when you meet this character. Show respect and admiration but not fear. No one likes a cringer. Listen carefully, look at him openly and honestly. Don't stiffen up with the jitters; senior businessmen are comfortable with men who are comfortable with themselves. You may be asked to repeat a part of your presentation or to encapsulate the essence of it briefly. Face the Man Kicked Upstairs relaxed. Look him in the eye, sit back, and get to the point.

The Consultant or Expert

The Consultant or Expert can be a serious obstacle, primarily because of the friction of egos that is implicit in the confrontation between you and him. You are a well-informed salesperson with solid product knowledge and a well-researched perception of your potential client's needs. Here comes this Consultant, who probably set up his own business because he couldn't get a job, and he is charging your prospect a hefty fee for doing things like interfering with your brilliantly mounted sale of the year. The dismaying thing about it is that you realize very early on that the Expert, who is supposed to evaluate you and/or your products or services, probably knows less than either you or your prospect. But you do not jump up and ask why your prospect's company has retained this person. You do not laugh in his face and throw him bodily out of the room. You listen attentively. You show fearless posture and eye contact. You take opportunities to recognize and appreciate the Consultant's expertise.

After all, his greatest concern is that you will reveal him for a sham. Move immediately to put the Expert at ease. Acknowledge that his role is warranted, and he'll back off immediately. You can conclude the confrontation with this character in an exchange of inoffensive generalities. Once he recognizes you're not the enemy, he turns neutral or even becomes an ally. Try to get these signals to him as soon as possible and try, of course, to make them subtle enough so the prospect won't pick up on your strategy.

Occasionally an Expert is intractable and unyielding and really needs a trophy head to show he's worth his retainer. When you find yourself face-to-face with this monster, you must move mercilessly but gracefully to fight fire with fire. (Presumably you have done your homework, and your knowledge of the business at hand is extensive and up-to-date.) Face him head-on. Focus on him entirely. Move in gradually. Ask him a question he can't possibly answer. Calmly. In control. If he bypasses your probe and attacks you on another front, you throw a hard, knowing, conspiratorial look at the primary prospect, and return to strip away the mask of the Expert once again. Ask him to compare two new developments in state-of-the-art manufacturing that would clearly improve ergonomics and product reliability. Make something up if you have to. Keep chipping away; once the Expert's shell is cracked, his credibility runs out rather fast. So he won't spend the next five months bad-mouthing you (if he holds on to this account that long), you give him a face-saving rabbit hole out: You allow that you understand that his expertise is in a slightly different area, and recent developments in your field are virtually privileged information.

In any case, once you decide to go to blows with the Expert, go for the jugular, but never lose control. Once you realize that the consultant is definitely going to kill your sale and put your butt in his trophy room, you might as well take the wraps off and get down to it.

The developing altercation is counterproductive, and the primary prospect will probably intercede and defuse the conflict. Even if you lose the consultant, you may have won some respect from the prospect, and you are more likely to find access to him again at a later date, perhaps after the consultant has drifted on to other pastures.

You feel tremendous pressure in your chest, like the weight of a piano, and you feel like you can scarcely breathe.

As a salesperson, you should recognize this as a simple anxiety attack. (At least you'd better hope it is, because if it isn't, then a) there's a piano on your chest; or b) it's a heart attack.) Relax. Breathe softly and easily. Close your eyes, if possible. Concentrate on any comfortable, secure fact or moment in your life. Concentrate on your courage key or the URY. The attack is all in your mind, as they say, so use your mind to vanquish it. I find there is much less likelihood of such attacks if I limit my intake of stimulants, such as coffee, tea, or anything else containing caffeine.

The point in all this is that you want to show that you are not intimidated personally by an attack on your product or services. You want to leave the door open for a future presentation when you will be selling the new, improved, updated, repriced whatever you sell. In other words, you are in there to sell two things: yourself and the product. You represent the product or service to a degree substantially beyond that of impersonal agent, enumerator of data, or demonstrator of equipment or techniques. To some degree or another, you are a part of the product. When the prospect has a strong and undeniable charge against the product, and there is no possible way to resolve the problem in that meeting, you must preserve *your* integrity, equanimity, and enthusiasm. The prospect may be dead set against your product at this point, but if he is still favorably impressed by you, you can get back in to turn him around. You get additional shots at him with your new or additional information or procedures. You remain controlled, resolute, and undaunted, under attack, either from a second party, or from the prospect himself, because *people will admire you for it*. No one likes a coward.

RESPONDING TO OBJECTIONS

No one likes a traitor, either. You do not betray your own company in the presence of a prospect. Ever. You probably know this intuitively or have learned it in sales training. And you may well have been careful to avoid verbally debasing or verbally agreeing with the thrust of a prospect attack on your product. But are you conscious of the nonverbal signals of betrayal you may transmit in the very instant you are verbally rebutting or denying the attack?

You are in the middle of being attacked. You signal silent agreement with the prospect's objections if you:

- tilt your head forward and/or slightly to the side
- look around or down with nervous eye movements
- swivel back in your chair, opening your arms and holding onto chair arms or back
- "collapse," that is, let your carriage and "upness" fall
- shrug your shoulders
- look at an angle (to the side and up), almost in apology
- make any facial expression that signals apologetic agreement
- start to make quick, jerky movements
- let your arms dangle over the arms of the chair
- scratch your head or face, stroke your chin
- blink excessively.

Be aware that the prospect is studying your reactions even while he is stating his objections. This is a crucial moment when, if you can control yourself, you will win psychological control of the meeting. This is when, even before you are saying anything concrete with your verbal response, you are saying it all with your nonverbal signals. This is when you pin the prospect's eyes with yours, when you carry yourself "up" and orient yourself head-on, when you slow down and control your deliberate gestures and expressions, when you "push" slowly forward as you respond verbally.

ANTAGONISTIC PROSPECT SIGNALS

Let's analyze the prospect's signals during a critical objection. They have some family resemblances to the initial antagonistic signs we discussed on pages 36 and 37, but there are some important differences and additions to fit the new situation.

Even if the prospect's voice is soft and he couches all his terms in gentle euphemisms, his nonverbals will let you know exactly what he is saying.

He may point at you, either with his finger or some object. Pointing is intended to "pin you down," and also is designed to test or belittle your status. He rubs his nose. He's hiding behind his hand with this gesture, giving himself a chance to work up a new mask to hide more intense emotions.

He will occasionally lean forward in his chair, palms down, a bellicose posture meant to intimidate.

His brows will knit and his eyes narrow, in spite of his best efforts to mask facial expressions. In unguarded movements, an antagonistic prospect's face will show flashes of stress in these two areas.

His mouth will dry, almost as if he has no taste for this business. He will frequently moisten his lips with a quick move of the tongue.

His body gestures are tight and uncomfortable. Muscles that are stiffened with discomfort and "armoring" are revealed in cramped, stiff movements.

There are three kinds of nonverbal signals transmitted to a salesperson by a prospect:

1. Those he wants you to read and understand.
2. Those he does *not* want you to read and understand.
3. Those he *subconsciously* wants you to read and understand.

A prospect who lets you catch him surreptitiously checking his watch obviously wants you to understand that he wants to get this over with as soon as possible. Either he is really running late, or he is trying to let you know he hasn't awarded you a high status factor and considers the meeting essentially lost time. He may have plenty of time and is using the watch-checking ploy to rattle your confidence. In any case, this functions clearly as a good example of a signal he intends for you to understand.

Signals a prospect does not want you to read would include any sign of vacillation or character weakness. When you score lots of points with significant new information that overcomes his major objection, and he realizes that he really ought to be buying your product—but he resists because he doesn't want to go through the hassle of breaking up with his present supplier—he will work hard to cover signals that would reveal crumbling resistance. Watch carefully for a quick flurry of covering moves and expressions right after you deliver a strong point or product feature. The prospect may not have any idea which gestures and expressions he is likely to "blurt out" at this moment, but he will normally worry that you might intuitively pick up on one or several of them. The prospect wants to run into the wings or jump behind a piece of scenery for a moment until he can regain control of his face and body. Covering gestures include:

- a forced cough with hand over the mouth and all the accompanying postures and gestures
- getting up and moving away from the desk
- turning away, looking away, picking up some item or paper on the desk and focusing attention on it
- rubbing or scratching a part of the face with a hand (a mask)
- an overly broad, exaggerated gesture or series thereof
- a sequence of quick, jerky, forced moves

- a sudden raising of the voice (frequently accompanied by a change of subject)
- a series of quick, forced head nods. *Only the first two or three are genuine;* the additional head nods are quickly added on to dissipate and camouflage the positive signal inadvertently sent by the first three nods.

Covering signals are intended to hide the prospect's softening and approach to surrender, so read them for what they are. Covering gestures are, of necessity, broader and more easily discerned than the minute, subtle flashes of uncamouflaged, involuntary signals of a weakening prospect. But the prospect worries that his true, involuntary signals will be received and easily decoded, no matter how subtle, so he erects a smoke screen of grossly obvious covering gestures. We see right through the smoke to the beginnings of a white flag being waved over the battlements.

Signals a prospect does not consciously send but subconsciously wants you to understand are by definition (if we accept that will is conscious) involuntary. We have a dichotomy: the prospect doesn't want to send conscious signals, as such, but he subconsciously wants us to receive and decode them. It's akin to a statesman speaking off the record, or one who wishes to communicate as an unidentified spokesperson. The audience (salesperson) is meant to get the message, but not so directly that the communicator can be held responsible or attacked directly for the content of the information.

For example, the prospect really wants to give you a chance, but he lacks the courage to tell his present supplier that the party is over. This prospect will subconsciously signal you to help him, to give him a real good push (a real solid reason would be nice, too). His signals will consist mainly of nervous jerkiness the closer he gets to saying "yes." He seems to ponder, stroke his chin, gaze into space or out the window. Then suddenly, a quick, nervous, but weak gesture accompanies another question or objection. His general body movements are characterized by hesitation. There is a pleading in the eyes. This prospect is begging for help. He really wants you to take the bull by the horns and force him to act. When you feel this sort of climate developing, go for the close fast and hard.

The prospect needs ammunition for the confrontation he dreads with his present supplier. You have to provide him with the goods, the facts and figures, and the unique product benefits, but you also have to give him the human, emotional ammunition; the willpower and resoluteness. Your credibility and enthusiasm have to more than offset the anguish and disappointment the previous supplier can potentially lay on the prospect.

Another example is a situation we discussed earlier, in which the prospect showed more anger than he meant to, but nevertheless wanted the salesperson to know just how angry he was. Consciously, the prospect didn't want to reveal a lack of control or excess of sensitivity, so he stifled some of the ire created by the late delivery of goods and consequent probable loss of promotion. If this prospect genuinely does not intend to buy from your company because of some incident or misunderstanding, he will never let you know that's what's bothering him. If you don't know what the problem is, you can't address and solve it. Thus, if you have a chance, if the prospect subconsciously wants to give you a chance, he will start to give you nonverbal clues to lead you in the right direction. Naturally, if you miss all the clues, he will eventually conclude you are not terribly bright after all, and he will discontinue helping you get to the root of his disaffection. As you probe verbally, watch his nonverbal signals at least as carefully as you listen to his words.

A prospect who consciously has no intention to buy, or who intends to make it hard for you for one reason or another, may, in spite of his conscious intentions, signal you that he can be persuaded; there is a chink in the armor, and you should keep on trying. Any one or several of the "opening up" or positive signals listed on pages 71–72 may provide the clue. They may be so subtle that reading them may depend more on your intuition than on your study of specific gestures and expressions. Knowing, somehow, that your prospect can be landed is an experience you may have called a hunch. Your hunch was most likely based on the array of nonverbal signals emanating from your prospect, signals you may not have been able to isolate or label but physical signals just the same.

THE AURA

But there are other supporting signals that may not be described physically. There is an aura, or personality field, that surrounds and emanates from the prospect (and from all of us, for that matter). Some call it "vibrations"—remember "good vibes" and "bad vibes"?

While we have lost the ability, at least on the conscious level, to "see" and read the aura, we find ourselves responding to something about the other person, something visceral that we sense like a dog "smells" fear. As with every other human faculty, your ability to sense and interpret someone's aura may be developed and fine-tuned. Start by accepting that the aura is there. Let yourself experience it.

Your interest in the aura is, first, in the one you generate around yourself, and, second, in the one emanating from your prospect. Although we are not fluent in the language of the aura, we can learn to pick up its essential signals—"Yes," "No," "I like you," "I don't like you," "I am weak and afraid," "I am powerful and not afraid."

You recognize that you have at times consciously controlled your own aura. You turn a corner in a strange neighborhood and find yourself face-to-face with a large, ugly, angry-looking dog. You immediately direct your aura not to show your fear, but to project friendliness or fearlessness. The dog heard or smelled your arrival before you appeared, so he had already prepared his ugly, angry, fearless aura to fend you off. Nine times out of ten, the beast is glad not to have to expose himself to direct conflict, so he happily receives your transmission of friendship or fearlessness, and he comes over to make friends, or he skulks off into the underbrush. If, on the other hand, you project abject terror, the beast will decode it immediately and will move to intimidate you further, may attack, and, in a natural environment, may turn you into instant warm lunch.

It *is* a jungle out there, and you must learn to receive and read your prospect's aura, just as any other predator that intends to survive and prevail.

Your prospect's aura will release signals he does not want it to send because it is difficult for him to control. He may not even be aware of it (ideally, you have read this book and he has not). He has to concentrate on his verbal fencing, on his gestures and expressions, and it is work enough just to keep these elements transmitting similar signals. If you feel a positive signal from the prospect's aura, trust it in spite of all the negative verbiage, covering gestures, and expressions he can produce. Even if you only sense a mild hint of a positive aura, hang in there. The aura is the most direct hot line to the deep-seated, "true" reactions and feelings of the prospect.

At this point, let us say the prospect decides to let the salesperson have it. He launches into the explanation of the event or circumstances that created and have sustained his aversion to the salesperson's product. The prospect drops all masks and covering gestures for a moment and lets it all hang out. His hands work into gnarled fists. His skin gets ruddier. He pins the salesperson with his eyes. Muscles in his face and neck stand out. Blood vessels swell. The array of body signals is familiar to anyone who has put a serious dent in Dad's car.

It would appear that this prospect is trying to make clear that he has absolutely no intention of buying your product. Actually, he is giving you a foothold. He is giving you a piece of information you can work with. At least you are no longer totally in the dark.

RESPONDING TO AN ATTACK

Your nonverbal response to a full-fledged direct attack is the single most important sequence in the sales confrontation. The prospect is unloading all of his most powerful ammunition in this salvo. It might lean toward a more exaggerated physical display of emotion, or it might be a quieter, but even more telling, verbal diatribe on problems for which you have no immediate solutions. In any case, the prospect is communicating from a level that is closer to the primitive, visceral entity than to the civilized, rational Homo sapiens. Consequently, he is going to tune in on your nonverbal response more acutely than your verbal one. Indeed, he may not even comprehend your verbal explanation or your promise to solve or remove the problem, so intensely is he concentrating on your nonverbal display at this moment.

Since he thinks he's really got you, he expects you to back off, lean back, look down or away, go limp or collapse body or limbs, open your hands and arms, as if in surrender and exhaustion, and move in faint, weak, nervous shrugs and flickers.

Whether he's right or wrong, whether your verbal response is a promise to effect a remedy, an easy righting of a misunderstanding, or a bit of instant flimflam that sounds like a solution, your nonverbal sequence is the same.

During the attack, you sustain your "up," but relaxed, general posture. You form a defensive bulwark with your hands and arms. If there are arms on your chair, rest your elbows on them, put your hands together in the classic log-cabin clasp, just in front of your solar plexus and collarbone— not too high, or it'll look like you're praying. If there are no arms on your chair, lay your clasped hands in your lap, still pointing the corner of the log-cabin clasp directly at the prospect. Don't let your wrists go limp. You do not, at any point, lean back, turn away or to the side. You maintain steady, unflinching eye contact. You may show attention to the prospect's words by facial expressions or positive head-nodding, but never by apologizing. What you are conveying at this point is: "I understand what you are saying and I appreciate how you feel, but you are wrong." Or "You may have been right in the past, but that's all been changed since then." Or "You have a legitimate problem, but it was based on circumstances I can and will change promptly."

You start to stammer and stutter when the pressure builds.

Slow down. Take a deep breath before you speak. Don't start to talk until you have laid out the sentence in your mind. Try speaking a bit louder.

At the end of his attack, you do not move back or look away, even for an instant. You launch into your reply immediately. As you make your verbal reply, you release your hands and arms to gesture. In your mind, you estimate how long your reply will take—ten seconds, twenty, whatever. As you reply, and ideally through the duration of your reply, you push your face and upper torso imperceptibly closer to the prospect.

This push or lean may only cover one inch over a period of fifteen seconds. You don't want to move more than three inches total, because then what you are doing may be noticed and become a distraction. As you get closer, your gestures must be slower and smaller in scope, since the closer you are, the bigger and faster they seem. At the conclusion of your reply, you shift subtly back to your original position.

You can effect the same push when you are standing, working to a standing prospect, and even to a sitting prospect. An example: You are making a presentation, standing, to a number of seated prospects. In your reply to an attack from one of the prospects, you approach and lean forward a bit toward the attacker as you respond. In this situation, the scope of your movement may well exceed three inches, and it may be perceptible. It will still be effective, however. Greater movement is expected at greater distance. Your shift back to the original position functions as a punctuation to your response. It says, "I am concluding now, because I am confident I have honestly and sincerely met and resolved your objections." Also, the shift back to the original position allows you to respond again to another assault.

The subtle push toward the prospect during the response to an attack is the single most important movement in your repertoire. It signals a sincere, fearless, confident reply. Even if the prospect doesn't want to believe a word you say, he still believes in you. You can bring him closer to your position. You can still sell him. No doors have been slammed. You didn't wave a flag of surrender—you are not beaten. If, in your response, you promise to come back with some verification of your explanation or solution to his real problem, he will see you again, and he is much more likely to accept and believe you. If, on the other hand, you respond to an attack by falling limply back, opening your arms, and letting them dangle in surrender, looking away and making faint, weak moves, you have signaled surrender and defeat. The prospect has made his point and, in the same sweep, eliminated you as a serious contender for his business.

Curiously, just after your gestures of surrender and defeat, the prospect will seem much more friendly and understanding. And why not? He has just beaten you, gotten you to throw in the towel, and doesn't have to worry about turning you down anymore. You relax in the warmth of this newfound friendliness, figuring you have somehow gotten the prospect to like you by agreeing that your product is overpriced or whatever. And suddenly he is showing you out, in a friendly way. And he probably will never see you again, in a friendly way. You don't want a friend (yet)! You want a customer. Respond to an attack, any attack, with the held position and the subtle, offensive push. Build your credibility and display your character.

To help yourself stay calm and relaxed when you are under fire, breathe long, slow, and deep. Make sure you have a good lungful of air before you initiate your verbal reply. If you're sitting properly, you'll already have more lung capacity than someone who is bent concave or slumped over. When you reply to an attack, you should either raise your voice slightly (without losing your deep, persuasive pitch), or lower it substantially for effect and then let it build gradually in volume through your reply. This is the auditory equivalent to the offensive push, closer to the prospect. As a rule, it is dangerous to lower the volume of your voice substantially, for fear of sounding timid or weak. But if you know what you are doing, if you feel in solid control of yourself, and if you are confident about what you are saying, lowering the voice level can be more effective than raising it.

Evaluate the prospect's voice. If he is roaring, on the edge of losing control, it's very effective for you to speak softly. Softly but clearly. You don't want a hollering match. On the other hand, if he's speaking softly in his attack, you ought to use a slightly louder volume. Speaking at low volume is a sign of status. Therefore, it works best with up-scale prospects. Don't speak softly to blue-collar or down-scale prospects; it'll be wasted on them. To lower-middle Americans, a soft voice is a sign of lack of conviction.

In any case, always speak loud enough to be easily heard by everyone present. It is an affectation, and a counterproductive one, to whisper so that people must strain to make out what you are saying. Yes, it does force them to be utterly silent and to concentrate on what you are saying, but it will also aggravate and cause their attention span to shorten.

EXERCISE: Always Being Prepared for Surprises

Are you prepared to withstand an attack on your veracity, an objection, sarcasm, or laughter, at any point in your presentation? Here's an exercise you can do that will help you learn to ride out sudden, unexpected squalls. All you need is a cheap cassette tape recorder.

Start the recorder. Wait a while, a minute or so, then record your voice saying "Bull! I don't believe that." About thirty seconds later, say something like "Don't be ridiculous." A while later say "That's not true." Then, later, chuckle or laugh. A minute later say something like "Not in my experience." And continue, with such interjections, until you've covered a time span that will equal your average presentation. Space the interruptions at odd intervals and don't overdo it.

Now rewind. Start your presentation, and start the recorder on playback. The "prospect's" interruptions may occur at any time, which prepares you for handling surprises without revealing your dismay. To vary the incidence of the interruptions, just start the recorder earlier or later with each exercise. And remember, it's not fair to turn the recorder off or hurl it down the cellar stairs.

THE TURNING POINT

Let us say the prospect's central problem has been revealed, and you have dealt with it. The prospect signals that a crucial turning point has been achieved. He leans back. He crosses his legs comfortably. Muscular tension slips from his body somewhat. He discontinues shielding his mouth and face with his hands. He begins to offer more reciprocal eye contact.

You have samples or articles of product-claim verification to take out of your briefcase. You do not lean and bend over to get things out but instead bring the case up onto your lap. Here you have easier access and better visibility. Because you placed the items you will need for this meeting in a special pocket, you find them instantly. You return the case to stand on the floor next to your chair, and keep the documents or items on your lap. You do not spread things out on the prospect's desk. Rather, you hand the papers or items to the prospect as you introduce them and explain what they are. The best time to pass something to a prospect is when he looks away from you and at the items in your hand.

Do not thrust things at the prospect; tender them slowly. Let him take things out of your hand and draw them into his personal territory.

When you take notes or make entries on a paper or pad, or read something that's on your lap or knee, don't tilt your head so far forward that your face is obliterated by your thinning crown. You keep your face "cheated" up so it is visible to the prospect. You will find good examples of "cheating" in TV newscasters, who keep their faces to the camera while reading a late bulletin, or in movie starlets, who somehow manage to keep pretty faces more or less turned to the camera—even while being attacked by werewolves.

If you must read something aloud to the prospect, look up from the printed material as often as you can without losing your place or chopping up your flow. This is something you can improve greatly with a little practice.

EXERCISE: Reading Copy Aloud

This is something that will also come in handy if you have to give a prepared speech. Anyone can read three or four words and then look up and repeat the words aloud.

What you want to do is push the amount that you can pack and hold in your memory, thereby reducing the number of times—and the duration of the moments—when you must eyeball the printed copy. The trick is to scan for the verb and the direct object of the verb. Once you have those two items in mind, the rest seems to fall into place easily. And who cares if you leave out an occasional adjective, adverb, or conjunction? By picking up verbs and objects, you will eventually be able to repeat two or more sentences without looking back at the copy or script. The intimacy you build with the additional eye contact you can offer is well worth the few hours of practice you should devote to this exercise.

When all the items, papers, or whatever else are on the prospect's desk or in his hands, you want to explain further, in response to his inquiries perhaps, but ideally, you want to do it from his point of view. Simple enough: Get up and circle around so that you are beside him, looking almost over his shoulder. Bend at the waist. Don't squat, even if you are a hardball catcher.

Your arm or shoulder may brush against the prospect's during this sequence. Fine. Don't avoid this contact. And when it occurs, use it to gauge his personal reaction to your personality. If the prospect is a member of the opposite sex, you're moving over very thin ice here. Physical contact at this point, especially on a first call, could be easily misunderstood. It has to really read as accidental and natural. Don't try to make it happen. If it does, accidentally and naturally, use it. Any inconspicuous, inoffensive, natural physical contact between you and the prospect can be functional in helping break down walls and relaxing inhibitions.

The prospect keeps touching you, but not in a sexual way.

Good! They like you. They are going to buy from you eventually. Don't rush, but move toward the close. Don't be intimidated by such touching. Your prospect's background and culture may have something to do with it. Don't try to touch back, especially if the prospect is older or above you in stature.

Once again, on the question of touch, it is helpful to weigh the background and nationality of the prospect. It is safer and easier to touch Southern and Eastern Europeans and Middle Easterners. WASPs and Northern Europeans are much less touchable. This corresponds with their sense of personal territory or space. Class also figures in the formula: Upper-middle-class people don't like to be touched by strangers or light acquaintances; lower-middles aren't so untouchable. People with status will touch underlings, but they don't want to be touched back. Their touch is used to remind the underling of the pecking order.

If you touch a prospect who doesn't want to be touched, you'll feel it instantly. There will be tension in the area touched, sometimes accompanied by an actual moving away, however slight. A mild flicker of discomfort may flash over the face. Most of these signals are too subtle to be seen as such. But you will recognize them immediately. Don't fret; it may be a mild case of bad vibes or personality conflict. The prospect may simply be one of those types who is uncomfortable being touched. Continue your presentation and refrain from physical contact.

Once the prospect has finished examining the papers or samples on his desk, you return to your seat.

> *You are in the prospect's domain. You bend over to pick up something, and your pants or skirt splits open in back. The noise of the rip is too loud to pretend it didn't happen.*
>
> If you don't have a tiny sewing kit (which you should), ask the prospect if he does, or if he would ask his assistant if he does or can get one. Somewhere in the office, someone should have a needle and thread. While you're waiting, be human and don't be afraid to laugh at yourself. Continue your presentation. When the sewing kit arrives, try to exit from the room by backing out of it. Go to the bathroom and sew up the split as best you can. Don't take a lot of time. If there was no needle and thread, you can rig something with tape. A woman may be able to cover the tear by rotating the skirt so that the seam is at the side and then tying a scarf to hang over it. If you are too mortified to go on effectively, ask the prospect for another appointment.

Should the prospect respond to your items of display or verification with a positive remark, you know from your sales training to repeat and support his remark. Augment the effect of this technique by supporting and encouraging with nonverbal signals also: Smile a bit, proudly and affirmatively, and open and close your repetition and corroboration with a positive double nod of the head. Remember, two or three positive nods look real and sincere, four or more nods are forced and phony. There is no exact prescribed moment when you should reward your prospect with a smile and positive head nod. Instinct and the content and style of your language will determine where to use these positive signs of approval and reward.

It is hard to accept that you can be rewarding, approving, and affirming a person who has just been ignoring, attacking, or rejecting you, but that is exactly what you can and must do. Through all the anguish, the flak and static of indifference, objection and antipathy, you must wait for, seek and find, the positive spark, the toehold, the crack in the door you must build on. And you must, in addition to your verbal approbation, encourage your prospect to continue on this positive train of thought with positive expressions and movements of approval and reward.

For example, the prospect says, "Well, you certainly are persistent."

You reply, "Yes, I am persistent, because I know our new franistan will solve your problem of (fill in the blank) and result in greater (fill in the blank)." You inhale and sit tall during the compliment, for that's what it is. You smile and offer solid eye contact as you initiate your reply. You also execute a subtle but unmistakable double-positive nod. At the conclusion of your remark, you punctuate with another double-positive nod, and a single or double hand gesture and facial expression that throws the positive surge of the compliment back to the prospect.

As a prospect moves from skepticism or hostility to "maybe," he will reveal this shift first in a number of nonverbal signals. Generally, his movements slow down a bit, his gestures are less concrete and single-minded. The muscular tension of the antagonistic prospect relaxes, as is apparent in muscles of the face, jaw, and hands. Posture changes from rigid and uncomfortable, from defensive hunching and fending off, to more relaxed positions. The prospect may cup or stroke his chin with his hand; he may scratch behind his ear. He may unbutton his jacket, loosen his tie, stretch his legs. He offers better eye contact. His expression mirrors yours more often, his single and double head nods are encouraging and indicate he is paying closer attention. He won't blink as long or as often. (A large percentage of blinking is a kind of editing you out. A prospect will blink less when he is less turned off by your image.) He assumes a more open body position. His eyes also seem to open a bit more. His lower lip will move forward a bit and therefore seem larger or plumper.

THE INFORMAL AREA

It is a very positive sign when the prospect invites you into the informal area of his office. If a prospect intends to turn you down categorically, he will almost always do it from behind a desk barricade. Whether the prospect invites you directly into his informal area, or after you have been flanking his desk for a while, try to let him sit first or at least indicate to you where he will sit. With low, deep chairs or sofa, and a low coffee table, you don't want to be seated directly opposite the prospect. If you do, you are likely to look as if you're all legs, topped by an undersize head. It's an especially clumsy situation for a woman with a male prospect. Even though she is trying to deemphasize her legs, they are placed on conspicuous, unavoidable display. In this environment, the salesperson should try to sit at a ninety-degree angle to the prospect. From this vantage point, you can lean into the prospect's point of view to see the printed matter or samples, or you can also turn your torso and neck so that your face is head-on to the prospect's, to add weight and conviction to serious statements. (We examine sitting position strategy in later sections on men selling to women, women selling to men, and conference-room selling.)

> *The prospect turns into a regular monologuist; he rambles on and on. You don't get a chance to ask a question because he'll answer them all eventually. How can you present to this prospect when he won't shut up? What should you do?*

Listen.

If you have to move papers or other material from his desk to another location in the room, gather and organize them carefully and deliberately. Do not sweep them up in a helter-skelter bunch and dash to the new location. Do not pack anything away that you or your prospect might conceivably want to refer to again. It is best, in fact, to leave much of your material in plain view for as long as possible. The weight of your verification and the impact of your colorful, brilliantly creative sales materials are burning their message into his brain longer. The prospect will not be constantly staring into your eyes. His gaze will wander, and it is clearly preferable if it settles on your sales aids than on an ashtray. If you have items to leave, hand them to the prospect; don't just drop them on a desk or table. The prospect is going to look at something you hand to him, and as you talk about it, it will have greater impact if it's in his hand(s), and he has to lay it down and open it up instead of you doing it for him. Obviously, if you have a clever sales gizmo that opens in special ways, pops up and plays "The Star-Spangled Banner" when you pull the little string, you do it for the prospect the first time. Then you let him play with it himself.

Beware of chairs and sofas in the informal area. They are usually much more comfortable and invite you to sprawl back and relax. It's almost impossible to sell effectively from this position. Sustain your "up," but relaxed posture. The prospect may have invited you into the informal area to get you to lighten up on him. He may feel that the casual, sociable atmosphere of the informal area will cause you to relax the energy and concentration of your sales effort. You, on the other hand, look on this environment as a place where the prospect's adamant sales resistance will soften up. In any case, an invitation into the informal area almost always indicates the lessening or disappearance of several layers of guardedness and reserve. The shields erected automatically at the outset of a first encounter are gradually dropped. The desk barricade is deemed unnecessary, and the new setting makes for less guarded communication. Consider that by coming out from behind the desk, the prospect is not only forsaking the barricade between him and you, he is also removing the one *you* may be hiding behind. He calculates that you are more likely to speak more sincerely in the informal area, that you'll reveal—even unwittingly, with your body language—more of the truth. He hopes you'll become friendlier and more sincere, and you'll tell or hint that he's right, there are still several serious bugs in the new distribution system or whatever. But you know what's on his mind, consciously or unconsciously, so you won't fall prey to this simple but effective ploy. You act friendlier, you assume more relaxed positions—without slumping or tilting to the side and without putting your feet up on anything—but you stay on course. He's brought you here to disarm you, but in the same stroke, he's dropping his own guard to some degree. Use it.

THE DOCUMENT OF COMMITMENT

Don't look to achieve a surprise effect by suddenly producing something from your bag like pulling a rabbit out of a top hat. Prospects don't like to be surprised. It knocks them momentarily off-balance, and they will overcompensate to regain their equilibrium. The prospect will feel manipulated and will reward you with increased resistance. If you feel the time has come to produce a contract or binding document of any kind, announce it first, just before you hand it to the prospect. Try to get him actually to take it in his hand; there is less of a tendency for him to recoil from it. If he lays it down on the table in front of him, leave it there until you have a reason to pick it up or touch it again. If you have any cause whatsoever to refer to the document of commitment, do make a point of touching it, handling it, and tendering it to the prospect to hold or touch.

If you see last-minute reluctance in the face of your prospect when you produce a document of commitment, lay it in plain view, but move the focus of the presentation back to some area of product benefit. Your goal at this point is to discover exactly why the prospect is still on the fence. As you review product benefits and verbally probe for the trouble area or obstacle, you must tune in very acutely to the prospect's nonverbal signals. If there is any chance of making this sale, the prospect will at some point slip across an invisible line into an area in which he will *allow you to sell him*. That is, he has not given himself over yet to making the commitment; he has not swallowed the hook, but he is circling the bait with interest. He won't say a word to indicate that he has come this far, but he will communicate it through nonverbal signals. He will underline his talk with broader, more relaxed gestures. He will offer more attentive eye contact. He will lean or turn his torso and shoulders toward you, and then suddenly lean or turn a bit away again. He will stroke his chin, pat his hair, scratch his neck or the back of his head. He will take an occasional deep breath.

THE CLOSING

The salesperson must not waver or offer any sympathy at this point. You are going for a close. You smell the close, you can practically taste it. You line up your shoulders and face with the prospect's, head-on. You let your cordial smile evaporate from your face. You pin the client with your eyes. You start your imperceptible push toward the client. In deadly seriousness, with not a hint of cordiality or friendliness, and all your concentration, you urge the prospect to make a commitment. There must be no embarrassment or hesitation in your character now, verbal or nonverbal, conscious or subconscious. You have no smile or cordiality in your demeanor, because such a display from you can be picked up by the prospect and used by him for his escape. He could easily smile right back, a wonderful covering expression, and say no. By being deadly serious in your approach to the close, you make it much more difficult for the prospect to turn you down. It is much simpler for him to deny you something that you seem to take lightly.

Your shift to earnest seriousness is very effective because you are moving from the earlier projections of "up" and relaxed but enthusiastic, controlled, and confident, warm and charismatic—to an intensely serious, direct request with no escape hatches.

This moment—requesting the commitment—is the one in which the pressure on you to generate positive and supportive sales signals is the greatest. It is also the one in which a reluctant prospect will be frantically searching your face, tone of voice, gestures, and posture for any hint of weakness, hesitation, or doubt. *You give him nothing.* If he is going to turn you down, let it be because of some prior, external condition, or some unanswerable, unsolvable fault of your product, *not because of you*. Even if you lose the sale, it's nice to know it was because of factors totally beyond your control. Great performers always give their best performance, even if the play or screenplay is weak, and they prevail in the end; they advance their careers and keep their fans. Even though the critics pan the show or film, they'll praise a good individual performance. The dedication to give the maximum performance, regardless of the conditions, is what makes stars stars. And it's what is going to make you a star salesperson.

If the prospect is on the verge of making a commitment, he will signal it by a combination of "opening up" gestures, but they will be hesitant, broken, indefinite movements. He will look at the document of commitment, then glance at the salesperson, then off into space as he ponders the pros and cons. He will move back, relax, and then sit up and forward to examine the document.

The prospect's glance is your cue to produce and proffer a pen, if one isn't lying there already. Do not offer the pen directly to the prospect. First, use it to make some prominent points on the contract or order form. If there are entries to be made or clauses to be added, you execute them. Put prominent Xs next to the spaces for the prospect's signature. The point in all this is to make the document seem less threatening. By writing on it, you reduce the cold, pristine, unfeeling legal instrument to an approachable extension of human assurances and guarantees. You wrote on it; now it's his turn to write on it.

Don't be surprised if there is a sudden, final show of resistance at this point. The prospect wants to elicit from you the strongest possible personal assurance that he will be satisfied, that you will deliver and the goods will be in order and above specs. He's asking you to assure him that you will personally take it upon yourself to make sure that your company doesn't do something to jeopardize his job. After all, you may be the only human connection this prospect will ever see representing your company. Whom will he call when something seems to be going wrong? Still, in all seriousness, you give the prospect the reassurance he wants. Your eyes must not flicker. Your voice must not waver or rise in pitch. You are sincere about your reassurance, because when you make it, you really mean it.

The prospect who balks at the edge of commitment is tripped up either by one snag that has loomed suddenly in his estimation or a general fear of making commitments. It is jarring to have this happen when you are so near the close, but you must not display your dismay. Go to work immediately to find out just what's on his mind. If you can't exactly pin it down (he may not know himself), you reiterate product benefits again, probe to find out if you have left any questions unanswered, and go for the commitment again. You must sustain your mood of seriousness throughout the wrenchings and writhings of the reluctant prospect-on-the-brink. Don't let him off the hook with a smile or a gesture of frustration or anxiety. *Do not sympathize with him or be embarrassed for your own pertinacity.* You only want one thing from this prospect at this point: a commitment.

Do not point or poke the pen at the prospect as you talk. Establish it, and then offer it for him to take. Pass it to him in such a way that when he takes it, the business end is pointing toward the document you want him to sign. Keep your eyes on the prospect's face. Hold the pen out there, in space, until he takes it. Do not withdraw your hand, even a fraction of an inch. And sustain unwavering eye contact. If your objective in this meeting is to get something signed, it is clearly advantageous to get a pen into the prospect's hand. If he puts it down, pick it right up again as soon as possible. Do not let it lie there until it is forgotten or becomes an object of intense focus. Pick it up again, use it yourself to make some notes or jots and scratches, and then offer it to the prospect a second time when you request the signature again.

Just as the prospect throws in the towel, he will exhale something like a sigh of relief. If he is demonstrative and is given to broad gestures, he will make the sigh a very clear statement, almost an audible groan. Get the pen in his hand immediately, if it isn't there already. Now shut up. Don't move. Don't make a peep. Fix your eyes on the prospect's, not on the document. He'll be looking down at the form or contract. If he looks up to see if you'll let him put you off, you are there, with your steady gaze, to block his escape. Let the moment be tense. Don't volunteer any further information. He may sit and look over the document for a minute and a half. Good. Let him take five minutes. Maintain nerve-racking silence until he signs. Of course, if he asks for further information or clarification, you give it to him. Then silence again. No small talk. This may be pure torture for you, but it's working on him, too. You've reached a point where additional verbiage is repetitive or unnecessary—nervous fill. There is nothing more to say; stop talking.

The prospect realizes that only he can terminate the tension of this moment. He will either sign the document or not. If you have done your homework well, and presented well and managed your sales signals well, he will buy whatever you have been selling. If, for some indiscernible reason, he backs out at the last minute, and is almost adamant about it, your new objective immediately becomes to preserve a line of communications and an open door with the prospect. *You do not act out discouragement or exasperation or ruefulness for the prospect who doesn't buy.* You move immediately to selling your second objective: to be given future opportunities to sell.

As you request an open line to present new information or demonstrate new equipment, you make no move to pack up or organize your body or belongings to leave. You maintain an unshaken, confident air. The prospect is likely to rise, signaling you that the meeting is over. He is embarrassed and wants you to leave as soon as possible. Rise with the prospect (unless you are a woman and he is a man), but stay where you are, and make no move to pack and leave until he has responded to your request. The prospect will grant your request for return matches, of course, presuming you have some new angle, product, wrinkle, improvement, or whatever that might cause him to change his mind. Once he has made this commitment, you move to beat an expeditious but dignified retreat.

You act toward the prospect as if the meeting were productive, and you are not crushed that he didn't order the ten thousand franistans in different colors. If you leave him with the impression that you think he is a fool, or boneheaded, or corrupt, he is not likely to want to see you again. Also, he will not want to see you again if he feels he crushed and destroyed you; he will be embarrassed for you. Your signals at this moment say: "I am a winner. I'll do just fine without this particular sale. It's his loss."

You pack up in an unflustered, controlled way, but don't stall—get it done. Shake hands warmly, go for solid eye contact. There is not a trace of disappointment, rage, or ruefulness in your face. Let your final note be an enthusiastic look-forward-to-your-next-meeting. And exit with a fully sustained *Up*, *Relax*, and *Yes* posture, expression, and carriage. The prospect will be left wondering if he made a mistake, rather than relishing the pleasant aftermath of having blown away another hotshot salesperson.

EXERCISE: Handling No-sales

A lost sale is not a catastrophe. You usually learn something from every one. If you have the right attitude, you can use the experience to your advantage. In any case, you must not let it break your spirit or make you gun-shy. The best way to prepare yourself to deal with the imagined Horror of Defeat is to purposely expose yourself to it. With this exercise, you can control the learning experience; you can set it up so you can lose a sale, but it won't affect your standing in the salesforce or your earnings. Here's what you do.

Try to sell your spouse on the idea of a vacation in Siberia. Try to sell a fellow worker a used typewriter ribbon, or a cup of water for a dollar, or your '75 jalopy for eight thousand dollars. Try selling last week's newspaper back to the newsboy. Walk into a bank and try to sell them on investing a million or so into your latest crackpot scheme. Next time you are in an elevator, try to sell your fellow passengers a ten-dollar bill for twenty dollars. You get the point; purposely expose yourself to the Horror of Defeat. You'll be amazed at how quickly the "horror" is deflated and neutralized. You walk away from each "defeat" stronger than before, because you know *it's not going to kill you after all.*

For a graduate-level experience with this exercise, try selling your product or whatever to that Impossible Prospect no one has ever been able to get, or hasn't even tried to get. Tackle that prospect who's so totally inconceivable and out of the question that your associates or supervisors will smile or laugh when you bring up the very idea. Go after this prospect with everything you've got. What can you lose? All he can do is turn you down, which is the point of the exercise in the first place. Then again, what if he *doesn't* turn you down?

Your closing sequence with the customer who *does* buy is much easier, of course. Your main task is to restrain yourself from leaping around the room in ecstatic joy. There is nothing wrong with this in and of itself, but there is the danger that the prospect may misunderstand your transport as an uncontrollable glee at having just put one over on him. Your attitude is, on the contrary, that the prospect has made an intelligent decision and will profit from or be pleased by having made it. If you are happy at all, you are happy for the prospect.

After the prospect has signed your document, you do not instantly snap it away, as though you have tricked him and he's going to catch on and take it back any second. Rather, you reinforce positive aspects of his decision and reassure the prospect that you feel he has made a smart decision. You want to get the document in your briefcase sooner rather than later, but you want to make it look like you're in no rush at all. We know one sassy salesman who often leaves the order form lying on the desk or table and lets the prospect notice that he is neglecting to take it with him. We don't condone such bravado as a rule, unless you're selling Krugerrands at half the price of gold. But the attitude behind such a tactic is what one tries to approximate.

On the human level, the prospect expects you to be warmer and friendlier now that he has bought from you. The contest and confrontation concluded, at whatever level, you are often now expected to drop weapons and shields and be the nice person the prospect knows is behind the relentless salesperson. That's easy enough to do. Sit back. Relax. Smile. Mirror the prospect's expression. If he launches into what's meant to be an amusing anecdote, pay attention and enjoy it.

THE EXIT

Successful people know how to use their time, and they don't like to waste it, but the few moments devoted to cordial social amenities with a prospect—now a new customer—are certainly not lost.

Let the customer signal the termination of the meeting. He's busy, too, or at least he wants you to think he is, so he should let you go fairly soon. If he doesn't, and he seems to be headed toward droning on for hours, you must actually tell him you have an appointment and that you are sorry to have to rush off, but you really must. You do not use body signals to transmit this information. The transmission of "I am late for a very important date" in nonverbal signals leaves you looking like a nervous Mad Hatter. No one enjoys having to receive and decode these signals, especially in the middle of a favorite story. Some communications are best made verbally, even though you are slightly embarrassed at having to make them that way. It is certainly better for the customer to know that you have an imminent appointment than to wonder if you: 1) have to go to the bathroom; 2) get nervous when people are friendly; or 3) hate him and can't wait to get out now that he's signed. Tell him you have to be across town in twelve minutes, and he'll understand and let you go, his feelings intact.

You rise immediately when the customer does. Ideally, you want to shake hands just before you exit, but if he offers a handshake now, you reciprocate, of course.

Pack up expeditiously but without frenzy. Your moves are controlled and deliberate. Do not diddle around with the sorting of things in your briefcase—you can do that later, on your own time. Get the stuff packed, grab your coat or whatever, bid the customer adieu, and exit. Do not put on your coat, hat, galoshes, or snowshoes in the customer's office. It looks extremely clumsy and takes his time.

You exit with the same confident stride you used for your entrance. Head up, brisk and businesslike; *Up*, Relaxed, and with a *Yes* attitude. A winner going off to make your next sale.

You call on a prospect and everything is perfect. There is a crisis, and he needs plenty of what you are selling. Fast! The prospect is familiar with your products, and it is just your good luck that you appeared at that moment. The prospect knows and likes you.

Forget selling; take the order!

PART THREE
Particulars

personally through 1930...
that everyone did the... all... were within...
happened in the same sense...
dental voices from the... house...

4

For Women Only

DRESS

Although this and the next chapter are labeled as being for men or women only, don't take that too literally. While we focus on the special conditions each sex encounters in selling, some tips and principles apply to both. For instance, though we stress clothes care on the road and body maintenance in Chapter Five, "For Men Only," women travel, too, and have to look neat and stay in as good shape as men do. Salespersons of whichever gender, read both chapters and pick up what you can use.

The subject of women's business clothes has been covered thoroughly in a number of excellent books. If you are a woman in sales, buy or check out one of these titles and read it. Try to get the latest book or revision, as styles and attitudes are clearly subject to change. Virtually every book on the subject comes to the same conclusion: Do business in a conservative, tailored, skirted suit with blouse and scarf. You are encouraged not to express your colorful, individualistic personality through your styles. You understand, of course, that if everyone did this, all businesswomen would be walking around in the same severe navy or gray outfit, unappetizing, identical cookies from the same mold. It is ironic that the authors, who have done years and years of research, are usually furthest from the mark. All their vast research took so long that most of it is old hat. Attitudes toward businesswomen and their styles in the early seventies don't help us much today. A modern woman uses yesteryear's rules only as a base. She is now free to exercise her own sense of taste and style to fit her look and personality. It is understood that she has the sense not to wear a pink gingham jumper to a meeting of the board.

If you are a passive, soft-spoken, ultrafeminine type, wear more serious, cut-and-dried clothes. Simple, well-tailored skirted suits in somber colors and unfrivolous blouses with little or no décolletage. Keep jewelry, fragrance, and makeup to a spartan minimum. Avoid soft, "feminine" hairstyles. In general, avoid clothes that accentuate your curves.

If you are a tough, persistent, unyielding, steely-willed rock, wear soft, feminine outfits, and don't be afraid of dresses. "Pretty" colors and feminine fabrics and prints are desirable. Moderate décolletage is acceptable. Wear soft, sensual hairstyles, lots of jewelry, and use fragrance. In general, wear clothes that heighten your femininity, and if you have curves, let them be curves.

In other words, *dress contrary to your character.* If you are a passive, easy mark, you don't want to announce it to your prospect the minute you walk through the door. Then again, if you are a pertinacious bulldog, you don't want the prospect to brace himself immediately to be bullied. This technique is especially effective on male prospects, who are still trying to "understand" women and who tend to jump to all sorts of conclusions about you based on your attire. The flintiest, most persistent saleswoman I know drifts into offices swathed in velvets and silks like Scarlett O'Hara before the war but doesn't leave until she gets what she wants. One of IBM's top saleswomen is the sweetest, most demure lady you'd ever find; she goes hunting in a severe black-skirted suit and starched white blouse so tight around her neck you wonder how she breathes.

The above approach isn't a hard rule; it's an option, another way to help you stay one jump ahead of your prospect. The point is, you don't all have to wear the same dark, conservative, skirted suit. That directive, issued primarily by male "image engineers" in the early seventies, is no longer the only way for a woman in business to dress.

> *When you use Winning Moves techniques, you some-times feel you're manipulating people, and it makes you feel sort of crass.*
>
> The crass is always greener for the professional sales-people who use the latest techniques. They feel crass all the way to the bank. When you take a shower, shampoo your hair, brush your teeth, and dress in clean clothes, you want to look your best. Are you being manipulative? Winning Moves are just another way to put your best foot forward.

You already know, no doubt, that red and warm colors make you look bigger; blue and cool colors make you look smaller. Horizontal stripes make you look shorter and wider; vertical stripes make you look taller and thinner. Dark colors make you look older and more serious; lighter ones have the opposite effect.

GROOMING

A saleswoman's grooming must be impeccable. Women have been doing such a fantastic job of grooming and "finishing" their image, especially in the last half century, that we have all grown accustomed to pristine, polished women with clean hair; healthy skin; neat, well-tended nails; clean, pressed clothes; well-maintained shoes; etc. Dirty hair, dirty or ragged nails, spots and stains on clothing—these things are simply unacceptable. It is not enough to be as well groomed as your male counterpart; you must surpass him in your attention to these details.

Every major women's magazine devotes at least one of its lead articles to makeup and hair. Still, thousands of women appear in public with improperly done makeup or unattractive hair. The problem, and it is a very old one, is that beauty is a subjective thing. The wearers of grotesque makeup believe that they have rendered themselves more attractive. The solution is to get objective second opinions. Not from your boyfriend (he's certainly not objective); not from your sister or best friend, who have preconceived ideas of how you look; but from a professional makeup person or cosmetologist and a professional hairstylist. Try to find a makeup person who isn't selling a specific line. Department stores frequently have visiting makeup people. Talk with several of them; let them make you up. Keep in mind that anyone who is selling makeup is trying to get you to use as many things as possible, so assess their recommendations accordingly.

SHAKING A MAN'S HAND

Normally, a man's hand is larger than a woman's. They usually feel coarser than a woman's hands. Women use more hand creams and moisturizers. So a woman frequently must concern herself with how to deal with the problem of the effect created by placing her fine, silk-over-bone-china, sparrowlike hand in the gruff grip of a beefy, coarse vise.

Surprise! Women's hands are strong. Very strong when they want to be. I saw a young mother catch and hold her three-year-old by his pants leg with one hand as the child dangled from the end of a tall pier. She held the child for several minutes until help came. Most effective saleswomen now use a firmer grip with men. Quite firm is quite acceptable—and effective. Remember not to wear rings on your right hand; when you squeeze, it hurts.

The best technique for making your hand seem bigger in a man's is to move your index finger forward—that is, spread it away from your middle finger—when you grip to shake hands. The larger male hand feels only the total width of your digits, and is not aware of the space between the index and middle fingers. It's a tiny move with a substantial effect.

POSTURE (SITTING, STANDING, WALKING, LISTENING)

A woman selling to a man sits up in her chair and leans a bit more forward than she needs to with a woman. Don't cross your legs immediately. Wait until you are relaxed and into the body of the meeting. The saleswoman wants to transmit that she is comfortable and self-controlled but not tired, complacent, or bored. Your skirt must be long enough that when you cross your legs, your top knee does not protrude like a bony skull. Avoid deep sofas or low-slung chairs that will put your knees close to your shoulder level. You want to avoid an unnecessary display of your legs and be able to stand up without having to have someone throw you a rope.

Even though you will lean forward at a greater angle in your chair when selling to a man, stay generally farther away than you would when selling to a woman, especially with new prospects. Sit straight; do not lean or tilt to the side. Do not tilt your head to the side; the effect is quizzical or flirtatious, neither of which you want to convey.

Men are still suffering the effects of antiquated perceptions of women. It is wise, therefore, to defeminize your stance when selling to men. Avoid *contraposed* positions, for example, with your hips on one axis and your shoulders on another. Do not put one of your hands on your hip; you automatically jut that hip out, as when you carry a baby. Do not put both hands on your hips; you look like you're angry, pushy, and demanding, and this is also a feminine gesture that calls attention to your hips and waist. Stand with your weight evenly distributed on both feet, with your feet a comfortable distance apart. Face the prospect. If you are taller than your male prospect, try to minimize the height difference as inconspicuously as possible. Do not stand close to the prospect for any period of time, as this accentuates the disparity. Do not try to reduce your height by slumping or rounding your shoulders. The effect is weakness, passivity, and lack of energy.

> *You go to shake hands with a seated prospect. He doesn't rise, and he pretends not to see your extended hand.*
>
> Stay there with your hand out, for fifteen minutes if necessary, until he or she shakes your hand. If they fail to rise, that's their problem. If you withdraw your unshaken hand sheepishly, you are at a disadvantage for the rest of the meeting. If, on the other hand, you hang in there until the prospect shakes, you clearly establish your character and pertinacity.

Your walk is an important facet of your impression management. If in high school you took a month to develop a walk that left flocks of boys whistling in your wake, now you can un-develop it. A saleswoman's walk is something she uses to get from one sale to the next, and nothing else.

There will be a natural rhythm and shift to your walk, the inevitable result of how you are constructed and the two-inch heels you're wearing. Keep it subtle in front of the prospect. Your walk should be businesslike, positive, and motivated but relaxed and self-assured.

Sometimes it may be hard to keep up with a tall, athletic male prospect who wants to take you on a fast tour of his plant. You don't want to slow him down noticeably, calling attention to your sex and the necessity of high heels, but neither do you want to trot or race after him. The solution is to walk, with control, as fast as you can; take larger steps and keep asking him questions—the more complicated the better. As he thinks through his answers, he'll automatically slow down his pace.

Don't try to walk like a man. You can't do it in heels. Also, it is unattractive. After you see your last prospect, you can put on your Nikes and walk home or to your car like Bigfoot. You know never to wear sneakers, clogs, moccasins, or slippers when making a presentation. Boots are, of course, acceptable if you will be working outdoors in snow, mud, or scorpion-infested desert land. Always walk with your head up, shoulders comfortably back, and a straight back. For the effect of an energetic mover and shaker, try taking a slightly longer stride.

The typically vain male prospect expects you to give undivided attention to his every precious word. To create the impression of intense listening, you lean forward when seated, arch your head and face slightly forward, and turn one ear *slightly* toward the prospect. Pin him with your eyes, and mirror his facial expressions. Be subtle with this; you don't want him to realize you're doing it intentionally. Punctuate his dialogue with an occasional positive double or triple nod of the head when appropriate. Don't stare at one of his eyes; shift from one to the other every once in a while. To listen closely when standing, you do not lean forward, but you still try for good eye contact; you mirror and use occasional head nods to indicate you understand what's being said. Most important, do not move, take steps, or fidget when your prospect is in mid-sentence. You move or approach the prospect *between* his statement and your reply or as you are beginning to make your reply.

Be especially careful not to lean your head to either side, whether listening or speaking. Women tend to do this routinely, especially in a meeting with a particularly dominant male type. The highest incidence discerned in the films we studied occurred in conjunction with the posing of questions by the saleswoman. It was remarkably consistent, especially among novice saleswomen; almost every question was accompanied by tilting one's head to the side. I suppose this is intended to look inquisitive or curious, and it well may, but it has the unfortunate side effect of also looking submissive and dumb. Watch an animal's head when it hears something it doesn't understand or can't place. The head tilts to the side. Watch a young dog or bachelor wolf try to ingratiate itself with the leader of the pack. The submissive one tilts its head to the side (sometimes to the point of rolling over and exposing its vulnerable underbelly), shows no resistance or fight, and throws itself on the mercy of the leader.

Men, aside from rarely eating quiche, almost never tilt their heads to the side. If you tend to, break yourself of the habit as soon as possible.

SEATING STRATEGY

Your priorities in seating strategy are to have the most unobstructed visual access to your prospect, to get reasonably close enough, to be at the side of his desk or at a ninety-degree angle in the informal area or at a table. Understanding that you must satisfy these priorities first, there are some other considerations that may influence your seating strategy.

Try for the seat with the brightest light or windows *behind* you. Generally speaking, you are better off keeping direct light off your face. Two kinds are particularly harsh: daylight (except at sunset) and "cool" fluorescents. Raw daylight is not as uncomplimentary as ugly fluorescent light. Incandescent lights are warmer (redder) than fluorescents and do nice things for your skin. Thus, if your prospect's office has fluorescents in the ceiling, a lamp to the right of his desk, and a bright window to the left, you would sit on the left side of his desk, with the lamp spilling some of its warm light onto your face and the window back-lighting you. You simultaneously save yourself from having to squint into the bright window light.

If you are a smaller woman, be wary of sitting in an enormous, high-backed, deep chair; it will make you seem even more petite. If you have a choice, don't sit in a seat that clashes with your clothes. Once again, if you have a choice, take a chair with casters, a swivel seat, or both, over a stationary one. The movable chair gives you additional options for angles and distance control. Remember, however, not to rock or swivel back and forth.

In the informal area or a home, avoid couches if possible. If you are alone on one, you will seem smaller. You will usually sink lower into a couch, and lose eye-height. Your skirt is more likely to ride up. If the prospect is directly across from you, you will present an image that is sixty percent legs and knees, and forty percent head and shoulders. This is because things appear relatively larger the closer they are to the eye; if you allow yourself to be swallowed up in the back of the couch, the closest thing to the prospect's eyes are your knees. Finally, it's harder to get up from a couch. Unfortunately, most of the time your prospect will gesture for you to sit on the couch, and he will sit at a right angle, or across from you, in a single chair. The way to avoid this is to stall for time, until you can see where he plans to sit (almost always a single chair), and then sit in the single chair at a right angle to his. If you have no choice, by all means sit on the couch without further ado. Just remember not to fall back into its clutches. Sit tall and try to play down your legs.

> *You are presenting to a male prospect in his office. You are both sitting in his semisocial area. He starts making passes, and loses the ability to focus on your presentation. You want to turn him off.*
>
> Uncross your legs. With your legs together, and your feet flat on the floor, sit up and turn your lower body away from the prospect. Stop smiling or laughing. Take out a pen and start summarizing for your close. Use eye contact only for emphasis or to conclude businesslike questions. Focus mainly on contracts and business materials. Speak a bit louder and more concisely. Ignore halfhearted double entendre passes. For heavier, more direct passes, you may have to resort to an upward roll of the eyes to signal your lack of interest.

VOICE

In a crucial presentation, or under pressure, many women start speaking faster, and slide into a higher octave. They start to squeak instead of speak, and increase the likelihood of stumbling over words, stuttering, or misspeaking themselves. As you feel the anxiety increase, purposely decrease both the speed of your speech and the register of your voice. Don't initiate a sentence until you have a full breath of air; tension causes us to breathe faster but more shallowly. Proper posture will help you take deeper breaths with less effort.

GESTURES

A saleswoman's gestures are expected to be less exaggerated and more graceful than a man's. When a woman gestures too broadly, the effect is often comic or low-class. Never point at any prospect, male or female, not with your finger or with any object, such as a pen. Avoid gestures or postures that play up limp wrists. Limp wrists are an atavistic hangover from earlier periods when women were expected to play weak, helpless bits of fluff given to fainting at the slightest start. Enthusiastic people rarely have limp wrists. Athletic, active women don't display limp wrists. Limp wrists can project a blasé attitude, exhaustion, or cowlike complacency, none of which effects you need in your presentation.

Perhaps due to cultural influences, or perhaps because of the generally narrower and less muscular shoulders of women, they appear to have less upper-body presence. This is even more apparent when the woman is seated behind a desk or conference table. When a woman is placed between several men at a conference table, she appears to take up less space. One technique to help offset this discrepancy is for the woman to use her arms, hands, and elbows to gesture a bit more broadly and support such broader gestures with her upper body and her posture (sitting tall). The effect is not dissimilar to the one created by an active couple on a dance floor; everyone around makes a little more room for them.

Don't allow yourself to be squeezed and dwarfed by two gorillas flanking you at a conference table. Immediately let them know you are there. Try putting your elbows on the table; spread out to stake out your claim. Sit up and a bit forward to make your upper body more prominent.

EXPRESSION

Women have very expressive faces, much more expressive than men. Men learn as little boys to hide the tears and expressions that will reveal their emotions. They are taught that to make a display of emotions is a sign of weakness unacceptable in a man. In fact, the little boy learns that allowing his emotions to show in his face will adversely affect his social life, career, and income. Little girls, on the other hand, are encouraged to express their emotions, to "have a good cry," and be generally demonstrative of their deeper feelings. That all worked very well when women limited their activities to domestic life and rearing children. For a woman in business, it is no longer functional. A woman making a sales presentation must learn (forgive us, Edith Bunker) to stifle her stream of spontaneous facial expressions and control the intensity of the signals she chooses to send. Generally speaking, she must minimize all her facial expression's. We are not proposing a poker face (although there are times when this is essential) but a face far less ingenuous than the one women are accustomed to using.

Prospects should not be able to read your face like an open book. It might well be transmitting value judgments or emotions that don't jibe with your verbal thrust. The best way to teach your face to send only the signals you want is to start with a clean slate. That is, the most important expression, the one you must learn first, is *no* expression.

It is not as easy as it sounds. You may be able to sustain an expressionless, emotionless face alone in front of a mirror, but it's a new game when you are involved in a face-to-face discussion with an important prospect. Can you resist raising your eyebrows the way you have been doing for years? Can you sublimate the smile you feel creeping onto your lips? Can you prevent your eyes from blinking and looking away when you really are dying to blink and look away? Once you have taught your face to stop disobeying you, you can start teaching it to assume the expressions you want it to assume, and you can work on controlling the level of intensity of the signals it imparts.

The object of all this is not camouflage or subterfuge, it's just to get your face to stop showboating and join the team. The main problem is that you don't see your face when you're selling (see the section on "Video Role-play," p. 189). When you look in the mirror, it's you looking back at you, and you lose critical objectivity. Your face probably has been doing quite a bit of independent signaling—overexaggerating your feelings, giving away feelings you don't want expressed, and possibly transmitting signals contrary to your verbal message. First teach your face how to shut up, then teach it how to help you say what you are trying to say.

TRUE LIFE STORY: The Sale Lost with One Look

I once had an assistant film editor who thought she was getting into a career rut and asked me if I wouldn't give her a chance to move into sales. Well, of course, anytime a bright, well-educated, attractive, ambitious person wants to try their hand in sales, you do all you can to make it easier for them. I gave her some homework for a couple of weeks, outside reading and digging through our sales files, and I started to take her along on some new business presentations. She ultimately worked out very nicely and moved on to other pastures. But on the way, she experienced one sale, or I should say a "no sale," which I am sure will stay with her as one of the most important nonverbal lessons of her life.

Through a contact, she had found a prospect and set up a meeting. She had sent a flyer and cover letter and a reprint of a recent article on us. The prospect, an older businessman in an industry in which he had little contact with women, had told the young saleswoman that he expected to meet "her boss" at the presentation. So I went along as an *éminence grise* (I actually was prematurely gray) to satisfy the prospect's expressed need. But I made it clear that the presentation would be in her hands, and I would not jump in until the prospect directed a specific question to me.

The meeting went very smoothly. The saleswoman was very effective, I thought. The older male prospect was clearly having trouble accepting the young woman. Yet she answered all of his questions clearly and without equivocation. She was "Up, Relaxed, and Yes." Enthusiastic but not gushing. Pleasant but not giggly or flighty. Carefully, patiently she coaxed him, nurtured him, led him to the close at the end of the road. All she wanted from him at this point was authorization to do some basic research and develop a rough treatment for a corporate image film. Very little money was involved. For us it was a very large step forward, because once we got to the treatment stage with a prospect, we never failed to produce through to completion.

She asked for the commitment. There was no document; at this stage all she wanted was a verbal okay. He stood up. He walked over to his window and looked out for a long moment. He strolled back to the informal area in which we were meeting. "I guess so," he said. He watched our faces. I felt the saleswoman look at me. I tried to keep my eyes on the prospect, to give him the approval and support he needed now. I glanced at the saleswoman, hard, to signal her to stop doing what she was doing. She was looking at me with a look that said, "See, I can do it! I even sold this carbuncular old coot. Ha! Aren't I something else!" I looked back at the prospect and tried to catch his glance. But too late. He was focused on the saleswoman's face. He saw it all. It was as clear as a bell. A funeral bell. I started to say something. He interrupted me.

"But I'd like to present your stuff to my board, and also my marketing staff, before you start anything. Give me a couple of weeks and then get back to me, okay?"

Yeah, sure.

One of the standby expressions you must learn to control first, especially with male prospects, is your smile. Do not paste on your party smile when you make a sales presentation to a businessman or a group of mostly men in a conference room. Most men are quite ready *not* to take you seriously; don't give them any ammunition. Businessmen laugh plenty and smile a lot at after-hours joints, cocktail parties, tailgaters, and Bob Hope specials, but they put all this aside between nine and five, especially in the presence of someone trying to sell them something. A man is likely to believe that if you smile too easily, you are just halfheartedly supplementing your income and don't really take your job seriously. When you keep a more or less straight face, his initial reaction will be to try to get you to smile. Fine—let him try. He's trying to get you to be jovial, genial, and playful so it won't seem important to you, or to him, when he turns you down or puts you off. Naturally, if the man says the funniest thing you ever heard, or Larry, Moe, and Curly charge in and eat his desk, you smile and perhaps laugh. After all, you are an intelligent person, and only human. Your prospect will be smiling or laughing along with you. Now you must return to earth rather quickly. Wipe the smile off your face *before it fades from his* and get back to business without hesitation or apology. The prospect will—must—follow your lead, however reluctantly. It is always desirable for you to terminate any tangential behavior or discourse before the prospect does. Then, once again, you are leading and he is following.

There are times when you can and should smile. You can use your smile as a reward. Whenever your prospect says something complimentary or positive about your products, company, services, or ideas, you reward him with a smile. Don't overdo it. Combine the smile with some positive head nods. However, if the compliment is directed to your person or accoutrements, you may respond with a quick, perfunctory thank-you, but do not smile as part of your reply (see "Cross-sex Selling," p. 117). A smile used as a reward can be as effective as any verbal technique you use to reinforce and encourage positive behavior, if not more so. Smiling, like anything else, has greater value when it isn't in overabundant supply. Especially for a woman selling to a man, a smile is a powerful resource that shouldn't be cheapened by overuse.

An easy smile suggests a bond of trust. As you get to know a prospect better (presumably he has become a customer), and you are convinced he takes you seriously, you may smile more freely.

There are two kinds of male prospects that present special problems; the "funny" prospect and the Man at the Top. The "funny" prospect is the one who secretly feels he missed his calling as a comedian or world-class wit. The Man at the Top has a warmer, looser personality, and he tends to smile regularly, no doubt because he's at the top. Both of these prospects want you to smile or laugh on cue.

The prospect who thinks he is the life of the party uses humor to sidestep and defuse any serious or consequential confrontation. You must try to keep this character down to earth and tuned in to the business at hand, your presentation, without hurting his feelings. Do not smile or laugh at his first couple of clever witticisms. Usually you can turn off would-be comedians in the first few moments of your meeting, simply by not responding to their efforts to be amusing. The prospect may be temporarily crestfallen, but so what? You're there to sell something, not to serve as a captive audience.

The prospect is chuckling, smiling, and laughing all through your presentation.

Worry. Either he's had a liquid lunch, there's parsley growing out of your ears, or he's having some kind of breakdown. In any case, people who are laughing rarely sign contracts. Try to bring this prospect down to earth if you can. Maybe it's your fault—you just can't resist entertaining a good audience. Resist. You can try for laughs at your audition for "Stars of Tomorrow."

You have a different sort of problem with the Man at the Top. You may already know that they are easier to deal with than their often churlish, insecure, or envious subordinates. Senior executives with power usually seem to be in a better humor than their underlings. Men at the top are enjoying themselves, and they project that to the people they meet with. It is very hard not to mirror their warm, relaxed good humor. After all, if you are a winner, don't you exude some of your own warm, relaxed good humor? Of course you do. And you should. Relax and smile more with powerful executives; laugh at their better lines. Don't force it, but let it come naturally. Rely on your natural charisma to determine how far to go. But beware: The senior power-wielder can switch from charmer to Grand Inquisitor faster than a chameleon changes color. You have to be prepared at all times to change gears rapidly to deal with a sudden, although frequently subtle, attack, or respond to a charged question. The chief executive will butter you up and get you smiling and then open fire.

Whether or not you can maintain equilibrium in the face of a sudden shift is a measure of your control, composure, and sincerity. Be prepared.

After eye control and overcoming expressions of fear or anxiety, the biggest problem with facial expression is the poorly sent signal. Because the poorly sent signal is not properly designed, it is likely to be misunderstood. For example, one of the most common poorly sent facial expressions is the one you mount to mean "I am fascinated but slightly perplexed by this information." It often looks like "I am quite irritated at this information, and at you for bringing it up."

How can we know that the expressions we display will be clear and understood by others? How many of us actually test ourselves or practice on videotape, or even in front of a mirror? Most of us rely on a mix of experience and our listener's response. After we hear from several friends and associates that our "look" of rapt attention makes us look like a psychotic murderer stalking his prey, we set out to redesign the expression. But "afters" are not good enough for a professional salesperson. You want to have all your facial expressions clearly worked out before your face-to-face. The best way to do this is in front of a video camera, in a full-face frontal close-up. Have an associate you are comfortable with feed you direction or motivation for a specific nonverbal expression. Record the verbal cues, then play the tape back and watch the facial expressions you displayed. Do they say, unquestionably, what you intended them to say?

Once again, video is more effective than working in front of a mirror, because the tape doesn't allow you to make instant adjustments to your reflection. Video shows you, moments later, the actual nonverbal performance you are presenting to your prospects. Your face and head, taken as a unit, is, of course, that element of your nonverbal equipment that is least observable by you in the moment of selling. This is unfortunate, because it is also the single most important nonverbal element you have. Perhaps all is for the best; imagine what difficulty you would have concentrating on the prospect if there were a mirror just behind his head, or a video screen reflecting a close-up of your face throughout your presentation.

You panic when you feel your little nervous facial tic starting up.

When you are alone, check in the mirror. The tic you think is as obvious as a hazard light may be completely invisible or practically indiscernible. You can work on trying to quell your nervous tic by reducing your nervousness. If you believe in mind over matter, try slowing or stopping the tic from within. In your mind's eye, try to isolate the little muscle that's in spasm, and persuade it to relax. I know it sounds ridiculously easy. It usually is.

CHARISMA

After our ideal saleswoman learns how to restrain, restructure, and control, what becomes of her natural enthusiasm, energy, and sense of excitement? Nothing, we hope. You keep these things intact, because they are an important facet of your emotional/philosophical base. In fact, if you are not a naturally persistent person, they may be the most important aspect of your character. Your enthusiasm will carry you over most hurdles; you don't want to let anything or anybody dissipate it in any way. What you will have learned to do, ideally, is to limit the external display of your enthusiasm to a level just below when you appear to gush, or be transported to a point beyond anything your prospects can relate to, based on their knowledge of the facts. You want to turn your prospects on, not scare them away with overbroad expressions of your wild enthusiasm. You must gradually bring them closer to your point of view.

The danger with externalizing enthusiasm, as with smiling, derives from antiquated male perceptions of the female character and her role. The danger is appearing flighty or girlish. It is unfortunate, because genuine enthusiasm is a rare commodity. Major corporations spend a fortune every year trying to instill a little enthusiasm in their salespeople. A salesman can display a rather large enthusiasm factor, and everyone reacts positively.

A saleswoman can be equally enthusiastic, but she must temper it and rein it in more in front of male prospects.

MANNERS AND THE MODERN WOMAN

A woman is still expected to be a lady, and a rudimentary knowledge and application of the social amenities is still appropriate for women in most business encounters, as it is for men—especially when they are dealing with women. Generally speaking, women are more careful about their manners than men, anyway, so they don't need to devote as much attention to this area. The greater danger is that in an effort to be ladylike, a woman will be too polite, understanding, and demure. In other words, she will be too easily put off by the prospect. You do not have to be rude to be persistent. There is no longer any reason, social or otherwise, to be ladylike to the point of providing the prospect a handy escape. You may change course when you find an objection or hostility on one front. You do not politely withdraw. You are not being impolite but persistent.

Think of the characters, the authority figures that women play routinely with men or boys: mother, teacher, nurse, telephone operator, airline stewardess, the clerk at the Motor Vehicle Bureau who makes grown men go to the end of the line. Boys understand the authority of a mother or a teacher. Powerful executives get embarrassed and look ashamed when female dental hygienists tell them they haven't been flossing. Chief executive officers buckle up quickly when they see the stewardess coming up the aisle. It is quite possible, even natural, for a woman to be strong without being obnoxious or rude. Inject your character with some of the authority of the mother/teacher figure. Be careful not to act patronizing. You want to be unyielding, firm, unintimidated.

When she is selling to very powerful, forceful male executives, one brilliant saleswoman assumes (in her mind, of course) the role of mother, and pictures herself cutting the prospect's meat and helping him blow his nose. In a presentation to three male executives, she actually got a clean tissue out of her purse and handed it to the overbearing one, who was sniffling with a minor cold. "Blow," she said. He was clay in her hands for the rest of the meeting. Obviously, it takes a certain flair and finesse to bring off such a stroke, and I would not recommend you run around telling male executives to blow their noses or showing them how to cut their meat. But it is very helpful for your attitude to appreciate that you don't have to base your character in a passive, overly polite, weak-willed, nineteenth-century shrinking violet.

You are in the middle of your presentation, and the secretary or receptionist rings in to tell your prospect that his next appointment has arrived.

Do not elide or speed up your presentation; it projects lack of stature. Conclude at your normal pacing. If anything, run over. Why would you rush to give more time to the competition?

CROSS-SEX SELLING

The strongest undercurrent in face-to-face selling to a member of the opposite sex is sex. The more attractive you are, the stronger the undercurrent becomes. Most men between thirteen and ninety-two will react to an attractive or interesting woman on a sexual plane, at one level or another. This is a perfectly natural reaction, and to it we owe such serendipitous conditions as the preservation of the human species. When an attractive, robust, important male prospect meets an attractive, vital, fascinating saleswoman, there are bound to be signals sent and received that are not essentially business-oriented. There is no doubt in anyone's mind that a prospect's psychological, emotional, and physical response to a salesperson of the opposite sex will color the response to the presentation being made. The question is, does it help to turn the prospect on to you before you turn him on to the product? The answer is almost always no.

Then again, you still don't want to lose the extra little

edge afforded by attractiveness and subliminal sex appeal. What you must do is walk that very fine line between maybe and no, between innuendo and inaccessibility. You dress and groom yourself and move attractively, but upon approach, your disclaimer signals must be unmistakable and clear. In case we have forgotten, or we aren't completely clear on what courting signals are, this is a good opportunity to define them.

1. "Making eyes." Looking too hard and too long, out of the corners of the eyes or from under heavy lids. Batting the lashes.
2. Showing an open mouth, pursed lips; licking or biting the lips, showing the tongue, especially the underside of the tongue. Sensual smiling.
3. Preening. Touching or stroking part of your body or hair. Fiddling with or removing jewelry.
4. Flexing the legs, rocking the top crossed leg rhythmically, extending the foot, kicking off a shoe.
5. Head tilted to the side, chest thrust forward, arms "open," nostrils flaring slightly.
6. "Mirroring." Reflecting the prospect's nonverbal ritual.
7. Touching the other party, other than the handshake or purely accidental touching.

Any one or a group of these signals may be taken as a more than ample invitation for the other party to pursue. If you send any of these signals, intentionally or unintentionally, and you don't intend to follow through, you must offset them with clear disclaimers. If courting signals are being sent to you, you are placed in the awkward position of having to turn him off (you) while you turn him on (to your product).

It is a delicate balancing act, requiring deep reserves of diplomacy, tact, and timing, to turn a man down and not permanently alienate him by crushing his sensitive ego. The best approach is, of course, to avoid the deep end of this pool in the first place. That is, you have to let the prospect know *as soon as possible* that you are not interested in extracurricular play. Once again, we face a push-pull situation; we want to make a good first impression and win the prospect over as quickly as possible, and simultaneously we want to hold him at bay and discourage his advances.

One of the most effective sales trainers I know advises her female charges to be totally, almost brutally, businesslike. They are careful not to send or even acknowledge flirting signals from male prospects. If the signals escalate to unadorned come-ons, the saleswomen are to resort to open and frank verbal clarifications of their lack of interest and a reestablishment of priorities, i.e., getting on with their presentation.

Be forewarned that when you do succeed in defusing a sexual overture and convince the prospect you are sincerely interested in doing business, he is likely to take revenge for being rebuffed. He will become so utterly businesslike so quickly, that it may startle you and throw you off-balance. Don't be put off. You can deal with this better than you can deal with a man on the make. And his disappointment won't last long. Once the prospect understands that you are not going to bed with him, he is more likely to start concentrating on the thrust of your presentation, rather than on your pulchritude or personality. In the final analysis, you will probably have earned the prospect's respect.

Subtle flirting can, of course, be used to get and hold attention and to help get someone rooting for you. There is no doubt in my mind that most cross-sex business relationships are substantially nourished by a mutual ongoing exchange of courtship signals. It works when the participants mix in the right amount of disclaimer and limiter signals to defuse any romantic or prurient inferences. One of the most widely used disclaimers is humor. Someone who is flirting can always control the flames with an occasional splash of levity. Humor adds objectivity and is an excellent antidote to the seriousness required to escalate sex or romance.

Other effective disclaimers which signal limits in flirting include breaking eye contact; bypassing signals sent to you; breaking mirroring, or "synchronicity"; or closing the body either during sending or receiving courting signals. If you must touch or are touched, intentionally or unintentionally, you can send clear I-like-you-but-I-won't-play signals by tensing slightly, breaking contact as soon as you can without appearing anxious or intimidated, and avoiding eye contact, except during the handshake sequence. Many attractive young women have been able to quell the savage male in pursuit by feigning ignorance and thereby bypassing his passes. For a woman in business, "playing dumb" is clearly not the technique of preference.

Using flirting effectively, with the proper blend of I-like-you and but-it's-out-of-the-question signals is one of the most delicate high-wire acts in selling, but it's worth trying to perfect. The tightrope leads to customers who like you and go out of their way to buy from you. They are complimented you find them attractive enough to flirt with (subtly, please), and probably thankful that you keep them at arm's length so they won't have to follow through.

THE EXIT

When a meeting is over, the male prospect, whether he has bought or not, tends to stop listening. Now he is just watching you. Everything you say will be lost, wasted, and forgotten. Get through your leave-taking as expeditiously as possible, without racing. Just as you hit the door, turn around and close with a pleasant remark, such as "Thank you so much for seeing me today" or "Have a wonderful day, Mr. Jones." It doesn't matter what you say, as long as it's executed with panache. You smile and exit immediately (close the door behind you), leaving him with the best possible image of yourself and the memory of your face—not the back of your coat. You've seen this exit in hundreds of films and plays, and it always works.

WOMAN TO WOMAN, IN THE OFFICE

Keeping in mind all the relative points we have treated above, let's look at a woman selling to a woman.

A female prospect is less threatened. She is more likely to be relaxed with you. Don't for a moment take this prospect for an easy mark; she's the sharpest of all.

For sales in the office, conduct yourself with the same reserve and distance you would with a male prospect in the same environment. Be businesslike—refrain from kaffeeklatsching or girl-talking (unless you know the prospect, and she encourages it). You may work closer to the prospect and sustain better eye contact than you would with a man. You can smile more. If you normally have honey in your voice in the company of men, take it out when you call on a woman. If this is an important meeting, and you have time to work out your makeup and costume, try for a stylish, smart, successful look. Eliminate anything sexy.

The woman prospect looks at you as someone who may have future contact with her superior, who may well be a man. (Sorry, but that's the status quo at the time.) If she sees you as a sex kitten, she may subconsciously (or consciously, for that matter) decide to protect him from his own baser impulses, get rid of you now, and squelch the opportunity for such contact. You want to "read" like a serious businessperson who just happens to be a woman.

A woman will be more objectively sensitive to your body signals than a man. A male prospect will, consciously or not, initially evaluate your face and figure on whatever scale of appeal he subscribes to.

The woman evaluates you also, but she is making harsher judgments on your taste, social status, and personal style. Her evaluation of your signals will not be obscured by your appeal to the opposite sex.

The saleswoman selling to another woman in a corporate or professional environment must move with deference to a woman with greater status. Such a woman will not relish being treated as just another "one of the girls." A no-nonsense expression and physical attitude are appropriate. If the prospect wants it less formal and "looser," she'll let you know. Sustain your best posture and manners at all times. Sit after she asks you. Smile politely—and sparingly. Maintain control of the speed of your moves; don't get flighty. Do not smoke, even if the prospect does. Do not chew gum. Do not fiddle with your hair or makeup. Listen attentively; sit up in your chair. Send all the signals of confidence and self-awareness that you would to a man.

When a woman invites a saleswoman into her semisocial area, she's prone to buy. Even so, don't take her for granted. Wait for her to sit. If you have samples and graphics to show, try sitting next to her on the sofa. Take your time. Let her set the pace. Try to get her involved in turning pages or helping you hold things up or open. If she signals she just wants to chat for a minute, stop selling for a minute and chat. A female customer who becomes a friend can be a long-term loyal customer indeed.

You don't have to make a brilliant exit for a businesswoman. Shake hands after you have packed up and are ready to leave. Smile, turn, and exit.

WOMAN TO WOMAN, IN THE HOME

Dress to or just above the level of the people you are seeing. Dress as lightly as possible, as if you live just across the street and you didn't have to get all bundled up just to drop in. Groom carefully, but keep your prospects in mind. You want to look as normal as possible.

When the prospect comes to the door, step back one or two steps so she can see you and won't feel threatened. Also, you want to leave room for the screen door to open; it inevitably swings outward. Stepping back also allows the prospect to see that you are alone. When you are plastered up against the screen door, or filling the entire view afforded by the peephole, there could be a parade of angry sumo wrestlers behind you.

Use full, neighborly smiles when you introduce yourself and explain what you are selling. Your mind-set here is that you have something that this woman really wants, and because you are a good neighbor, you are stopping in to tell her how to get it herself. A good smile is essential to distinguish yourself from the swarms of door-to-door people who are on serious missions for charities or organized religions. A full smile is highly recommended; a half-smile is a mistake. A half-smile looks phony and forced, and projects your nervousness. If you can't muster up a full smile, don't smile at all.

Although your goal is not to sell anything in the first few

seconds of your opening, you should have in your hands, or clearly visible, samples or a brochure of the item or items you intend to sell. Don't rush the prospect; you are giving her plenty to look at. A moment earlier, she was completely comfortable and relaxed in her private cocoon—her domicile. Suddenly, you show up, a stranger perhaps, an intruder in any case, and surfeit her with a barrage of new images and words.

Your goal in the opening moments is to be let inside. To accomplish this, you:

1. Convince the prospect you are friendly and easygoing (nonthreatening).
2. Tempt her with the emotional appeal of the excitement, newness, effectiveness, or value of your most tempting item.
3. Send body signals that you fully expect to be let in. When the time is right, you cue the prospect to open the door.

The body signals that will essentially force the prospect to open the door are:

1. If you have some large or heavy item (like a vacuum cleaner) that has been standing on the ground next to you, when the prospect is on the brink of letting you in, pick up the item or items as if you expect the door to be opened for your entrance. Step to the side to allow the screen door to open. You can even ask the prospect to open it for you, if she hasn't already. Out of politeness, she will feel compelled to open it and hold it open as you enter.
2. If you have a tote bag full of samples, a brochure, and a handbag, struggle with these things as you try to show the prospect something in the brochure. The point of your struggle is that it would clearly be easier to show her this or that if there were a table to put things down on. Have your finger in the brochure, for easy opening to your hottest item. If there is a screen door between you, move the brochure slowly

up or down as the prospect tries to read or see what
you are pointing at. The screen will create a moiré
effect with the horizontal copy in the brochure, making
it difficult to focus on, and the prospect will open the
screen door to enable her to see better.

3. Hand the prospect something. Preferably the most
   valuable item in your bag. She is quite likely to open
   the door to receive it.

4. If you are separated by a screen door, try squinting and
   shading your eyes with your hand in order to see
   through the screen. Your prospect will eventually be
   made to feel uncomfortable for hiding from you.

5. If you're selling a fragrance, hold it as if ready to spray
   it, or apply it to your wrist. It's inconvenient to smell
   through a screen door; she will open it.

6. If you have some small premium giveaway or sample,
   she will have to open the door to receive it.

7. Ask if you may come in. Assure her it will only take a
   minute and that your own house is much messier than
   hers.

8. Ask if you may use the phone or bathroom. A prospect
   who won't let you in to sell her something might well
   do so for a priority matter like calling the baby-sitter or
   using the bathroom. She may change her mind about
   seeing your merchandise once you're inside and she
   begins to relate to you as a human being.

9. Wipe your shoes like mad on the welcome mat.

If the prospect adamantly refuses to let you in, try
conducting the sale right on the doorstep. Some prospects are
genuinely embarrassed by the condition of their homes and
simply refuse to let anyone see how bad it is. If the prospect
comes *out* to meet you, that is probably the case. If possible,
launch right into the body of your presentation. If your
products or services really require an in-home presentation,
try to arrange a time to come some other day.

If you are turned down categorically, do not show your
disappointment by looking away, frowning, or collapsing your
posture into a loser's slump. Smile bravely, leave your card or
brochure, promise to be back again, turn, and walk off

confidently, as if you had just sold everything in your line. This makes you feel better, and it leaves the prospect wondering if maybe she made a mistake by not taking advantage of your offer. Do come back again and again. You never know when a tough prospect will turn around, or why, but they frequently do. In any case, the prospect will come to admire your pertinacity. Eventually, she may reward you for having a quality she prizes so highly.

Let us assume, as is more likely, that your prospect lets you in. If you have a coat or outer boots, and you don't see immediately where they go, ask the prospect. If you are in a mobile home or small apartment, there will be only one room or area in which to make your presentation. In a home or larger apartment, the prospect will probably try to steer you to the living room or some formal, more public, space. If you are selling vacuums, living room furniture, fine art, or Oriental carpets, the living room is a wonderful place to be. If you are selling health and beauty aids, kitchen items, life insurance, membership (in anything), vitamins and drugs, or cleaning materials, you want to be in the kitchen, eating nook, or dining room. The kitchen is your first choice. The way to get there is to suggest that you have samples that might spill, your shoes are dirty, etc., and you don't want to risk messing up your hostess's lovely living room.

Once in the kitchen or eating area, ask the prospect where you might sit; these seats are generally reserved by family members, and you don't want to sit in one that may put the prospect on edge (like the one Grandpa passed away in last week). If there is an expensive-looking tablecloth on the table, and there is any risk of one of your samples staining it, ask if it might be covered or folded back or replaced with something less fine. Even if the home is a tumbledown mess, the prospect will appreciate your consideration for her property.

If the prospect offers you a cup of coffee or tea, thank her and refuse. How much time do you have to waste while coffee brews; how much time do you want to waste going to the bathroom on every call? Also, coffee and most teas contain caffeine, and will increase anxiety and tension.

If you are selling from a brochure or with small samples, and you are led into the living room, go for the couch that faces the coffee table. Invite and signal the prospect to sit next to you. You will use the coffee table for a display counter. Be careful if it is wood or some scratchable surface. If your bag or case has metal nubs on the bottom, put it on the floor rather than the tabletop.

Facing the couch, try to sit on the right side (on the left if you are left-handed). Gesture for the prospect to sit next to you. With the prospect on your right (or left, if you are left-handed), she is better able to see what you write in the order book. You make the entries in the order book or form to expedite the process and serve the prospect, but it is important that she be able to see what you write as clearly as possible. Another advantage to positioning the prospect on your right (or left) is what Maris Johnson, former sales training director of Avon cosmetics, calls "finger selling." This is the use of your fingers to direct the prospect to items in the brochure you think will appeal to her. Your right hand (if you are right-handed) will be a more adept guide than your left one.

Let the prospect open any attractive packaging that is easy to open. If it's a utilitarian outer package or something difficult to open, you open it and hand it to the prospect. Put everything you show out on the table rather than back in your tote bag. This helps the prospect recall what she has seen, and also signals her that you will be staying for a while.

If the prospect is not interested in something you hand her, she will move more slowly to take it, and she will put it down rather soon. At this close range, you will actually be able to see your prospect's pupils. When a product turns a prospect off, her pupils will narrow down to pinpoints. If something turns her on, you will probably be able to discern pupil enlargement.

If the prospect takes every opportunity to get up and putter around, she is either hypertense, or she is trying to signal you that she wishes you would hurry up and go. Don't be dismayed; chances are she wants you to go because she has very low sales resistance, and she knows she is probably going to buy more than she should. You settle right in and let her buy as much as she wants. Of course, there is always the possibility that your prospect actually does have something better to do, in which case, once you are inside, she will buy something from you quickly to get rid of you sooner. If you work in the late afternoons, it is a good idea to time your calls to fall on the half-hour commercial breaks between soap operas. The breaks between shows last up to five to six minutes, ample time to get in, show your best-sellers, and fill in the order form before the next show starts. Once the program is under way, your prospect will sign the order form expeditiously.

Some of the obstacles that are likely to come with the territory are babies, pets, and husbands. To babies and pets you are an event, a new amusement, an interesting guest who may provide entertainment. Or, if your timing is inopportune, you may divert Mommy's attention away from baby and provoke a jealous rage. Do not underestimate a mother's ability to hear, think, and make decisions in spite of a three-hundred-decibel blue-faced tantrum. Be patient and calm; you may help lessen the din by rocking the carriage or murmuring lullabies while Mommy looks over your wares. Cute and cheer-ful toddlers seem far more civilized—but beware, they are as curious as cats, and you must be on one-hundred-percent alert to prevent them from eating, drinking, spilling, or destroying your samples.

The family dog wants his head scratched. The family cat expects you to let him use you for a heating pad. (Naturally, Molting Morris is yellow, and your skirt is black.) Keep in mind that these little creatures are members of the family, and treat them with the proper friendly deference. If you find it difficult to present with pets climbing over you, do not pet, scratch, or pay attention to them. They will drift away soon for greener pastures.

Most husbands believe that they have great sales resis-tance and that their wives do not. If a husband is nearby when you are presenting, or moves in and out of earshot, his implied signal to his spouse is that he is bearing witness to her weakness. Your options are: 1) speak softer, so he can't hear; 2) bring him in and sell to him also; or 3) find out when he's out and reschedule.

One highly productive cosmetics saleswoman I know sends husbands scrambling by bringing up subjects with her prospects that husbands don't care to discuss.

You know, of course, never to flirt with the husband of a prospect. If he flirts with you, bypass his signals totally. If he rushes into the street, throws roses at you, serenades you with a guitar, and throws himself in front of your car, run over him.

> *You have a strong suspicion you are really wasting your time.*
>
> Leave. Cut your losses. You *are* wasting your time.

If you are a woman selling essentially women's products and on a cold call, and a man answers the door, you immediately ask for the lady of the house. If you are told that she is not in at the moment and asked if he can't help, look at your watch as if you had an appointment, beg his pardon for disturbing him, and beat an expeditious retreat. If you can find out when she is expected to return, that will help prevent another wasted visit. Don't go into an apartment or house occupied only by a man (or men) unless they are over seventy, you look like Ernest Borgnine, or you have a black belt in karate and a pair of skittish Doberman pinschers.

I appreciate that many thousands of real estate saleswomen go into empty houses alone with male prospects every day. One hopes that the saleswoman has thoroughly qualified and identified the male prospect before taking him out. My wife was a realtor for quite a few years, and I worried every time I heard she was showing properties to a lone male prospect. Overly paranoid, I'm sure. It is not, however, a wild assumption to anticipate that some percentage of able-bodied males alone in a house (especially a furnished one) are likely to throw some gratuitous courting signals to an attractive female broker. Augmenting the likelihood is the prospect's knowledge that the broker would really like to have him buy from her. The broker's best bet is to ignore and pass over courting signals categorically.

The prospect is not going to buy a house he doesn't want because you climb into bed with him, no matter how fantastic you are. He will buy the house he intends to buy, whether you sleep with him or not (see "Selling Residential Real Estate," p. 171).

To recapitulate and summarize the essential nonverbal behavior for women:

1. *Selling to a man or men.* Be firm, direct, persistent, not passive, sweet, and ladylike. Cut way down on smiling and laughing. Avoid provocative clothes, gestures, postures, and makeup. Bypass courting signals sent to you. Work farther back. Speak slower and lower. Dress simply and seriously in well-tailored clothes with a minimum of jewelry and accessories. Sit up, a bit forward, your head straight. Listen intently. Avoid complicated, new-wave, "kicky" hairdos. Touch only in the handshake.

2. *Selling to a woman or women.* Relax more; let more of your personality and enthusiasm show. You can smile and laugh more. Work closer. Adopt a stylish, smart, successful look, not a sexy one. Move with deference to a woman with greater status. Sell to her almost as you would a man.

3. *In the home.* Dress like a next-door neighbor. Smile. Step back at the door. Get inside. Try for the kitchen. Get the prospect to sit next to you. Show admiration and respect for the home, its appurtenances and inhabitants, including pets. Learn how to deal with husbands. Try not to arrive in the middle of *General Hospital.* Don't go into a house with a lone man or only men.

5

For Men Only

DRESS AND MAINTENANCE

Salesmen must be clean-shaven. Don't wear a beard unless you have no chin or have something serious to hide. Most people don't like people with beards as much as they like people without beards, except at Christmas. A mustache is more acceptable, but beware of weird mustaches. Pencil-line types are categorically out. So are Hitler types. Waxed handlebars are okay if you are in a barbershop quartet. Droopers that dangle into your mouth are quite unattractive. Don't wear a Chinese ancestor mustache unless you are a Chinese ancestor. Don't wear a Mexican bandit mustache unless you are a Mexican bandit. Don't wear "lamb chop" sideburns unless you wear Edwardian clothes. Don't wear Edwardian clothes.

Your clothes must fit. This is self-explanatory. If your clothes don't fit, do something about it. Stop eating. Stop wearing your brother's clothes. Go to a tailor.

Your jacket should not feel like steel cables under your arms when you reach forward. Your pant cuffs should not hover somewhere above your shoes. They should *touch* the tops of your shoes lightly. Tailors call it "breaking" on the shoe. That means a horizontal dent will appear along the front of the pant seam just above where the cuff rests on top of the shoe. Your pants should be on the snug side, unless you've gone to pot. Voluminous baggies look great in a harem, but not on a salesman at work.

Your shirts will crawl and wrinkle less if you buy them slightly tapered, European style. American shirts off the rack still tend to have about a yard of unnecessary fabric in the torso, as if we all had gargantuan livers. I don't know why; I suppose it's easier to make them that way. Look for shirts with some shape. Blends are best, 65 percent cotton, 35 percent synthetic, for all-around serviceability. Your shirt collar should be comfortable, not constricting. If your neck pinches into little wrinkles when you button the top button, your collar is too small. You should be able to get two fingers down the inside of your collar (along with your neck, of course) without strangling yourself. It's better to have it a hair on the loose side than on the tight side. You can always take up a little slack with your tie.

Wear a tie of average width, giving way a bit to current fashion one way or the other. Avoid synthetic fabrics. Do not wear a bow tie unless you are:

- over sixty
- under thirty
- a resident of New York or San Francisco
- an art director, juggler, or clown
- in a dinner jacket or tails
- a bow-tie salesman.

Do not wear a string tie unless you are:

- southern (deep)
- carrying a basket of fried chicken
- a real cowboy over fifty.

A Yankee should never wear a string tie, unless he is the firstborn son of Senator Claghorn (which I am, and I *still* never wore a string tie).

On clothes in general, you want to be a bit on the conservative side. Successful conservative. See how your prospects dress, and then aim one step higher. Not a big step.

You're probably not going to make a friend of the buyer in a polyester suit when you come in adorned in custom-tailored silk and cashmere.

A dark suit is always safe. Navy or gray. Pinstripes, used sparingly, are de rigueur for financial circles, insurance and the like. No fluorescent colors. No brown suits. The only acceptable light-colored suit is off-white or light beige, and then only in the summer. You must have at least one perfect navy blue suit. Not black but navy. Use this for any important prospect. This is your maximum for power and status. No shiny synthetics—ever. Wool or light wool gabardine or a blend with not too much synthetic in it. Silk is fine for warm climates.

You need a blazer—navy and wool or a primarily natural blend—which you wear with gray or pale beige slacks. This is slightly less formal than a suit but still has some status, and suggests an active, sporting life-style.

If your customers are given to sports jackets, add a couple of them to your collection. In the East and North, you want wool tweeds and camel hair; in the South and West, you can explore various lighter fabrics—linens and silk and blends that are light on synthetics. In the West, a beautifully cut leather or suede is acceptable anywhere a sports jacket is worn.

TRUE LIFE STORY: Dressing for Your Prospects

My director of sales and I were flying to Cedar Rapids to spend the day convincing an insurance company that they should sponsor a series of public relations newsfilms for national TV release. Their ad director and marketing director were going to pick us up at the airport and stay with us for the rest of the day. Leaving from New York, I assumed that a marketing director and ad director of an insurance company would both be in sedate suits.

I could see them from my window seat on the plane as we taxied up to the unloading area. They both were wearing sports jackets. The ad director even had on a golf shirt with an open collar. I suppose they had dressed for us "creative" types, and we had dressed for them. I was wearing a navy blue three-piece suit. My sales director had on a charcoal-gray suit. "Give me your jacket!" I said. We swapped jackets. Mine was a bit snug on him but not noticeably so. I stuck my vest and tie into my carry-on and opened my collar. The bit of white T-shirt exposed was removed by ripping a healthy tear down the front and folding back the two flaps. When we met them inside the gate, two guys with sports jackets met two guys with sports jackets. Everything went smoothly from the outset, and we got the account.

Coordination of textures and color is easy if you follow these simple rules:

1. *Socks.* Black, period. Over the calf or close to it. (I know they won't go with your white shoes. Don't wear white shoes.)
2. *Suits.* Navy, gray (or off-white or beige for summer).
3. *Shirts.* White, pale blue, pale yellow, pale beige, tattersall, blue stripe, beige stripe. That's it. Don't wear colored or patterned shirts with white collars unless you flunked out of prep school.
4. *Shoes.* Black, cordovan, and something to go with your off-white suit. Oxblood works well with the navy blazer and a burgundy tie, and a white shirt, of course. Boots are acceptable for certain people with certain kinds of customers. Boots must be kept up and shined. They don't look good when they're dirty and cracked.
5. *Sweaters.* A light V-neck looks good with a jacket and tie for cool weather. Crew necks don't sit comfortably over a tie.

   Solid colors are best. Leave the fancy patterns to the guys in *Gentleman's Quarterly.* Beige, blue (dark and light, but not iridescent), off-white, burgundy, a controllable yellow, gray. Don't wear black, bright red, hunter green, or pink sweaters.
6. *Vests.* Be careful about the color and texture of the vest vis-à-vis your shirt, tie, and jacket.
7. *Overcoats.* A full-length wool, navy or gray, with a

tweed fabric, or camel hair. Cashmere, if you've had a particularly good year. No three-quarter lengths. No parkas or sporting coats unless it's below freezing—well below. No fur coats. Leather is a possibility if it's extremely well tailored. Your raincoat or trench coat must be beige, not black or white or any other color.

8. *Umbrella*. Black with a wooden handle. If you have one of those collapsibles, hide it.

9. *Briefcase*. Leather, period. No vinyl. No artificial leather of any kind. Dark brown, not black. As thin as you can live with. If possible, avoid those squarish things that resemble midget suitcases.

If you have to carry a sample case that you think is ugly or cheap-looking, try to get someone at headquarters to do something about adding some class to the case. If you have to, get yourself a case you like and put the samples in that. If the people at the home office complain that it isn't in keeping with corporate image, explain patiently to them that they're wrong and you are right, and they really ought to upgrade their act. Remember to agree with them just before they fire you.

PUTTING IT ALL TOGETHER

Once you know what suit or jacket you're going to wear, the rest is easy:

1. *Dark suit*. Light shirt, dark tie.
2. *Dark jacket*. Light slacks.
3. *Light jacket*. Dark slacks.
4. *Patterned suit or jacket*. Solid shirt, patterned or striped tie.
5. *Solid suit or jacket*. Striped or tattersall shirt, solid or solid knit tie.
6. No patterned or striped slacks, ever.
7. Experiment with vests. A plaid vest over a striped shirt with a striped tie is a no-no.
8. Use solid V-neck sweaters to provide a buffer between a sports jacket and a striped or patterned tie.

9. Do not mix brown and gray.
   Do not mix brown and burgundy.
   You can try to wear a brown sports jacket with a solid blue shirt, but you'd better have a good eye.

Some other guidelines:

1. If you wear beige slacks with a navy blazer, try to find a tie that has a bit of both colors in it.
2. Don't wear black shoes with beige slacks. Try brown, cordovan, or oxblood.
3. Don't wear brown shoes with gray slacks. Try black or cordovan.
4. Never wear jeans on a sales call, unless you are selling farm equipment, livestock, illegal substances, fruit and vegetables, or stolen guitars.
5. Never wear a white tie on a dark shirt, unless auditioning for *The Godfather.*
6. Never wear a black tie unless you are horizontal in a pine box. French cuffs are very impressive, but don't wave them in people's faces if the cuff links cost more than $1,000, or less than $25.
7. Only two articles of men's clothing are permitted to shine: your right shoe and your left shoe.
8. Do not wear your high-school ring. Do not wear your college ring, unless you are still in college, and then someone else should be wearing it, anyway. Do not wear the diamond pinky ring your uncle Herb gave you.
9. The only acceptable jewelry for a man, other than the aforementioned cuff links, is a wedding band and a gold wristwatch.
10. Do not carry a pocket watch on a fob unless you have a title, earn over $100,000 a year, or are over 65.

You are on an important call for a big piece of business. You wear your new $475 suit. On a tour of the plant, your pants snag on a piece of machinery. The rip is irreparable. The prospect didn't see it happen.

You probably could win the price of a new suit back in a lawsuit. And lose the account. If you are going to get this piece of business, eat the suit. It comes with the territory. If the client knows what happened and insists on having his insurance pay for it, you may choose to accept graciously.

Glasses

If you wear glasses, don't get into the habit of looking over the top of the frame for distant objects (anything farther than reading distance), such as the prospect's face. It makes you look *old*. This move is a virtual trademark of grandfolks. As people age, they tend to get more farsighted. They wear glasses for all the close work, like reading. But rather than take them off for distant objects, they look up over the top of their glasses.

Bifocals are now available with no line in the lenses. Ask your optometrist. Or get into the habit of taking your glasses off when you have finished with the close work.

In your selection of glasses, don't underestimate the importance of finding frames that suit or complement your face. Don't trust the optometrist or yourself—bring along a tasteful, honest friend and try on everything in the store. If you don't find exactly what you want, look elsewhere.

You want frames that go with your face, rather than stand out from it. Don't try to compensate for a narrow face by wearing wide glasses. Don't buy aviator frames unless you fly to work or drive a Porsche. Consider the color of the frames; does it go with your skin and hair? And will it work with your basic clothing colors?

Don't get tinted lenses unless your ophthalmologist has prescribed them. They don't make you look cool. They don't make you look prettier or more intellectual or more sensitive. They make you look weird and affected or sick.

Glasses can be a wonderful prop. You can gesticulate with them. You can use them to look meticulous and intelligent. You can take them off at a crucial point (a kind of unmasking) to underline a sincere moment. At an easel, you can use them as a pointer.

Still, it is an exceptional pair of glasses on an exceptional face that enhances the overall look. If you can wear them comfortably, contacts are probably a more aesthetic way to correct your vision. The danger with contacts is what to do if one of them falls out in the middle of your meeting. Naturally, your important prospect will have a real thick rug. It's a jungle down there. You know you'll make a great impression groveling around like a pig rooting for truffles. Do you write the lens off and continue selling to a slightly blurry prospect, or do you grovel and run the risk of making a fool of yourself? It depends, of course, on the circumstances. If it looks like you are going to make the sale, wait till after the prospect makes a commitment. If you are sure you are looking at a stone wall, you might as well at least retrieve your lens. One positive facet of this nightmare is that the prospect is not likely to forget you soon. If the prospect is a contact lens wearer, too, he will certainly be more sympathetic to your plight. Then again, if you have the right "up" personality, and the prospect is a member of the opposite sex, you might be able to turn the lost-lens catastrophe into an effective flirting ploy. There are not many more effective inhibition relaxers than crawling around on all fours with someone.

Maintenance: Your Clothes

Hang your pants on genuine pants hangers, full-length with the waist down. Do not hang pants halved over a hanger bar. If you are on the road and have no pants hangers with you, jam the cuffs into the top drawer of a bureau and let them hang full-length. If there is no way to hang them full-length, lay them on something flat in preference to hanging them halved over a hanger bar. For an emergency pressing, put your plants flat under the mattress and sleep on them.

Hang your jackets on a hanger, wood or plastic, the thicker the better, whenever possible. Never hang your jacket on the back of a chair or on a wire hanger. In an emergency, you can use three or four wire hangers together to create a satisfactory hanger. Try not to hang your jacket on a hook, especially for a long time. It is preferable to lay a jacket on a clean surface than to hang it from a hook.

When you go on the road, pack your suits, jackets, and pants in a folding clothing bag rather than a suitcase. Use a flexible under-the-seat bag for additional space. The folding clothing bag is kinder to your jackets, and if you don't enjoy hanging around airport baggage-claim areas, you can carry it on. If you don't know where the closets are on the plane, the steward or stewardess will show you.

Stuff socks into packed shoes, so they won't collapse and crack or wrinkle. Fill the collar of a laundered shirt with either a pair of socks or shorts, so the collar doesn't get totally squashed down.

Don't pack aerosols, or anything that might leak, with your clothes, especially in baggage that will be checked. The baggage compartment on a plane may be subject to different pressures and temperatures than the passenger compartment. A five-hour swim in Foam-O-Shave will leave your best suit looking like a discarded welcome mat.

When you reach your destination, and it's too late for valet service, there are a few tricks you should know to spruce up your wardrobe.

You can take a lot of wrinkles out of clothes by letting them hang in the bathroom when you take a hot shower.

A synthetic-blend shirt will dry nicely overnight and be essentially wrinkle-free if you get it on a hanger immediately after washing it and hang it over, under, or in front of a heat or air outlet or a radiator.

Almost all socks can be washed (in tepid soapy water in the sink for about ten minutes, then rinsed well) and dried by the following morning. You dry them by rolling them up in a dry towel, then walking barefoot over the towel for a minute or so. Take the partially dry socks out and hang them near a heating outlet or radiator.

The best organic spot remover is still saliva, and you

always have some with you. For oil or grease spots, use salt or talc to absorb the grease, or try to remove it with lighter fluid. Gasoline is good, too, or vinegar or club soda. Some spots respond well to tepid soapy water. You probably already know to use cold water on a coffee spot, and salt and cold water on a red wine stain. Lemon juice and salt are best against a rust spot. Kerosene or lighter fluid followed by soapy water is good for tar. Use alcohol for a shoe-polish spot remover, and very hot water under pressure for a fruit stain.

You are at lunch with the prospect, and a blob of cocktail sauce falls on your shirt or tie.

Don't try to clean it at the table. Excuse yourself and head for the bathroom. Use cold water. Dry the water out by squeezing the area between two layers of tissue paper. Those electric blowers are fast driers also. When you return to the table, come armed with an interesting story or hysterical joke so everyone doesn't sit around talking about what a slob you are.

Maintenance: Your Body

Getting in Shape

If you were typecasting a successful, energetic, go-get-'em salesman, would you cast a sloppy, fat slob, or a trim, firm, fit-looking type? Film companies make it easy on themselves by casting people who *look like the role they're going to play.* Make it easy on yourself, and make sure you look like the role you're playing: successful salesperson.

Being fit and trim is, quite simply, the best way to look fit and trim. Overweight, out-of-shape people can of course be good salespeople, but they're always bucking the odds. Two things work against you. One, you don't look good, so prospects are less inclined to enjoy seeing you. Two, you are not performing at your peak potential, because you've let yourself fall apart physically; you tire sooner, and it takes more effort to do things.

If you tend to put on weight, get yourself on a diet and an

exercise program, and stay with it. Selling takes a lot out of you. Exercise, especially involvement in a sport, helps put a lot back in. Sports, exercise, yoga, aerobics, martial arts... physical fitness definitely improves your psychological outlook and tempers you for the rigors of selling, such as rejection, depression, and self-doubt. Physical fitness helps you keep everything in perspective. Get lean and mean, and stay that way, so when you go into the head-on combat of a sales confrontation, you feel forceful, alert, fearless, invincible.

The prospect invites you to tennis, golf, racquetball, or to crew on his racing sloop.

Do go out of your way to play sports with the prospect. Friendly competition in a sport is one of the best ways to build and solidify a strong social bond. Remember to let the prospect win at least half the time. Avoid crewing on his racing sloop at all costs. Say you have congenital terminal mal de mer. Crewing in a race will cut your stature irreparably. You become a sort of slave, a swabbie to his admiral. And God help you if you do something wrong, like run up an empty halyard during a sail change.

Skin

Your skin is the litmus paper of your body. It will show emotional or psychological imbalance as well as a physiological one. Extreme tension or unalleviated worry will start to express their adverse effects in your skin. And when you break out, you worry even more, further exacerbating the problem. If you or your doctor is convinced that stress is the root of your skin problems, you must, of course, find and pursue a program that will alleviate that tension or its effects. It may be psychiatric therapy, body therapy, TM, biofeedback, religion, hypnosis, old-fashioned-do-it-yourself willpower, or any combination thereof.

Usually, however, an occasional dermatological disruption is caused by a simple intake of too much this or that, an allergy, or overexposure to sun, wind, or cold.

You probably knew what substances were bad for you by

the time you got out of high school. Sugar, oily, fried foods, and nutmeats are fairly common sources of pimples. Some kinds of skin are aggravated by acidic foods, such as citrus fruits.

Let us assume that you are smart enough to do what you must to keep your skin looking its best. Still, the best-laid plans aren't always enough, and you might see a pimple brewing before an important meeting. If it is the night before, steam it. You can do it with the hot tap water in your hotel or motel and a washcloth. You dip the corner of the washcloth into reasonably hot, but not scalding, water, and you press it gently to the affected area. Use a gentle circular motion, with the skin moving with the washcloth. Do not scrape the cloth across the surface of the skin. Patience is the key. If you can salt the water slightly—so the salt is in solution, not granular—that's even better. The instant the pimple gives up, apply water as cold as you can get. Keep up the application of the cold water, on a washcloth, with absolutely no rubbing, for a minute or so, longer if you got impatient and bruised the area. Then apply a small square of tissue and hold it with gentle pressure over the area until you fall asleep or simply can't stand it anymore.

If it is the morning of the meeting, attack the pimple with a direct application of the white paste formed at the damp end of a styptic pencil. As the paste dries, it absorbs evil substances from the pimple in ten to fifteen minutes. Remember to rinse and dry your face.

If you are at home and you need a deep-pore job, squeeze half a lemon into a pot with an inch of water and add a spoonful of sage, rosemary, or thyme (hold the parsley). Cover your head with a towel, let the towel hang down around near the sides of the pot (watch out for the fire or heating element), and turn up the heat to make steam. With your face about a foot from the pot, close your eyes and hang in there for about ten minutes. Close the pores up with several splashes of cold water. You'll feel great, and look about five years younger. Don't do this too often, however; it'll desiccate the skin.

The simplest and most effective way to treat a shaving nick is with immediate application of very cold water for about thirty seconds. Place a dry piece of tissue about four layers thick over the nick and apply steady pressure for several minutes. Exercise caution when removing the tissue. You may have to dampen it slightly just an instant before removing it.

Women are expert at using makeup to cover blemishes; men who are not professional actors should never do it. Not because it doesn't look better, but because other men will think you are weird or effeminate if they detect that cosmetic cover-up. A sincere shaving nick that you can't stop or hide, even a sincere blemish or small pimple, is more acceptable on a man than detectable makeup.

Teeth

It is absolutely crucial to have well-maintained teeth. Stained, cavity-ridden, pitted, chipped, and missing teeth are unacceptable. We agree that painless dentistry is a contradiction in terms, but failure and poverty can hurt you even worse. Find a good dentist, with a dental hygienist on staff, and use them both. If you need major work, or have a particular tooth that is ready for a root canal, and you don't think you can afford it, you should know that you can have the decay stopped and the tooth immobilized while you raise the money. Chipped teeth can be evened out cosmetically with the new technology of bonding, which is fast, inexpensive, and painless. When your teeth and gums are healthy and clean, it makes for fresher breath. *You can destroy an otherwise perfect presentation with bad breath.* Brush and floss regularly, and carry a breath spray when you are on the job. Avoid garlic and onions for at least eight hours before a face-to-face meeting. Quit smoking. If you must drink, vodka is the least noticeable on your breath. Don't get into the habit of taking minty candy to cover up; it does even more damage to your teeth.

Hair

Your hair should be neatly groomed and recently cut or styled. Hippie-length hair is unacceptable, unless you work with rock musicians, pro football players, or disciples. There must be no straggly fuzz creeping down your neck (where you can't see it). If you don't live with someone who can tell you it's there again, get a small hand mirror. If you don't live with someone who can shave it off for you, try it yourself. With a safety razor, how much can you lose?

If you have a bald spot that's beyond hiding, don't try to hide it. Men get bald, and that's the way it is. If it's any comfort to you, most anthropologists believe that prehistoric men didn't go bald. That's the price of civilization. It's okay to have a bald spot as long as the rest of you looks healthy and vibrant. Look at Yul Brynner. In any case, it's better to be stone-bald, or shave your head, than to wear a toupee. Don't think for a moment that you are going to fool all of the people all of the time. You're not even going to fool the majority. And keep this in mind: Once they know you wear a toupee, it's on their minds every time they see you. And all throughout the call, your prospect has a little voice in the back of his head that keeps repeating, "This guy is wearing a wig!"

You can expect a toupee to look essentially unnoticeable at the stylist's, when you get your final fitting, and when he painstakingly places it and styles it into your own receding wisps. But will you be so careful each and every morning? Then let's see you at the end of the day when the back of the rug sort of hangs away from the back of your head. Or, even better, let's see you a couple of seasons later, or years later, when your hair color has shifted and the toupee's hasn't. Exposure. Mortification. Derision. Is it worth the constant dread? No.

You should not wear a hat. Hats have been "out" since JFK. Obviously, if you have to work in subzero weather, a warm hat of some kind is called for. Just remember to leave it in your car or take it off in the lobby or elevator or reception area. Never wear a hat into an office.

Emergency Tactics

You are on the road and you forget your blow-dryer. Dry your hair more thoroughly with towels, then use the heat lamp as you brush or comb, or stand with your head in front of a heat or air-conditioning exchange.

You forget your comb and brush. Use a matchbook with every other match removed.

You forget your toothbrush. Use a washcloth and your finger. Salt is a good substitute toothpaste. Floss with a piece of thread from a sewing kit.

You have no soap. Use shampoo.

You have no shampoo. Use soap, but rinse it out thoroughly.

You forgot to buy shaving lather last night or you didn't pack it to avoid danger of accidental discharge on your clothes. In preference to making a harsh lather with hand soap, use any oil, suntan or hair, or Vaseline.

For hangover bags under the eyes, apply cold compresses made from tissue, cotton balls, a washcloth, or damp tea bags.

You forgot your nail brush. Use your toothbrush. (I don't recommend the reverse.) Later, buy yourself a new toothbrush and a nail brush. And don't ever forget your nail brush again.

MEN SELLING TO WOMEN

Most of the material in this book is applicable to some degree or another in a cross-sex selling scene. In this section, therefore, to spare repetition, we shall confine ourselves only to those differences in technique that apply to men selling to women.

Due to average heights and muscle mass, a salesman today will usually have an edge in physical presence over his female prospect. This generalization applies if the salesman has good posture, carries himself tall and confidently, and is trim and fit. Let us say he has at least the wherewithal for greater physical presence.

In the initial "sizing up" of the other party in a one-on-one sales confrontation between men, there is a subconscious vying for the dominant role. The dictates of civilization and better business behavior do not allow the two men to start arm wrestling, jousting, dueling, or trading blows, but on a subconscious level there is a definite confrontation of adversaries taking place. Three elements determine who takes the dominant and who the recessive role: pure physical prowess, implied power, and willpower.

Pure physical prowess is the possession and display of size and muscle volume. When you are in a discussion with a pro football tackle or a prizefighter, you are always aware of the fact that he could, if provoked, reduce you to a pile of broken bones. Of course, if you are at the same level of physical might or skill, you balance and cancel the power of that threat. Implied power is the power that is implicit in the possessor, due to his position at the head of an organization that will act on his orders or in his behalf. A title on the door and a Bigelow on the floor are generators of implied power. Limousines, bodyguards, imposing mansions, elegant clothes, powerful friends, or a full-grown Doberman at your heel—all contribute to an aura of implied power. Willpower is, of course, the inner strength of the will that allows a scrawny shrimplike Mahatma Gandhi to force the hand of the British Empire, or a pint-size Napoleon to conquer Europe.

A man selling to a man will feed all three factors into the equation to determine the other man's power. And although physical prowess seems such a coarse and primitive attribute to weigh, it is still a substantially important component in the dominant-submissive struggle. (Look at a room full of corporate executive officers; most of them are tall or big. The short or scrawny ones have the gleaming, powerful eyes of Genghis Khan, a testament to their strong willpower.) A man selling to a woman doesn't factor in the threat of her physical prowess. He is at a loss, therefore, because he has honed his skill at dueling with épeés, and suddenly he is in combat with an opponent who will only use pistols. The female prospect has, through the effects of civilization, refused to allow physical prowess to enter into her assessment of a salesman's power. In fact, an obvious display of physical prowess will probably work *against* the salesman. The female prospect will find it immaterial or, worse, a repugnant signal of lower-class origins or lack of manners.

This is not to suggest that you try to hide or minimize your height, broadness of shoulders, or well-developed pectorals. It is to suggest that you do not use your Superman grip when you shake the hand of a female prospect. Firm is good, but your vise-grip is a mistake. You may try pulling the prospect toward you slightly; let your intuition guide you. If she is terribly shy and fragile, it may be too intimidating. In any case, you must terminate the handshake immediately when she signals it is to end.

Lower the volume of your voice. Women generally are discomfited by a commanding voice. To a woman, a lower voice probably signals more confidence than a louder one. The snake in Eden spoke, I imagine, very softly.

The prospect speaks so softly you can barely hear her.

Fine. This is a wonderful excuse to work in more closely and speak more softly and deeply yourself. A soft-spoken prospect is usually not a phony and is generally nicer to be around. Don't for a moment think, however, that a soft voice signals a weak character.

Sustain solid eye contact. A woman will usually look away first, because she doesn't want you to read her steady gaze as a courting signal. However, if you keep avoiding her eyes, you look nervous and insincere (see more on courting signals in the section "Cross-sex Selling," p. 117).

Work farther back in the beginning, then move closer *gradually*. You may find the limit of her personal space is farther away than a man's. However, her space perimeters will shrink and become blurred rather quickly if she responds positively to you. If you feel this softening and relaxation of the distance barriers, move closer. Your nonverbal signals will have more impact, and hers will be easier to read. As you get closer, gesture more slowly, in a smaller way, and with more control. Your facial expressions should be less broad.

Smile. Good, full smiles are quite acceptable and will show you are at ease. It is unfortunate, since today's women have a marvelous sense of humor, that many middle-management women in business feel compelled to act even more serious than their male counterparts, perhaps to compensate for their presumed flightiness, as women, on the part of stodgy male superiors. If you find yourself in a meeting with a woman who is working very hard to stay deadly serious throughout, it is wise to appreciate her goal and to cooperate as much as possible. She is likely to loosen up in a subsequent meeting once she trusts you.

Don't be patronizing, even if you are forty-five and have three daughters in college, which your prospect looks like she just dropped out of. All you need to know is that this prospect has the power to say yes or no, to buy or not to buy. The fact that she is twenty-one is immaterial. Look at it this way—if she becomes a loyal customer, she'll be buying from you for a *long* time. A patronizing perspective will especially show in your face and in your tone of voice. Once it creeps into your nonverbal performance, it is virtually impossible to eliminate. Get rid of it up front, immediately.

Neither should you be obsequious and fawning. Even if she is chairperson of the board, a woman won't like you if you show that you are intimidated by her. Women are comfortable with people who are self-confident, just as men are. Do not offer false flattery not based on fact. A woman knows her strong points well, so if you fabricate something, you are likely to miss the mark, she will know you are flattering only for effect, and she will distrust you. Flattering is one of those activities wherein your nonverbal display must be one hundred percent supportive of the sincerity of your communication. If you fake it, the chances are it will show.

Listen very closely. Don't ever interrupt. Men have a habit of interrupting women, or cutting off the ends of their sentences. If this is a habit you have, break yourself of it.

Relax. Don't rock, squirm, twitch, jerk, or fidget; you'll look uncomfortable, and she'll think it's because you're uncomfortable with her because she's a woman. At the same time, don't be too casual, because it will project presumptuousness or a lack of respect.

Never look at a female prospect's breasts or legs or derriere. At least, never get caught. Never give a woman a head-to-toe once-over with your eyes; it reads like a rude and insolent invasion of privacy. It does not "turn women on." You might look briefly at her hair or hands. This shows you are interested in her, or attracted to her, but is less forward and shows respect.

Don't touch. Outside of handshakes and accidental brushing, don't consciously touch a female prospect. Even if she touches you.

The more attractive a female customer is, the less you should flirt or flatter. Attractive women get gratuitous come-ons from males constantly. Believe it or not, it rather rapidly gets to a point where it's boring. Don't jump into the ship of fools with all the other predictable Lotharios. Try your best not to react to her appearance at all. Relate to her on an intellectual level. You must, of course, stifle the body language that's crying out, "You're gorgeous! I'm mad about you. I'm going to jump your bones in about three seconds."

You can be resolute and enthusiastic, but women don't respond to pushiness in a salesman. Persistence, yes; pushiness, no. The minute a woman feels you're high-pressuring her, she will produce an obstinacy that will leave you wondering how they were ever labeled "the weaker sex."

You may lose the battle, but don't give up the war. Since the first hominids skulked upon the face of the earth, women have, after all, reserved the right to change their minds.

You are at an out-of-town convention. Your job is to try to get the such-and-such account. The prospect from such-and-such is an attractive, bright member of the opposite sex. You meet, and the prospect tells you that he or she expects you to take them to dinner later.

Make reservations.

6

Bridging Age Gaps

THE WHIPPERSNAPPER GAP

If you are quite young and are selling to people substantially your senior, you may find it difficult to get them to take you seriously. You like to get enthusiastic about your product, but when you do, you feel and appear even younger. Even though almost everyone wants to "give a kid a break," it's not enough to depend on for a livelihood. A prospect who has been in a business for fifteen years and knows his stuff is likely to resent the six-month wonder, who presumes to talk with authority but is, by definition, short on experience and depth. There is usually an automatic distancing between the prospect and this upstart. Let's call it a "Whippersnapper Gap."

To compensate for it, you do what any other actor would do; age your character. Not a lot, but enough to dry the moisture behind your ears. You don't want to overdo it— you'll look like Dorian Gray just before the fall.

You should dress more conservatively.

Consider readjusting your hairstyle; does it look too trendy? Is there a style that will make you look less youthful?

Slow your moves down. Sitting down and getting up shouldn't be done in a quick and easy snap.

Salesmen, you can safely dust a little unscented talc into your sideburns. Don't do it if you're under twenty-two.

Smile a bit less. Young saleswomen must particularly avoid gratuitous, openmouthed smiles. Facial expressions should convey a deeper level of seriousness than would normally be expected from someone of your tender years.

Don't squirm or squiggle impatiently in your chair.

Slow down your eye movements. Quick, flitting eyes are a product of the shorter attention span of the young.

Listen closer. You recently got out of school; you knew how to make a professor think you were really hanging on his every word. Do the same thing with your prospects. Paying attention implies respect, and everyone likes that.

Salesmen, watch your grip. Very young salesmen frequently have an indifferent handshake and smooth, tender hands. Strengthen your hands with exercise, and toughen the skin with some heavy manual work (or play); this is a crucial element in your first impression.

Young saleswomen, this may surprise you, but cut way down on the "sweetness and light." You are always courteous and attentive, but leave the lion's share of ladylike demureness to the nineteenth century. Shrinking violets do not make sales. Be direct, clear, and deliberate. Female prospects will rather enjoy your courage and the fact that you know how to get to the point. Older female prospects may enjoy seeing in you that all their pioneering wasn't for naught—you represent the new order, new opportunities. Male prospects are likely to be knocked temporarily off-balance by having someone they typecast as a sweet young thing suddenly coming on all business, flinty and persistent and not to be intimidated. Your direct assault immediately dissipates any impression your prospect may have of you as a young, shy babe in arms.

Young salespeople must, in any case, develop a most extensive product knowledge, and that includes knowledge of the competition's product. All salespeople are wise to sustain a thorough product knowledge, but a very young salesperson must compensate for his lack of experience with an exceptionally well-funded data bank. Learn your products, their background and benefits, cold. Then augment credibility by becoming well informed on competitive products. Then learn as much as you can about the businesses you are selling to. Before your older prospect has a chance to discount your opinion, you floor him with facts and figures he's forgotten or never knew.

And that's how to bridge the Whippersnapper Gap.

TRUE LIFE STORY: Not Letting Bad Luck Deflate or Flatten Your Presentation

I had a commercial film studio in Stamford, Connecticut, in 1969, when it was commonly understood that the only places to have a decent film studio were New York, Hollywood, and maybe Miami and Chicago. It was a very hard sell. New York ad people wouldn't even talk to me (there was nowhere close by where you could get an exorbitant, exotic lunch). I went after industrial film prospects. I finally succeeded in luring up a likely prospect from the city. Everything went smoothly, but the man was not relaxing and opening up to me. He was a great-outdoors, male-chauvinistic, quiet type. I had the feeling he had pigeonholed me as a callow, artsy-craftsy, intellectual upstart. I sensed he didn't "like" me. During the tour of the studio, I considered being rude to one of the female employees, or challenging him to arm wrestling, so he would understand I was just one of the guys. But I didn't, and by the end of the presentation I was sure I had lost him.

I had to drive him back to the station so he could catch the train for New York and not miss an important afternoon meeting. It was pouring, a deluge of Niagaran proportions, when I hustled him into the Mustang. It was a fifteen-minute drive. One-quarter of the way there, my left rear tire blew out. We shimmied onto the shoulder. I told him to stay in the car; no point in two of us getting drenched. I leaped from the car and put on the spare in about three minutes. When I climbed back in the driver's seat, the guy couldn't believe we were ready to roll again. He was visibly impressed. I told him I had spent a few summers pit-crewing so I

could get into races. We started talking about racing.
We talked about sailing. We talked about the service. All
of a sudden, his train was coming, and he had to break
off a terrific story about a marlin that pulled him overboard
off Mazatlán. The next day he called and said he was
giving us the job. Anyone who could change a tire
that fast couldn't be all bad, he joked. I laughed along,
but behind my laughter I was soberly calculating that
if I hadn't made short work of the tire—if I had bitched
and whined and bemoaned my fate and called Triple
A so I wouldn't get wet (while he missed his train and
his meeting), I wouldn't have gotten the account.

THE GEEZER GAP

On the other end of the age scale, as inevitable as taxes
and death, is the oldness syndrome. The problem isn't grave
(poor choice of words) if your prospects are as old as you, or
in some lines of work where there is increased stature implied
by ripening years—statesmen, judges, philosophers, some
writers, some lawyers, some artists.

If you are not one of the above and you find yourself
routinely selling to prospects who are twenty years or more
your junior, you will have to take steps to bridge the Geezer
Gap.

Look at your clothes. If they are yesteryear's styles, give
them to the Salvation Army or Goodwill Industries, who will
see that they go to some deserving statesman, judge, or
philosopher. Out with the funny-width ties, the outdated
lapels, the skirts of improper length. Out with "tired" clothes
of any style. At the time of this writing, baggy pants and
padded shoulders are totally "out" for men, but "in" for
women. Next season, the reverse may be the fashion.

Update your hairstyle if there's enough of it left to style.
Consider coloring your hair. Women have been doing it routinely
for thousands of years. Women "of a certain age" should not
darken their hair, but should go for a *lighter* shade. The extra
light reflected and diffused into the face is soft and will help
minimize tiny wrinkles.

Men of advancing years should also think about coloring their hair. But they should think twice. There is still a certain stigma attached to it in America. It's considered either a dishonest or nonmacho act. You must consider if you can get away with it, if you're willing to put up with the hassle of messing with the chemicals, and if you can handle the trauma of being found out. (Daddy, is this black toothpaste?) Graying is frequently accompanied by the development of a growing bald spot. As bad as it is, gray or white hair calls less attention to your bald spot than hair colored darker.

Avoid heavy, ponderous moves that signal tiredness and ennui. You don't want to project a frayed-collar jadedness, the loss of energy and enthusiasm. Don't collapse into chairs with a groan or an *ooof*. Inject your moves with some spontaneous spirit and lightness. Let there be some wonder and excitement in your eyes; the eyes of older people sometimes seem dead. The best way to project a vital, vibrant, vigorous you is to stay involved in an active-life sport—swimming, tennis, running, aerobics, golf, dancing—whatever. Then you don't have to project anything; that's what you are.

Beware of phony smiles. Fake smiles really look contrived on older faces. On the other hand, *real* smiles are especially disarming on an older face—look at Santa Claus.

Listen more closely. Senior people have the problem of having heard it all before. They must make a special effort to tune in on the prospect's communications. This young prospect may just come up with a new wrinkle. (Sorry.)

For older saleswomen, it is more effective to be more of the lady the young saleswoman is trying to bypass. Forwardness is unappealing in an older saleswoman, who is likely to appear cronelike and strident. Mature women can command a lot of respect and power, but they do it through dignity and equanimity rather than pushiness. The older saleswoman is, ideally, not stubborn, but firm; not insistent, but persistent; not loud, but clear. She is courteous and expects to be treated courteously. And if she sticks to her guns, she is almost impossible to turn down.

The essential characteristics of advancing years other than changes in skin and hair are a bent back; heavy, slow, weak, and broken moves; and a "catch" or hesitation in the voice.

Heavy, slow, weak, and broken moves are counteracted by keeping up your body tone and coordination with active involvement in sports and exercise. Your body is perfectly willing to fall apart if you let it. With no use, your muscles will dwindle away to feeble vestiges of their former selves. Overindulgence inevitably results in the accumulation of fat. The weight and volume of the fat pulls you into new and uglier shapes. Your moves are slow and heavy because the muscles are weak and the burden of movement is greater. Gestures are broken because coordination and strength are lost. All this can be avoided by the enjoyable pursuit of any active-life sport—dance, aerobics, or a program of exercise, and a sensible intake of food and drink.

The catch in the voice is usually not discernible until you are into the sunset years. But we trust our ears enough to guess someone's age merely from hearing his or her voice; and the guess is usually reasonably accurate. To take years off your voice, you want to speak with the self-assuredness of a younger person. Once you commit to a chain of words or sentences, it should flow evenly from the first syllable to the conclusion of the communication. Older people hesitate, I believe, because they are more cautious about what they say and the way they say it. When you become so cautious that it interferes with the flow of your speech, that's too cautious. Perhaps as we age, gray matter gets a little sluggish, and we can't think on our feet so fast. We want to respond, but we don't want to blurt something out that offends, makes no sense, serves no purpose, or is an incomplete response. The solution is to think for a second longer before you speak. One technique to give yourself some time, without an uncomfortable moment of silence, is to repeat what the prospect has just said or asked, in slightly different or simpler terms. Since you're just feeding information back to him, you can start laying out your response as you speak. Your repetition may serve a far more important function than stalling for time; it augments understanding of exactly what the prospect is saying. Also, hearing his thought back in slightly different terms often leads the prospect to add or refine his original thought with an important qualifier or further information.

For example, your prospect says, "I had a fairly high opinion of your computers until I heard how hot they ran."

You respond, "You're saying, in other words, that you decided against buying our computers when you heard that they put out more than average heat?" As you do so, you are formulating your response, you show that you are paying attention, and that you don't want there to be any misunderstandings.

You are in mid-sentence and lose your thought utterly.

Go back immediately to something the prospect said and ask a question about it. Never roll your eyes and smack yourself in the head like an escapee from bedlam with a hole in his marble bag.

What can you do to lessen the effect of time on your face and skin? Some measures are inexpensive and simple. Avoid lots of intense direct sunlight on your skin. If you are often outdoors in sunny climes, use lotions or moisturizers with a sun block such as PABA. People with a serious interest in their skin seem to have nice things to say about skin preparations that also contain vitamins E, A, and D. Grandmothers often rave about the preserving powers of glycerin and rosewater. It is said that Porcelana, and lots of patience, will help banish dark aging spots.

There doesn't seem to be much you can do to stave off the advent of wrinkles, other than to moisturize and avoid direct sun. Men generally let the lines come and call them "character lines," or "smile lines." Women generally get rather more upset by the inevitable advent of wrinkles and battle them bravely with lotions, creams, baths, massages, and masks or packs of earth, organic matter, and god knows what it was the mysterious gypsy lady told them to put on their faces.

Still in the category of simple and inexpensive is the icy water bath. It works for both sexes. First you clean the facial skin with mild soap or a nonsoap cleanser, and rather warm water. Get the pores completely clean and as open and relaxed as possible—no scrubbing! Now run the water as cold as possible. Splash it on your face with your hands, or apply it with a washcloth. Just *hold* it to the skin, no rubbing. (There is a scene in *Mommie Dearest* in which Joan Crawford uses a bowlful of ice for the cold half of this treatment.) After about fifteen to twenty seconds, your skin and face will look about ten years younger. Unfortunately, the effect doesn't last very long, but repetitions may help the skin regain some of its tautness. It's wisest to ask your dermatologist. Just before a call, a salesman can use the technique to firm up his facial skin anywhere he can find a sink with hot and cold water. It is harder for a woman, naturally, once she is fully made up. But she can approximate the effect by carefully patting cold water to her forehead and cheeks.

One of the typical characteristics of older men is the assertive growth of facial hair on the eyebrows, and in the nostrils and ears. If you want to look younger, you will have to carefully trim the burgeoning hedgerows above your eyes, the whisk brooms being spawned in your nostrils, and the weird little feelers your ears sprout. You must be careful to trim eyebrow hairs one at a time, and at different lengths, so as not to create the effect of two caterpillars with crew cuts. Nostril hairs are best cut with tiny, blunt-tip scissors available in most drugstores. Get the most expensive ones you can buy, and hide them where little Billy can't find them to cut the feet off his plastic soldiers.

No longer in the realm of simple and inexpensive, but incontrovertibly the most effective way to take a giant step backward in time, is plastic surgery. Not long ago considered a risky option only for the malformed or truly homely, plastic surgery is performed today as routinely as having a tooth pulled or having bodywork done on your car. Common procedures are the miniface-lift for the areas around your eyes, the nose job, and the reduction of sagging chin or chins.

I have seen miniface-lifts that were remarkably successful at causing the march of time to do an about-face. They can take the droop out of the lids, the puff out of the bags, and substantially reduce the set of deep wrinkles. Additionally, the entire mask of skin is sort of pulled back up, lifting the tissue and musculature of your face back to where it used to be. Normally, you are out of the doctor's office that afternoon. Local anesthetics may be used, lessening the risks associated with general anesthetics.

The nose job, increasingly popular on both coasts, is equally simple. The important thing to remember if you opt for this procedure is to keep in mind "less is more." Don't replace your hulking, bulbous tomahawk with a tiny, pert pug nose. Find a normal-looking compromise that fits your face. Also, talk with people who have had it done. In spite of doctors' assurances to the contrary, people who opt to take off too much always seem to have stuffed-up noses. Also, with time, the nose seems to constrict into an even tinier, sharper little blip, and the ski-jump effect seems to intensify. A nose job should be subtle; don't be greedy.

There is no longer a stigma attached to corrective surgery. All sorts of people are having one procedure or another done to make themselves more pleasing to the eye. Debra Sue Maffett, Miss America of 1983, freely admitted to a nose job, and she probably wouldn't have won without it. For anyone whose appearance affects their performance, and everyone in face-to-face sales is obviously included, corrective plastic surgery is certainly an option to consider. One of the benefits is the psychological shift you will experience in your attitude toward yourself. You will feel better, knowing you look better or younger. Consequently, your self-confidence is augmented.

TRUE LIFE STORY: Remaining Cool and Confident No Matter What

A once-admired, rather flamboyant advertising man had left a creative directorship to start his own agency. It folded after seven months and ninety thousand in unpaid bills. He couldn't skulk his way back into another salaried position; it wasn't his style. So he had gone into consulting. There were ups and downs, mainly downs. Years passed. At age 57, he initiated a final push to earn enough to retire on. He had succeeded in setting up

a meeting with a large New York financial institution,
to win a substantial new product introduction and plug
into a retainer on some ongoing business as well. This
one account could put our friend back in the pink for
many years. He had asked three bright younger people
into the presentation of his campaign, to pose as his
full-time executives. I was the director of broadcast
marketing.

We met at their offices (he didn't have one), in a
prestigious paneled boardroom with a monolithic, twenty-
foot-long oak table. We sat on one side of the table,
the financial people on the other, a formidable wall of
navy blue and dark gray interrupted only by pinstripes
and a flash of gold cuff links.

Our "boss," at one end of the table, rose ebulliently
to speak. "Gentlemen," he said, "it gives me great
pleasure . . ." And suddenly, like a piece of Puffed
Wheat bursting from the end of a General Mills cannon,
as brilliant and shiny as a shooting star, one of his
teeth exploded from his mouth and went skittering across
the table, some eighteen feet, and rolled to a halt like
a malignant curse in front of the chief executive officer.
Everyone looked in horror from the ugly hulk of a
gold crown, still wet, to the face of the once-flamboyant
ad man. He never missed a beat. He didn't waver from
his positive posture and confident expression one iota.

"Gentlemen, it's easy to get someone's attention,"
he continued. "But then, does the way we get their
attention turn them off? Is the hard sell relevant when
what we have to offer is pure gold? We submit that the
advertising for your new investment program be low-
profile and dignified. There will be no ugly pitchmen,
no strident sideshow barking to offend the conservative
investor. After all, this is a prestigious investment firm,
not a sideshow!" And with that, he retrieved his tooth
and dropped it in his pocket as though it were one of
his standard openings. And they bought it. Maybe they
knew what had happened, but figured anyone with that
kind of presence of mind and moxie couldn't be all

bad. They gave him most of the work he was after, and last time I saw him he was having lunch at "21." He had a completely new set of teeth that looked like Chiclets. I wondered if one of them was removable for effect.

7

Selling to the Emotions

Emotions motivate.

People buy what appeals to them emotionally, from salespeople who appeal to them emotionally.

You cannot force people to buy.

You cannot trick people into buying. (That's illegal.)

You cannot turn a prospect on with a cold enumeration of product features.

You cannot sell with pure logic.

Years ago, salespeople talked about finding a prospect's "hot button." That was the topic that seemed to turn the prospect around and make him into a customer. In the beginning of modern selling, salespeople weren't quite sure what the "hot button" was, or how it worked. They weren't even sure how to go about finding it; trial and error was the recommended technique. The proverbial "natural salesperson" was thought to have some innate intuition and be able to discover a prospect's "hot button" quicker than mere mortals. Once the hot button was found, the rest of the sale was expected to flow to its conclusion without impediment.

Today we recognize that the "hot button" is nothing more than the moment of emotional impact or implication of the product on the prospect. It is the moment when the prospect experiences a positive emotional reaction engendered by the effect of the product or its capabilities on his self-image, or his idealized self-image. It is the urge to possess the product in response to the compelling force of emotions such as fear, envy, or greed.

Your job is to find and know the kinds of emotional appeal your products are most likely to have, then to find and use the prospect's sympathetic chords or emotional keys to turn him on.

If you sell a high-glamour item, it is obvious that the product will enhance self-image, public image, style, and stature. It will provoke envy, admiration, and respect in the prospect's peer group, and additionally may help satisfy his need for pleasure, power, or love. Is there any emotional appeal in a brass-tacks item like a cinder block? Certainly. The builder who buys your cinder blocks is going to build stronger buildings that will enhance his reputation, leading to more and larger contracts, resulting in greater profits with which he can satisfy most of his heart's desires. In other words, there is no sale, no product, and no prospect in which the reading, understanding, and use of emotional appeal and emotional response does not play a principal role.

Nonverbal communications are crucial in selling because they play such an important part in determining the prospect's reaction to you and consequently to your product. Your winning moves shape and color the emotional environment and will influence the prospect's emotional state and sensitivity. It is clear that you will have a much easier time discovering the emotional appeal of your product if your prospect is emotionally for you, or at least not against you. This is what master salesman Joe Girard is talking about when he holds forth on "selling yourself." You sell yourself by projecting a terrific, friendly, honest, sincere, bright, direct, successful personality. You un-sell yourself when you stimulate negative emotions such as:

- fear, by coming on too strong
- resentment, by being patronizing or snobbish
- distrust, by using mechanical clichés, exaggerating, or evading questions

- anger, by thoughtless faux pas, such as telling an ethnic joke that may offend
- nervousness or distraction, by sending heavy courting signals
- revulsion, by displaying some distasteful action or habit
- indignation, by insulting the prospect's intelligence or taste
- disesteem, by exhibiting low-class signals to upper-middle-class prospects
- "bad vibes," by not tuning in and paying close attention.

If you are able to sell yourself, you're halfway home. All that remains to do is to find that emotional need in the prospect and let him know how your product is going to satisfy it. Frequently, your product does most of the work for you. It shouldn't take you long to figure out which emotions a product stimulates.

A woman looks at an evening gown and she sees herself making a grand entrance into a roomful of people she wants to impress. She uses a full-length mirror to help her imagine exactly how smashing she is going to look. She experiences warm little zickers of premonitory delight just thinking about how all the women are going to be consumed with envy, about how all the men are going to be filled with longing and desire. The gown is perfect, it compliments her figure to a *T*, it's an eat-your-heart-out dress. She can't afford it, but she'll buy it because she *must* have it. The smart saleswoman in this situation doesn't have to say a word about how well made the fabric is, how strong the zipper is, or that the colors are fast. All she has to say is "Wow!"

A man is about to buy a set of professional ratchet wrenches. He looks at them all, gleaming neatly in their bright metal box, and sees himself, a genius engineer, capable of fixing or constructing *anything* with that set of wrenches. He sees his wife impressed that he even knows how to use such things, and her look of admiration when he repairs the garage door. He sees the look on his mechanic's face when he says, "Oh, you can forget about resealing the head on my motor, I did it myself." He can see the undying gratitude of his next-door neighbor when he repairs his lawn mower with three turns of one of the new wrenches. The man doesn't really *need* thirty-two wrenches in a shiny red box, but he buys them because he is turned on by the image of his owning them.

Do you think a couple buys a house they need? All you *need* is a square cement cinder-block shelter with a tin roof and adequate plumbing and utilities to support your family. People buy a house that appeals to them emotionally. They want a house that makes them feel something: warmth, power, status, permanence, or peace.

A product or products will normally have some intrinsic emotional appeal that prospects will respond to. Assume that the prospect who is looking very hard at the racy red sports car is responding to fairly obvious emotional appeal in a fairly predictable fashion. Almost everyone wants to own a racy red sports car, and for essentially the same reasons. This is convenient for you because you know which emotions and self-images to support in your selling. Everyone in sales isn't so lucky, and it usually takes a little digging to find the emotional link between him and the item he wants or will want to possess. Let's run through a list of possible buying emotions, so we know what we're looking for.

1. *Pride.* Appreciating personal worth or making a statement of personal style.
2. *Vanity.* A heightening or enhancement of self- or public image.
3. *Status.* A sense of accomplishment, social recognition.
4. *Cupidity.* The joy of possession, for show or for security.
5. *Love and libido.* The feeling that such and such an item will bring or earn love, or lead to libidinal gratification.
6. *Fear.* Fear of loss of social approbation, station, security, friends, respect. Fear of loss of life sells many items beyond the obvious insurance policies, health aids, and medical services. Fear of the hereafter motivates expenditures for monuments (of one form or another) and bequests to charitable and religious organizations.
7. *Pleasure.* The absence of pain. The desire to be entertained, amused, soothed, thrilled.
8. *Envy.* The compulsion to surpass the Joneses, or at least keep up.

9. *Power.* The sensation of being able to influence the lives of others. Being in control.
10. *A sense of mission, or conscience,* such as patriotism.

To find the aspect or product benefit of the product that stimulates one of these buying emotions, you:

1. Establish a positive, nonthreatening emotional environment by projecting your own "up, relaxed, and yes" emotional state.
2. Listen to your prospect. Watch your prospect.
3. Probe with general questions.
4. Listen and watch.
5. Probe, with specific questions that carry your best guesses about what you believe will appeal emotionally to the prospect.
6. Listen.
7. Watch.

It would certainly be handy if prospects would just blurt out what product benefit or approach would get their juices flowing, but they don't. They conceal these things as part of their natural sales resistance. And, just as frequently, they may not know themselves what motivates them to buy one thing over another. It may be so deep in their subconscious that they are unable to wrestle it to the surface where they can recognize and define it—for themselves, let alone for you.

Modern testing techniques have shown that a customer may choose an item because of any number of characteristics that are not mentioned at all in the subsequent verbal response to explain the choice. A shape, color, sound, smell, texture; an image of an appealing scene, aesthetics, a childhood memory. Any number of product features, including packaging, advertising, and public relations, may trigger an emotional response that will become a buying impulse. Frequently, that trigger is provided by the salesperson, especially in the sales of controlled or regulated items where the only substantial differences will lie in the character and personality of the salesperson.

If the prospect will not, or cannot, communicate verbally

to us what will turn him on emotionally about a product, we turn, of course, to a careful reading of his nonverbal signals. As he talks, or as you talk, and you examine or explore the item to be sold, you watch for the following signals to indicate a stimulated emotional response:

1. The facial expression lifts or brightens. Eyes open more, seem to moisten or glisten; there is less blinking. If you can see them, watch for pupil enlargement.
2. The prospect inhales deeper, holds breaths longer.
3. He grins, especially on one side, a mischievous or Cheshire-cat grin. Or he smiles, sometimes ruefully (How am I going to pay for this?).
4. He carries himself better, as if "putting on airs."
5. He poses, struts, or preens.
6. He touches the product with interest.
7. He moistens his lips.
8. He touches or strokes part of his body.
9. He looks long and hard at the product, shifting his point of view often.
10. He looks away from the product and then looks back immediately out of the corners of his eyes.

You present brilliantly, but you know this prospect is slipping through your fingers. Somehow, the vibes are all wrong.

Try something completely different. Try appealing to a different emotion. Alter your style. Go bigger or smaller, faster or slower. If you have been smiling, try a serious look, or vice versa. It may surprise the prospect, but then it may be a pleasant surprise. At any rate, once you're certain you are losing him, why not try something new?

If you see one or any combination of these signals, note what direction you are moving in, or what aspect of the product's benefits is under discussion. Whenever you feel the prospect girding up his resistance or stalling, reintroduce the element that seemed to turn him on the most. That is, lead him again to consider or imagine that image or fantasy that stimulated him emotionally. The power of a strong emotion will almost always triumph over logic. All you have to do is keep the fire warm under the emotion. Your job, once you have found and opened the emotional "window," is to reinforce frequently the prospect's image of himself owning the product. You must say sincere, positive, and honest things about how the prospect's image is enhanced by the product, keeping the prospect's uniqueness in mind. You must support the prospect's notion that he deserves the product. He looks better, it suits him perfectly, it will make him happy and his peers envious, members of the opposite sex will find him irresistible, people will be awed and show more respect. For your assurance that his projections will be satisfied, your nonverbal signals must be one hundred percent sincere. When they are, the prospect feels you are a sensitive person who understands his point of view and shares his goals. If signals are not sincere, he feels you are manipulating him only to make a sale, and you will lose.

This is not to imply that you should gloss over or neglect any of the important product features and benefits. The prospect needs the features to address the questions and doubts mounted by the logical, rational side of his mentality. The emotional response, the urge to buy, will almost always carry a buying impulse through its conclusion with the purchase of the item, but the rational voice frequently has veto power. Once the prospect has decided he wants the product, emotionally, he wants you to assuage the qualms of his businesslike, rational side, which clearly simplifies your work. When the prospect wants to be sold rationally, his rational investigation of the hard facts will be less intense and certainly less critical. In any case, he will need the rational backup for himself or his boss, associate, or spouse. When the other party, back at the office or the home, reacts with "You bought *what!?* For *how much!?*" the prospect is armed with a logical, rational reply based on the information you provided him.

EXERCISE: Finding the Hot-button Emotion

This is so easy it's hardly an exercise. Keep a pad and
pen or pencil handy when you watch TV. When the
commercials come on, grab your writing instruments,
watch, and try to isolate the emotion the TV spot is
appealing to. If you can't find any, it's not a very good
spot, or you're not terribly perceptive. Additionally, if
you have time, you might also jot down *how* the advertiser
(read *sales agent*) appeals to that emotion. Sometimes the
emotion they're after is rather well concealed, and sometimes it's simply understood and accepted, as with a
charity spot. This exercise will help you find the turn-on
emotions of your prospects and will also serve to give
you some ideas, nonverbal and otherwise, for how to
stimulate and arouse those emotions.

8

Selling Residential Real Estate

When walk-ins enter a retail establishment, usually they want to be left alone to browse. Almost no one welcomes the salesperson who rushes over and offers to help the customer. Prospects will ask if they need help. They will search out and find a salesperson if they need one. The opposite is true in a real estate office. Walk-ins want to be helped. If there are several salespeople at a number of desks, walk-ins expect to be told or signaled which desk to approach. The broker "on floor" should get up immediately, step out into the foyer or reception area, and introduce himself. A really alert broker will see prospects approaching the office, or looking at house pictures in the window, and when the prospects are deciding whether or not to enter, he opens the door for them. If there is a secretary up front, he can direct the prospects to the broker who is "on" but who is momentarily tied up on the phone.

In almost every other type of sales situation, the salesperson does not shake hands with walk-in prospects. With real estate, there is no rule. You must be alert to the prospect's moves. If prospects are warm Southern or metropolitan types, they may very well offer a handshake as part of their introduction. You will sense that a handshake is coming by the proximity of the prospect and a slight lead with the right shoulder.

People who have not bought or sold a home before have a minimal knowledge of how a broker works, what obligation are incurred by talking to one, how referrals are handled, etc They don't know what to say and what not to say. They know they don't want a bunch of strange salespeople bothering them at one in the morning. If they are looking to buy in the area, they may worry that they will be stuck with a salesper son they don't like. (Yes, it is possible that someone may no like you, no matter how lovable and filled with life you are. Consequently, walk-ins are a mite uncomfortable in the beginning. It is your job to put them at ease.

Lead them into an informal area, if possible. Your office should have some sort of small conference room or lounge Offer them chairs. Move slowly and without tension. If there is coffee or tea, offer them some. Hand them the appropriate pictures and brochures or flyers. Use maps and charts. Pic tures and printed material break up the forbidding starkness of the table and the tension of the meeting.

Your primary goal is, of course, to convince the potentia lister that you will do a great job of selling his property, or to qualify potential buyers as to seriousness of intent, the type of property sought, and their financial ability to follow through You probably make some quick assumptions about prospective buyers, based on their nonverbal signals. If they are dressed like bums, the man unshaven and the woman with sock rolled down over mismatched shoes, you may have to do some very creative financing to get them a mortgage. Try no to jump to conclusions, though. These are sometimes the people who drive away in a chauffeured Rolls-Royce.

Beware of prospects who respond to financial question with a no-problem wave of the hand, and expressions that are designed to lead you to believe that money is no object Unfortunately, such people usually don't have enough object to put together a down payment. Perhaps they have been deluding themselves. Don't let them delude you. Serious customers will think hard and come up with responsible answers to financial questions.

Beware of prospects who come on very friendly right away. Not because they are flirting (which is, of course, a possibility), but because people who lay on unwarranted warmth are frequently compensating for the fact that they know they are wasting your time. They may be sort of looking for a house—or not. They are likely to have a large number of salespeople taking them to a large number of properties. The only way to tell if they are just spinning their wheels is by a sensitive reading of their nonverbal signals.

You qualify the potential buyers according to the guidelines set up by your office. You show them pictures of homes that fall into the range between what you calculate they can afford and what they conjure up in their delusions of grandeur. Watch their faces and hands when they look at these pictures. The longer they look at one particular listing, the better. If they are looking through a book, watch the speed with which they turn the pages. The slower they turn, the more interested they are. When prospects see a place they think they'll love, they will be anxious to see it as soon as possible. If a property is clearly beyond their means, it is a waste of your time to show it. You must learn to be firm, friendly, but clear with prospects that want you to show them such a listing. Not only do you lose time, but then everything you subsequently show them they *can* afford looks worse by comparison. You probably know which house is perfect for your customers before they do. Do *not* try to sell it in the office.

Take prospects in *your* car. Insist on it. You want to be close to them, to watch their reactions, hear their comments. Let them decide who in their party will sit up front and who in the back. You drive. The need for complicated and knowledgeable driving precludes one of your customers' party driving (see "Your Car," p. 180). Don't try to be the Salesperson of the Year while behind the wheel. Your first priority is safe driving. Confine yourself to responding to questions and making general comments about neighborhoods you are driving through. The best thing you can do is *listen* to the prospects.

Show your worst house first. This is the monster they can afford with no sweat. But, of course, it's far below their projection of a home they see themselves living in. They'll hate it. Watch their reactions, and file this information for future use in decoding their nonverbal signals. They will get back in the car quickly (they may never get out) and be anxious to get on to the next property as soon as possible. Once you detect a strong negative emotional reaction to a property, do not continue to show it "to be fair" or to be thorough or polite. This is a waste of everyone's time. Get on with the next act.

Your strategy is to show your best bet at the end of the period you have given this prospect. You do not, however, want to show your best house in the dark. Watch the time, and start showing it no later than twenty minutes before the sun sets. Homes look their best in this light; it's like seeing everything through rose-colored glasses. Greens look darker, so the foliage looks fuller, and shadows are longer, so the house look bigger. And the dying light doesn't play up all the little cracks and crevices and peeling paint. There is also a sense of time running out, which may remind your customer to act quickly before someone else puts a binder on the property.

Park across the street from the house. This affords the widest and probably most impressive view of the house and shows how it fits into the street and neighborhood. If you have a choice, park on the lower side of a rising or cresting slope, to make the house look bigger. Do not park directly in front of the house, but favor one end or the other, whichever offers the most aesthetic perspective.

Bring prospects through the front door, even if you have to go around to another entrance to open it for them. You should enter the house first, to make sure no one else is in it (kids, vandals, another broker), or to let the occupants, if there are any, know you are there. Then let the prospects explore the house, rather than taking them on a guided tour. You follow them into the rooms, letting them discover while you answer questions. Let them set the pace. If they are about to miss the guest bedroom over the garage, or the sleeping porch, then lead them to it.

You are showing a residential house with a lock box on or near the front door (the lock box contains the key to the door). You get out the key and try to open the front door, and it just won't work. The prospects are standing there getting restless.

First you should try to get to the lock box and front door alone for a minute. If the street is nice, encourage the prospects to stroll along it, to get a feeling for the neighborhood. If the yard is nice, send them on a short turn through the yard or the new garage or the beautiful view from the terrace. Now you get a moment to tackle the sticky lock alone. Calm down. The reason the door won't open half the time is because you are panicky and the door knows it. Relax. *Pull the door toward you as you turn the key.* If that doesn't work, pull the door toward you *and up* as you turn the key. If you simply can't open the lock, as a last resort you can let the prospects try. One of them will get it, naturally, on the first attempt. If not, before you throw in the towel, remember to try the back door.

Turn on every light in the house. A well-lit room looks more spacious and cheerier and constitutes a brighter, more positive environment for positive emotional reactions. The most important light for you to illuminate is, of course, yourself. Buyers may think they like a house, but it is human nature for them not to trust their own reaction. They will use you as a source of third-party objectivity and of expert testimony. You see so many homes in the course of your work, they reason, that if you really like this one, it must be quite special. It makes sense, therefore, for you to be especially "up" and enthusiastic when you show them "the right house." This doesn't mean that you sell harder or talk faster. You show that you sincerely like the property through your nonverbal communications even more than your verbal ones. Feel and enjoy the special character of the house. Let it envelop and embrace you. Let your positive, happy, comfortable aura fill each room you enter. Your prospects will pick up on your signals and will inevitably mirror them. Your emotional state will make for a similar positive mood in your prospects. The house will assume a happier or more hospitable ambiance or spirit. People definitely respond to the "vibes" of a house, although they may never admit that they are responding on that level. Your positive living energy and charisma may totally offset the ominous, baleful vibes of a room that seems to contain memories of evil, anguish, pain, and death.

If your prospects break up and move to different parts of the house, you stay with the one you believe is the stronger decision-maker. It's not necessarily the chief breadwinner of the family. Clue: The principle decision-maker is the one who looks mainly at you during crucial decision-weighing discussion. The secondary decision-maker will frequently look at the stronger partner for a lead, a reaction, or approval.

If your prospects walk around the outside of the house, this is a strong sign of interest. It's a sort of territorial staking-out. Also, if customers look out of windows often, into the yard and neighborhood, it's a positive sign of serious interest. If they take off their coats, they're obviously making themselves at home. Watch for signals of stimulated emotional response (see "Selling to the Emotions," p. 163).

When the prospects start asking questions about the taxes, assessments, mortgages, cost of utilities, and so on, you start hustling them back to your office. Use the excuse that you have all the pertinent data there, as well as your handy desk calculator. You do not want to start negotiating in front of the owner, if the owner is in the house. An important aspect of your work is to act as a buffer zone, a great mediator between the two parties. You can do this best when they are physically separated. Primarily, you don't want the potential buyers and sellers to be able to see one another's nonverbal signals as negotiations are taking place. The parties involved are better off this way because there is no danger of their nonverbal signals giving away their true positions, or being misconstrued by the other faction.

When you get back to the office, park as close to your door as possible, and preferably not near their car. If they get into their car and say they want to go home and think about it, you lose. You must get them back into your office to sell them on making a commitment and authorization for you to negotiate on their behalf (a pleasant euphemism for "signing a binder"). You do not lead them to your office to "get a binder," or have them "make an offer." You are going there to provide your prospects with more information and to answer questions you were not able to answer on the road. Once in the office, you move on obtaining a commitment, of course. For your nonverbal strategy in this situation, see appropriate sections throughout this text.

Communicate your prospects' primary offer to the owner in person. You cannot tell enough about a reaction over the phone. You really must see a full nonverbal display to know how far off or how close you are. As a rule, try to conduct any important negotiations in person. After all, how many of your nonverbal techniques can you use in a letter or over the phone?

Finally, it is important in real estate sales to know when to stop talking. As a rule, stop talking when you have said all there is to say, or when your prospect is talking, reading, or writing (especially a check). And don't talk again until someone asks you something.

TRUE LIFE STORY: Not Showing Your Feelings When They Won't Help Your Sale

My wife is a real estate broker. We were dressing for a party we really didn't want to miss. The inevitable last-minute opportunity suddenly cropped up, as it is wont to do. A couple who were frantic to find an estate on the water, who had been looking for two weeks solid, and who were going back home tomorrow in despair, simply *had* to see a house that just came on the market, *now.*

"We're just going out," replied my wife, to let them know the dimension of her sacrifice. "So are we," responded the couple, unimpressed. We met in front of the house half an hour later. My wife had talked with the owner the day before, and he had urged her to come

by anytime with customers. Most of the lights were
on, and the TV was on in the den. We rang and rang,
but no one came to the door. The owner was a widower.
His wife had passed away some months before, and the
kids had all moved away long ago. It was understood
that Mr. Tod (not his real name, of course) was given
to drinking in excess, and we assumed he had passed
out somewhere. We went around to the side entrance
and knocked until the windows rattled. The next-door
neighbors' window opened.

"Are you showing the house?" he called.

"Yes."

"Well, go right in. You'll find him on the floor
somewhere, dead drunk. Just step over the body."

He chuckled and closed the window.

We laughed in unison.

"Do you really want to see it?" asked my wife.

"I think I love it," answered the lady.

The door was open. We went in.

We were in the kitchen. It was very hot, about eighty
degrees (the temperature outside was in the fifites).
Hot and moist and close. There was an enormous load
of groceries on the kitchen table and on the floor in
front of the refrigerator. A honeydew melon had been
sliced open and left out on the counter. Three fat
houseflies were having a meeting on the edge of the
largest slice, trying to decide if they should eat the
whole thing themselves or if they should go get some
friends. All the frozen food was standing in puddles
created by their own thawing. There was an open bottle
of vodka on the table, half-empty.

The couple loved it.

My wife suggested they wait a minute while we found
Mr. Tod and told him we were showing his house. I
went upstairs. My wife was going to look on the ground
floor and downstairs. Mr. Tod wasn't upstairs, or in
the attic bedrooms. I returned to the kitchen. My wife
was there ahead of me. She told us Mr. Tod was in
the den and had fallen asleep watching TV.

So she showed the house, floor by floor, room by room. The couple liked it more and more and were already getting decorating ideas. My wife supported their enthusiasm and gave them background on what a terrific neighborhood it was, etc. We looked into the den, with Mr. Tod sitting there in his shorts and undershirt, asleep in front of the TV, his drink still in his hand on the edge of the sofa.

The couple was going to make an offer, and we had a little powwow in the breakfast nook to discuss what moves were to be made next. The oppressive heat and the parties awaiting us made it a short discussion. The couple gave my wife their out-of-town number, we shook hands, and went our separate ways. When we reached our party, my wife asked me if I would call the police and report that we had found Mr. Tod dead.

"Dead?" I said.

"I'm afraid so," she replied queasily.

"But he was sitting. Up. He had a drink. In his hand. Watching TV."

"Rigor mortis, I guess," she said.

"But you were smiling and charming and enthusiastic and..."

"I wasn't really sure."

"Sure you were sure."

"Well, maybe. Sort of..."

"You knew."

"Look, there wasn't anything to be done for Mr. Tod. His last words to me were to sell his house. Now I could say with certainty that it was available for immediate occupancy."

"You showed that house and never stuttered or looked sad or got sick or seemed depressed or rushed them through, and the owner was sitting there dead?"

"I guess so."

"Do you know what I am going to do?"

"No, what?"

"I am going to put you in my book about the body language of selling. I'm going to give you as an example of hiding your feelings when they don't support your sale."

"Oh, horsefeathers," she concluded.

YOUR CAR

Keep it clean and shiny. You can make a brand-new Rolls look like the old gray mare with a thin layer of grime. Keep the interior clear of debris. You never know when the prospect will suddenly suggest you drive over to the plant so he can show you what he's talking about. Frequently he suggests going in your car, because he knows it's another statement about your character. If you have a sports car, you can score points by offering to let the prospect drive. If he accepts, it puts you in the position of director/supervisor, as he will probably be unfamiliar with your car's idiosyncrasies.

If you are driving, *don't* show off. Even if it's a recently tuned Ferrari, don't "open her up," or demonstrate your racing turns. Prospects really won't appreciate your cavalier attitude toward their lives. And stay calm when the little old lady cuts you off at the intersection. It might be the prospect's mother!

When you are a visitor, be careful where you park. It's better to be in Lot Z, half a mile away, than to leave your wheels in the sacrosanct reserved space of an irritable senior vice-president. Imagine the effect on the middle of your close when you hear, over the PA or intercom, "Will the owner of the pink-and-green Buick bearing the plates NUM-ONE come directly to the security office. You're being towed," and you bolt from the room like a rabbit with a hotfoot.

If you have a dog or cat that likes to ride to grandma's on Sundays, take them in the car you don't use for sales calls. Many people are allergic to animal hairs. *Everyone* is allergic to getting annoying animal hairs all over their coat or suit. If you have had Spot or Morris in your car, vacuum the interior completely. Then go over the seats and carpeting with a piece of duct tape or something that will lift the hairs out of the fabric.

It's smart to keep a couple of kids' toys visible in the back, say, on the shelf behind the rear seat. Enhances your image as a responsible family man.

If you find yourself selling in your car, which is a matter of course for real estate sales, try to avoid serious selling on unfamiliar roads. You'll start driving slower and slower, you'll make wrong turns, and the prospect(s) will start to worry that you aren't paying proper attention to your primary goal: keeping them alive until they sign the contract.

When you are selling while driving, don't try to sustain good eye contact with the prospect. He'd really rather you kept your eyes on the road. If the prospect is driving, put your serious selling on hold—he's really not concentrating on your patter. Limit yourself to recapping points already covered or easily digested, pleasant observations about the environment you are driving through. Don't stare at the prospect as he drives; it makes him uncomfortable because he can't defend himself by staring back or avoid your eyes by turning away.

If you take multiple prospects in a car and you will be selling during the drive, the best place for you to be is in the middle of the backseat. Try to put your primary prospect in the front passenger seat, and install his or your subordinate as driver. A secondary prospect goes next to you on the backseat. This accomplishes several things. It gives the primary prospect the best view. It delegates the mechanical task of driving to the least important player. It upgrades the backseat, since you choose to grace it with your presence. It frees your mind and body to concentrate on your sale. It frees the primary prospect to concentrate on what you are saying. You don't have to keep craning your neck or twisting around in your seat to look at the prospect. Everyone thinks you gave up the front seats because you are courteous and well-mannered.

Try to avoid pointing at everything you describe. It's very effective to use words to describe where you want your prospect(s) to look. It underlines your facility with language, and it enables the prospect(s) to see the sights without having to keep looking back at your hands and gestures to figure out where you want them to look.

Don't smoke in a car (don't smoke, period). And be attentive to the comfort/temperature range for your passengers. Do not play music. There is rarely a station or type of music that will be enjoyed by all. Do not play the radio; why complicate your sales message with all the jumble of sales messages on the air? Do not take or offer coffee from a thermos in a moving car. Why risk scalded prospect lips and dangerous spills?

Finally, make sure you have enough gas, oil, antifreeze/coolant, etc., to get you where you want to go and back. And a spare and, at night, a good flashlight with fresh batteries. If you get a flat in the middle of nowhere, and you are really good at changing flats, don't hesitate to do it yourself. Try not to let the prospect get dirty, but if he really wants to help, let him. If you are a ninety-pound woman who has never seen a tire iron, and the prospect is a two-hundred-pound mechanically inclined gorilla, let him do it. And let him know you're very happy he was along.

If anything mechanical goes wrong with the car, move immediately to get some new transportation as soon as possible. Don't try to fix it. While you're waiting for AAA or your partner or the taxi you called, use the time to sit in the car and do some gentle selling. If the car is stalled anywhere on a highway, in any position where it could possibly be hit by another vehicle, get out of it and stay out of it till help arrives. Don't freak out, bitch, whine, or curse your evil ancestors. Take it in stride, with humor and equanimity, and your prospect will pick up on, and reflect, your disposition.

9

Winning Moves on Camera

With the proliferation of inexpensive video equipment, increasing numbers of companies are installing video centers to produce internal communications and tapes for sales and service training. Local cable outfits have increased the chance that your products or services, or your company's reputation, may come under media scrutiny—and you may be the party responsible for representing and defending your company when under pressure. Video teleconferencing is growing rapidly. And, more and more small businesses are using local TV as an advertising medium. In any case, as your career advances, so does the likelihood that you will find yourself nose-to-nose with a relentless, cold, all-seeing zoom lens. Every element of your dress, grooming, posture, gestures, and expressions will be under close scrutiny—thoroughly illuminated and enlarged for anyone to see. If you don't come off well, with controlled, calm credibility, your career may well be in trouble.

It is quite possible, and even likely, that someone who seems relaxed and in control in regular meetings and presentations will fall totally apart upon their first exposure to a film or video interview. They are prone to stutter; twitch and tremble; make faces they don't mean to make; perspire profusely; gesture clumsily; slump or slouch; stare nervously up, down, or all around; or make jerky, broken moves.

The simplest way to avoid this first-appearance-on-camera nightmare is to make it *not* be your first appearance. As with anything else you want to do well, you must practice. No one walks up in front of a live camera and does as well as someone who has done it several times before.

The thing that makes a film or video camera so intimidating is the way it looks at you. It never relents in that unblinking, all-seeing stare. And there's no way on earth you can stare it down. You have the additional dread afforded by the knowledge that the editor is in a position to make you look even worse by using those pieces where you really blow it.

Once you agree to speak or appear or be interviewed before a live camera, once it is crouched before you like a steel-and-glass triceratops ready to spring, you must face the fact that you are about to be electronically captured in every detail. Remember the old saying "The camera doesn't lie"? The motion picture TV camera is even more sophisticated; it makes it very hard for *you* to lie. If you do, the camera faithfully records all your traitorous signals, and you might as well have a neon sign over your head, flashing "LIE!" And it can be played over and over again.

This environment demands that your subtext, your key, your character, and your externals be rehearsed to the point of second nature. The most trying on-camera appearance is the press conference or media grilling where the reporters are out for the sensational truth, and it is your mission to smooth over and minimize in order to project confident credibility. If you have to think on your feet, anticipate where the interviewer is trying to lead you, and cleverly circumvent the really dangerous issues and defuse the potentially volatile revelations, you must be free to concentrate one hundred percent on the content of the interview, not on your conscious nonverbal performance. In other words, you don't have the time to be self-conscious. This means you rehearse, plenty, on camera, with at least two hot lights aimed at you. And have associates lambaste you with questions.

Let's dispose of this tense confrontation before going on to the more mundane kinds of video selling you may have to do. If you have a choice, try to meet the video press on your own turf. You feel more confident, and they are never entirely sure you won't terminate the interview by having them thrown out with the forklifts.

Dress conservatively. Solid colors. Solid shirts and blouses. Stripes and checks buzz and bleed on video screens. Avoid large blocks of stark white. White sets up what's called white noise on TV. Women can wear their basic business makeup, carefully applied, of course. Avoid a hairstyle that requires spray; it'll wilt under hot lights.

Check what's behind you. You don't want a leaf or smokestack in the background to look like it's growing out of your head.

Practice saying "no comment" in a friendly, matter-of-fact, guilt-free way.

Blot the perspiration off your forehead and nose just before they start shooting. If you are off-camera for any portion of time in the body of the taping, use a discreet tissue to blot any new perspiration from your brow and nose. Are you aware that you can apply a little mild antiperspirant to your forehead and brow just before the taping? *Don't get it in your eyes.*

If your mouth tends to go dry, put a little Vaseline on the tip of your tongue and spread it around the inside of your mouth and over your teeth, especially the front teeth and gums. This, incidentally, facilitates a ready smile.

Use Visine or Murine on bloodshot eyes; on camera, they make you look like a drunk. Don't wear sunglasses unless you are blind. Tinted lenses will look like sunglasses, so don't wear them, either. Wear contacts or regular glasses, or go without and talk like Mr. Magoo. Men, shave closely. A five o'clock shadow looks terrible on a TV screen. The lights make it look worse than it is. Have your hair cut and neatly groomed.

If you're going to be taped by one unit or interviewer, try to go over with him beforehand what areas he will be probing. If you see that he intends to move in directions that are outside your expertise or responsibility, you can try to steer him clear of them before the cameras are rolling.

Remember that the audience will be seeing everything *only* from the point of view of the taking lens. In a multiple camera situation, that's the one with the *red light glowing*. The director or producer or interviewer himself will apprise you of the format of the show, and tell you whether you are supposed to look at him only, the camera only, or at either as you choose. Do what you are told. If you may look at both, start your statement and replies looking at the interviewer, then look into the lens for the body of your answer, then back to the interviewer. The camera lens is the eye of ten teleconferencers, or ten million viewers of network news. You must look right into the lens itself. Sometimes, in an effort to get you to play to the lens but still give you something to relate to, the interviewer will sit as close to the camera as possible. Don't keep your eyes on the interviewer—*focus on the lens.*

When you are asked a tough question, don't look up (you look dumb, or like you're whipping up a lie) and don't look down (looks like you're ashamed or guilty). If you must look away from the lens or interviewer to gather your thoughts, sweep your eyes slowly across an imaginary audience standing behind the camera. Or gaze casually at two or three points behind the camera or interviewer. To the audience this will look like you are facing a real crowd of inquisitioners and looking at them squarely without fear or reservation.

If you are asked a question you cannot or will not answer, and you don't want to use "no comment" yet, do not hesitate to tell the interviewer that you are not best qualified to answer that, but Mr. So-and-So is. Or use the old standby that all the information isn't in or is still being digested, so you or your company haven't come to a conclusion on that point yet. When you feel you have said enough and don't wish to volunteer any more information, smile pleasantly and stop talking. Just stand there and don't say another word, even though you feel strongly compelled to do so. Local TV news has to be fast-paced to keep up the ratings—they'll cut away from you to something else pretty quickly when they realize you're not going to expand on your remarks. Remember that a viewing audience will trust your image over your words. If your nonverbal presence and array of signals transmit sincerity, honesty, and equanimity, the audience will tend to believe almost anything you say. If, on the other hand, you give them the pure, unadulterated truth, but you look uptight and panicky, no one believes a word of it.

Let's get back to less intense on-camera situations: teleconferencing, internal communications, TV advertising, and sales training films or videotapes.

You may begin by taking from the above material any elements that are germane. You always want to look your best on-camera. You will always go out of your way to rehearse beforehand. If your company doesn't have any video equipment, look into video and public speaking courses in the nearest large town or city.

PREPARATION FOR YOUR ON-CAMERA APPEARANCE

Rehearse, with video equipment, if possible.

Get a good night's sleep. Get up early and take a leisurely breakfast with no coffee or tea. (You don't want to stimulate the adrenals to fill your system with adrenaline. It only aggravates your tics and makes your hands and knees shake more.) Take B complex vitamins or a C and B complex combination, a natural tranquilizer, with your breakfast. If you smoke, try to smoke as little as possible. Even if it did calm your nerves (which it doesn't), you aren't going to make a good impression by coughing and clearing your throat.

Don't drink any alcohol. Even at lunch. Even if the taping or filming or teleconference is at four P.M. It may loosen you up, but it may loosen you up too much. It will slow your reactions after a time, and rather a short while after drinking. It's not worth the risk. You want to be completely clear. Use some other technique to deal with your tension and stage fright—exercise and rest, autosuggestion, TM, or one of the many innovative psychotherapies. As FDR said, you "have nothing to fear but fear itself."

Ask the director or camera person how much of you they will see. If the material will be almost entirely medium close-ups, you don't have to worry about your legs and hands. If they will be doing lots of close-ups, you know to slow down your eye and head movements.

If you are sitting or standing, don't rock or sway back and forth. Don't make any fast moves; you'll go right off-camera. If there is a makeup person, don't hesitate to avail yourself of his services. Women will almost always profit by having an objective professional add the proper finishing touches or redo an entire face, for that matter. Men who are very pale will always look better with a light application of slightly darker foundation. Bald men must get some dulling base or powder onto their crowns or risk the inevitable halation or hot spot of reflected light. At the least, a makeup person will blot and dry your glowing brow and nose between takes, especially if you are cordial and ask them to keep an eye on you. Don't feel silly for a moment. Presidents, premiers, and anyone else who uses TV as a communications medium use makeup to improve their appearance.

There will be some loss of acuity in the audio track, from transmission, re-recording, or in the amplification system on the other end or in playback, so you compensate for it by speaking slower, lower (in pitch), and a bit louder and clearer than you do face-to-face. If you are miked with a lavalier (a little mike that's pinned to your tie or the front of your blouse), be careful not to bump or rub it with your sleeve as you talk. Get a decent lungful of air before you speak; it adds "projection" to your voice and helps prevent stammering or stuttering.

THINGS TO THINK ABOUT FOR YOUR ON-CAMERA APPEARANCE

Whatever is closer to the camera appears bigger.

If you are out of the light, you are out of the picture.

"Cheat" your face to the camera when you are not playing to it directly. Don't ever turn your back to the camera.

Always look alert, even though you may not be speaking; anyone in the audience could be looking at you at any time.

The tighter the shot (or the closer the camera), the smaller and slower you make your gestures.

If there are any "cold" fluorescents in the room or area, insist that they be turned off; they make you look green around the gills, and they phase unpleasantly with the frames-per-second of the camera.

Sudden moves toward or away from the camera are likely to get you right out of focus.

Make friends with the director, say something nice to the camera person or whoever sets up the lights. For your little extra ounce of charm, they will make you look especially good.

If you are in control (if you are paying for the taping or filming) and something is happening you don't like or understand, stop everything and speak to the director or senior person on the crew. If you have even a tiny twinge of an idea that something is wrong or could be better, act on it. Don't stifle. Tell the director immediately what you're after or what your problem is. Don't wait until all the equipment is wrapped to mumble something about the fact that the chairman was misintroduced or the product packaging was not the latest mock-up.

When you are speaking in a close-up, try desperately to avoid licking your lips. Never chew on anything, like a pen or pencil. Use facial expressions sparingly, especially in close-ups. The slightest nuance will do the trick, as the screen will isolate and magnify it. Do smile, but be careful if you have a few gold crowns in there; it is not classy to have one of them reflect a dazzling sunburst of light into the camera. You know, I assume, never to chew gum, betel nuts, or tobacco. And never to smoke on-camera. Even Johnny Carson, a self-avowed nicotine addict, tries to hide the occasional cigarette he can't resist while taping his show. One likes to think he does this because he knows how bad it looks, but it may be just because he doesn't want to hear about the dangers of smoking from Tony Randall again.

VIDEO ROLE-PLAY

Many larger companies have upgraded the role-playing exercises of sales training by investing in video recording systems. These can be tremendously effective. They show you much more about yourself than a mirror can. Videotape is more objective and has the advantage of limitless replay for closer examination. We can save it to look at later and measure progress. The special value of videotape recording is that it allows us to see ourselves as others do. Mirrors can't do that as well, for the same reason that you can't tickle yourself. When you look at your image in the mirror, you know that it's you looking at you, and you don't really get outside yourself to see yourself objectively.

Role-play without video focuses entirely on the verbal aspects of selling. You go through the maze of probes, advance alternates, countering objections, bypassing, cushioning, trial closing, clarification, verification, repetition, and whatever other twists and verbal turns your particular brand of sales training prescribes. Sales trainers or observers from your peer group critique your facility at wending your way through this sales word-puzzle. But no one tells you that you point at the prospect when you counter objections. That you frown when met by indifference. That you jiggle your leg and pull your lower lip when you get ready to close. Even your best friend may not tell you that your hair is ridiculous, that your clothes should be donated to the Smithsonian Institution, and that your smile is phonier than a promise in Hollywood.

There are three things you can do to give your video capability even more depth: 1) move the camera to the prospect's point of view; 2) play back the tape with the sound off to evaluate nonverbals; 3) try some tight close-ups on specific body parts.

Almost every setup I have seen for videotaping sales role-play had the camera positioned to the side of the players, in a two-shot. This is clearly not the best place from which to observe the presenter's technique. First, he is reduced in size, as we must pull back to include the prospect. Then, all we can see is a side view. Third, the presenter gets only a partial idea of how he looks to his prospects. Move the camera to a position over the shoulder of the prospect. Place the lens close to the prospect's head, approximating his eye level. You don't have to see any of the prospect's head, ear, or shoulder. If you worry that a prospect will bash his head against the lens, move the camera farther behind the prospect's position. The prospect's chair should be a fixed-back thing with no swivel base or wheels, to prevent collisions with the camera or tripod. For an interesting variation, the presenter can sell straight to the lens. The prospect stands behind the camera or out of view entirely. This technique will give you footage that will show you *exactly* how your winning moves look to your prospects.

Playing back the tape with the sound turned off is always an effective way to isolate nonverbal signals. You and your associates and trainers can observe and critique while the tape is playing back. You will be stunned at how much information you are transmitting with nonverbal signals. You will learn a lot about degree of intensity in your expressions and moves, and how, in most cases, "less is more."

Focus the lens on the presenter's hands for the entire presentation. The camera operator may have to follow some of the broader gestures. Try a tight shot on the presenter's face only. Or his legs and feet. Obviously, the presenter will be aware of the camera's focus on some isolated part of his body (if it is away from his face), unless you are shooting through a two-way mirror. Still, you accomplish a lot simply by calling the part or system to the presenter's attention. Naturally, if you can tape a close-up of a presenter's hands or feet without him seeing or knowing what you are doing, it will more effectively reveal any counterproductive behavior.

Trainers and participants in video role-play must go out of their way to be very positive and encouraging, especially to newcomers. Videotape is a startlingly revealing reflection, much more powerful than the first time you heard your voice on a recorder, and it can be bruising to the ego. Experienced hands must assure the novice that everyone is disappointed with their first few videotape role-play performances and encourage him to stick with the program.

10

Winning Moves with Audiovisual Aids

If the company you work for has prepared visual or AV aids, use them. If you are self-employed, you can put together a binder of visual aids yourself. With the help of a printer and an artist friend, you can get fairly fancy for very few dollars. In any case, your binder and its contents must be neat, clean, and new-looking.

If the binder is small and is to be laid flat on the desk or table in front of the prospect, hand it to the prospect closed, and right-side-up from his point of view. Continue your verbal presentation and then lead into the information that is visualized, simplified, or detailed in the binder. Let the prospect open the binder. You direct him what page to open to, if it's other than page one. If there are pictures, diagrams, or anything that you will want to point out, move around to the prospect's position, so you share his point of view. You stand next to his chair and bend at the waist to get closer to his eye level. If you are a woman selling to a man, be careful to avoid brushing arms or shoulders with the prospect (if it's completely accidental, don't worry about it). Keep your eyes primarily on the visual aid; this directs the prospect where to focus his attention. If he looks up from the binder to check your face for signals, you offer reciprocal eye contact briefly and then redirect the prospect's focus to the visual aid.

You must use your peripheral vision to pick up on the prospect's signals. You can't watch him while he's reading or examining the visual content. He'll be aware of it (he has peripheral vision, too). He'll feel uncomfortable and will not be able to concentrate on the content of the visual aid.

If the binder is one of those that forms its own easel, you should set it up, with the first page oriented to the prospect. Try not to plant it uninvited like the Great Pyramid falling onto the middle of the prospect's desk, but tender it to him. He will usually gesture to you to go ahead and put it down. You may signal a "May I?" both verbally and with an expression plus a gesture. Work either from the side or from the prospect's point of view. Avoid continuing your presentation from right behind the upright binder or display. Your face right above or beside the visual aid is distracting and, once again, the prospect is made uncomfortable by your watching him while he is compelled to focus on the visual-aid item, scale model, video monitor, or rear-screen projector. Always try to position yourself so that the prospect does not have to worry about you studying his face. Failing that, make sure not to get caught studying his face.

Slide presentations, filmstrips, and 16mm and Super-8 films are all fairly common AV aids. The Super-8 cassette, shown on a portable rear projector, stole the limelight from the slide show in the late sixties. The very mention of slides conjures up the unpleasant memory of sitting through your neighbor's two-hour pictorial record of his exciting trip through the Plains States. Filmstrips aren't much better. There is simply something terribly dated about a procession of stills. All the boring, flat, industrial photography, the inevitable pies and static, uninspired charts. The overwritten voice-over and hackneyed stock music don't help. How can we present such unappetizing fare to an audience that is so sophisticated, it is rarely impressed by the production value and professionalism of network TV? Yet major corporations spend millions of dollars annually on slide and filmstrip sales software. I suppose they rationalize that it's a step up from printed materials. I may be in the minority, but I would rather look at beautifully designed, printed color graphics than a filmstrip or single-projector slide presentation.

If you have a professionally produced, well-written short film or videotape, you have a powerful, dramatic sales tool. The film can be shown to larger audiences (over fifteen) in the 16mm format, and works well for smaller groups or one prospect in the Super-8 format.

If you will be selling to a group large enough to warrant a 16mm setup, you must find out beforehand if they have a projector, screen, or operator. If they don't, you may find yourself on your own, with the responsibility for setting up and operating the projector. Whether you use theirs, rent, or bring in one from your office, familiarize yourself with the equipment before the screening. Don't try to wing it. Murphy's law applies twofold in the world of motion pictures. Bulbs burn out. The sound dies or is unintelligible or blows everyone out of the room. The film tears, burns, scratches, piles up on the floor, falls off, and rolls up the middle aisle. If you are not prepared for it, it'll happen.

You substantially cut down on the threat of contingencies by breaking yourself in on the equipment. Thoroughly. Be prepared to administer instant adjustments, such as focus, framing, and volume—in a darkened room. If you are pinch-hitting as the projectionist, stay near the projector. If the projector is in a booth, you leave the booth and join the prospects in the conference or screening room during projection, so you can watch for nonverbals that will signal interest, indifference, or hostility. The clumsiest moment is when the film ends and you are obliged to scramble back into the projection room to turn the projector off. If you gotta do it, you gotta do it. If there is any possible way to avoid it, take that option. Ten dollars slipped to a kid from the mailroom. A nearby secretary, who is asked nicely and is given the approximate completion time of the screening, will usually be glad to turn off the projector, just out of the mercy of his heart. Ideally, you want to be able to stay with the prospects at the end of the film, to ride on the crest of the energy and excitement it has created and not lose a beat in moving nearer to your close.

If you have a portable Super-8 projector that has a captive rear-screen assembly, you obviate many of the problems of the 16mm screening, but you also inherit a set of new contingencies.

The projectors aren't as reliable. The sound is tinny and lacks highs or lows. The music usually sounds "funny," because the units are not driven by constant-speed hysteresis motors. Scratches on the film cover more of the relative picture area, which means that they look worse. Dust and dirt collect in the cartridge where you can't clean it, even if you knew how to. The fragile cartridges crack and break rather easily. The "gate," which is part of the cartridge, is often bent a fraction of an inch out of shape, causing "roll" when the claw can't quite reach the perforation. Picture and sound can get out of sync. The screen looks washed out unless you can get the room really dim. The Super-8 print, which is "looped" in the cartridge, often jams and piles up on itself in a spaghettilike tangle. The print starts to look like it's raining (fine scratches) after about twenty-five screenings. The cords are never long enough to reach where you have to go. The motors are noisy. And so on. But it's still better than showing a filmstrip.

As with any screening, you pretend to concentrate on the show, but you tune in, peripherally, on the audience reaction, which is (until the lights come up) nonverbal. We'll look at some of these signals at the end of this chapter.

Plugging in, setting up the projector, and dimming the room are all awkward, distracting activities. Hold off until you have made a solid impression and put the prospect more at ease. Let the prospect know that a film is part of your presentation and that your "briefcase" is the projector (he is probably already familiar with the equipment).

Your prescreening preparation should have included asking the prospect or his secretary if there are blinds, shades, or drapes in the room, and if they are still functional. That is, is it possible to cut off most of the daylight coming through the window? If that's not possible, try to schedule an alternate office or conference room with fewer or no windows. It is important with Super-8 rear-projection units to get the room as dark as possible and to center the prospect in front of the screen for maximum brightness.

The two most terrible moments with the Super-8 projector are plugging it in and packing it up. Plugging in is a hassle because the outlet is never where you would like it to be.

First, you can't find one on your side of the desk or table. The one the prospect knows about is hidden behind a heavy cabinet and is already overloaded with more plugs than Johnny Carson's show. The only accessible plug will require you to grovel on the floor and work your way under a plant or piece of furniture like a beagle with a bone. You don't want your prospect to see you like this. What do you do? You get him involved in the task of darkening the room. While he's trying to get the recalcitrant drapes or blinds to close, you grovel and plug in. When the drapes crash to the floor, at least it wasn't by your hand.

You want to sit on the same side of the screen as the prospect, to watch the show with him. This will help you determine where to set up the projector and in what direction to point the screen. If there is still light coming in, you want it to originate *behind* the screen. Then, the rear projector's own shadow helps keep light off its captive screen.

Videotape is moving rapidly to become the medium of preference for AV sales aids. The advantages are manifold. The technology doesn't rely on the erratic stop/go motion of film and the scratch-prone recording of images on a fragile emulsion. You can screen the thing innumerable times without noticeable image breakdown. Picture and sound are physically "married" on the same piece of tape, so there is no drifting out of sync. You don't have to worry about framing or focus. The track sounds pretty good, and the music doesn't wow and flutter.

The equipment is not really portable yet, so you will be screening on the prospect's setup. That is good news and bad; you don't have to drag around a heavy, fragile piece of electronics, but you may be disappointed with the colors you see on their monitor. Have your fingers on the "color" button or "hue" control as your first scenes hit the screen; with a minor adjustment you should be able to put your green or purple salesperson right back in the pink.

Make sure you find out before a tape screening that you are *absolutely clear* on what tape format you will need to play on the prospect's equipment—three-quarter inch, VHS, Betamax 1 or 2. Then recheck with someone else. It's amazing how little people know about video equipment they use frequently, sometimes sitting right in their own offices. Most disheartening is when you are assured that the prospect's office has a U-matic (three-quarter-inch) playback setup, and you drive sixty miles for an important presentation, only to find out it's a microwave oven! (Laugh. I did.)

If there is a serious interruption during your audiovisual presentation, such as a phone call your prospect must take, or something he must attend to for a few minutes, definitely stop the projector or tape deck and wait for his return. Don't try to back it up a few feet—you are just asking for a jam. If the prospect is gone for more than a couple of minutes, you might briefly recap for him the material the show has already covered. Then start the thing up again. Caution: With 16mm film you can't just stop the projector dead; the gate gets too hot from the high-wattage lamp, and if the film is stopped with no cooling time, the film will burn or sort of cauterize in the gate. That wouldn't be so bad, but then it breaks, nine times out of ten, and that is bad. If you must stop a 16mm screening mid-show, turn off the *lamp* first, count to six or seven, then turn off the drive motor. After a second or two, throw the drive motor into reverse and count eight or nine seconds back—*with the lamp still off*. This will save your film and rewind to a little bit ahead of where you stopped the show. Sixteen millimeter projectors don't like to run in reverse. Pray when you do it. And remember to switch the motor to forward when you restart the screening.

If a film or videotape breaks, or smoke and sparks start flying out of the equipment, *don't try to fix it*. Wrap the show, get it out of the prospect's sight if possible, and go right on with your backup materials as if nothing happened. Don't fume about lousy engineering, your bad luck, etc., etc. Forget it. Use the missed show as a reason for a return visit if you can't close him on this one. Remember, the prospect will take his lead from you. If you moan your fate and gnash your teeth in an ill-concealed rage when the film snaps or green fluid starts seeping out of the TV monitor, the prospect will pick up on your anguish and get sour himself. Wait until you are well away from the prospect's offices before you throw the videocassette into the incinerator or make mincemeat of the film print. Do not jump up and down on your projector in front of the prospect. And certainly not on *his* projector.

When a film or video tape is running, you must make your best effort to appear absorbed in it, even though you know it by heart. Backward. The prospect is audience-empathetic, and he will be tuned in to your responses to the program. Look how much effort the networks put into building a laugh track behind all their sit-coms. Things seem funnier to us when others in the audience are laughing. And sadder when everyone around us is weeping. On the other hand, if you're watching a show or movie, and the rest of the audience is asleep or walking out, you don't feel much like rolling in the aisles in hysterical laughter. If you appear interested and absorbed in your AV piece, it will shape your prospect's attitude and response to it also.

You stay aware of your prospect's responses to the program without staring at him. Here are some of the clearest signals and what they mean.

- He coughs and crosses his legs or shifts position often. (You are losing him.)
- He blinks a lot or blinks overlong. (He's not thrilled by what he's seeing.)
- He lifts a hand or finger slightly from his thigh or a flat surface. (He disagrees with that point or section.)
- He tilts his head to one side. (He's not following completely.)
- He cradles the side of his head in his hand. (This isn't turning him on.)
- He crosses his arms high on his chest. (Looks like bad reviews.)
- He looks at you every once in a while. (He doesn't believe the claims in the film or tape.)
- He rubs or scratches his head or the upper part of his face. (This is going to be a tough nut.)
- He strokes his chin occasionally. (Now you are starting to cook.)
- He sits up or forward a bit in his chair, and his torso lines up with the screen. (Yeah!)
- He breathes out audibly. (He's bored.)
- He breathes in audibly. (He likes that part.)

- He tenses his jaw muscles. (Bad news. He disagrees.)
- His mouth opens slightly as he watches. (He's paying attention. That's good.)
- He points and darts a glance at you. (He's going to want to discuss that part of the program in greater detail after the show.)
- He glances at his phone, his desk, or the door. (He's getting bored.)
- You hear Zzzzzs. (Get your firm to hire a different producer.)

When the show is over, you turn the lights back on and open the blinds or whatever. Let the prospect help you if he offers. Do *not* immediately pack up a projector. Turn off a video monitor—its hum is distracting—but leave the videocassette in the player. Continue your presentation. Leaving the hardware and software in place signals the prospect that you intend to stay awhile. Pack up prematurely and it looks like you are ready to be dismissed. If a rear-projection unit was assembled on the middle of the prospect's desk, and you can't see around it easily, fold the top part down and move the unit to one side, but don't close the cover and don't coil up the cord until you are about to leave.

Always pack a spare bulb with a film projector and have a backup reel or videodub in your bag. Always pack a fifteen-foot extension cord. The one from the projector is never long enough to reach where you want it.

Handle film or videotape cassettes with care. Keep them in the case provided. Try not to crush them into a tightly packed suitcase. Store and pack film cartridges in cellophane bags with twist ties, to keep out dust. Keep any film projector away from dirt, dust, and moisture. A piece of dust in the gate means a long, ugly scratch on the film. Keep video and audio cassettes and reels away from magnetic fields (loud-speakers, electric motors, and those metal detectors at the airport).

Glue a heavy piece of cork or felt to the plastic, metal, or hard rubber nubs on the bottom of your projector, player, or any heavy unit you want to put on a prospect's desk or table.

EXERCISE: Working with Your Sales Aids

Virtually everyone in sales uses various sales aids in the course of making a presentation, especially one that involves a demo. For an exercise that will enable you to keep your eyes on the prospect and which will make you very smooth with your sales aids, try this.

Go through every phase of handling your sales materials or equipment *blindfolded*. Or in darkness, or with your eyes closed, if you can trust yourself. The first time you go through your presentation and use of sales aids blindfolded, you will discover a whole new world of shortcuts and different ways to present and deal with materials and machines. You will find features, positive and negative, of your props, samples, and equipment that you overlooked with your eyes (there's some irony here), features that will expedite and simplify how you deal with such items.

Rehearse working blindfolded with your sales aids until you are as completely comfortable with them as a concert musician is with his instrument. Now, when you present in a natural environment, you won't have to fumble with things, look away from the prospect, or break your train of thought to wrestle with sales materials or demo models. And why not? If you had to, you could do it blindfolded!

Note: Do not rehearse plugging in any piece of electrical equipment while blindfolded.

11

Winning Moves in
Public Speaking

Let's say you've perfected selling one-on-one. You're not at all intimidated by presenting in a conference room, before a small group, or even before the unfeeling lens of a teleconference or motion-picture camera. What happens? Your career moves into high gear. Your earnings increase substantially. You develop charisma. Less successful salespeople start to use you for their role model. And, as inevitable as spring follows winter, you are asked to make speeches before large groups. Industry associations, conventions, award ceremonies, civic and fraternal groups. They want to hear what you have to say. And you want to leave town and change your name.

With a chain of innovative excuses, dodges, and lies, you can avoid making a speech for your entire adult life. However, with every speech you get out of, you are throwing away another rung in the career ladder above you. It's a simple choice: If you want to climb to the top of your profession, you *must* acquire the ability to speak in front of a large group. Like anything else that looked impossible at first, you will find public speaking a skill you can handle and even come to enjoy, once you commit yourself to it and apply the guidelines given in this chapter.

I have never met a person who was not filled with dread at the prospect of their first public speech. There is little you can do to quell the inevitable queasiness. For your first speeches, fluttering butterflies will always act up as you approach the podium or microphone. Actors learn to use that rush of excitement. They channel it to add energy to their performance. You can, too. But first you must accomplish the two crucial basic steps of preparation:

1. *Prepare your material thoroughly.* No one wants to hear you speak if you don't know what you are talking about. Organize the material so it makes sense, and make sure it is absolutely clear. Rehearse aloud. Record yourself and listen back with objective ears. Reading material aloud is an effective acid test for overwrought or unclear material. Dull parts will suddenly seem terribly dull. Confusion will proclaim itself as if in boldface. Non sequiturs will catch you smiling. (Did I write that?) Rework your material, pare it to the essentials, and then rehearse more.

2. *Speak.* In public. Any public. Try out your speech on any group of people who will hear it, including your daughter's Camp Fire Girl group. Sign up for any available public speaking course *before* your first real speech. Attend every session, take every opportunity to speak. Like anything else, it becomes easy when you're used to it. It isn't enough to rehearse your material alone or to a videotape camera. You must work before a living, breathing audience. Imagine a frustrated actor who has never appeared before an audience. He spends, let us say, three years alone in his attic, learning the entire script of Hal Holbrook's *Mark Twain Tonight*, a one-man show. He knows the material cold. Now take this man and smack him down in front of a full Broadway audience, and tell him to play the part. Chances are he'll freeze on the spot. And even if he is able to force the words out, he will be so stiff and uncomfortable his performance will certainly be far from compelling.

There's something other-dimensional about an audience. It is, somehow, more than its parts. A great, seething, breathing, all-seeing, all-hearing, strange-smelling monster. Many but one; the combined aura of a crowd, its attention focused on one point. It can drive a man irrational, blank out his mind, or send him scurrying to the wings to be sick. An audience reacts very much like a large dog; unless it's simply out to eat you, it depends on you to govern its attitude and behavior toward you. An audience's first impressions of you are very strong, and are evaluated long before you have started to make any verbal sense: Your walk to the podium. Your bearing, grooming, dress, character "mask," the mood of your expression. How you carry or take out your paper or notes. How you look at the audience. How you relate to the microphone. (Do you adjust it when you don't know how to adjust it? Do you blow in it a couple of times, or say "Testing, testing two three four"?) Do you cough and clear your voice? Is your voice even and clear, or is it pinched high in your throat? All these questions are resolved; all the signals are transmitted to and deciphered by the audience before you have completed your first sentence. It doesn't seem fair, somehow, after all the work you put into the body of your speech, to be judged so much on the first few seconds you appear. There's an obvious way to deal with the first-impression syndrome: Make a great first impression! Block out and rehearse your entrance, from the moment you appear until you are several sentences into your speech. Go through the actual moves. Watch yourself moving through each separate piece of business.

Walk to the podium or microphone at an even, almost brisk pace. Don't race—you'll look nervous. Conceal your paper or notes if possible. If people see a script, they immediately anticipate a long, dull, unspontaneous speech. No one enjoys having someone read a prepared piece of copy to them. Everyone, on the other hand, respects and admires a speaker who is so confident, and knows his stuff so well, that he's going to speak only from notes. Spontaneity—that's exciting. That means a speaker an audience can relate to, because the speaker doesn't have to concentrate on reading copy. He has time and attention for the audience. He goes through the material with them, not at them. He can make mistakes and be human about it, and we like him better for it. He can jump forward in his material or repeat appropriate points as the need or inclination strikes him. I'm not recommending you wing it—do work from notes—but whatever it is, don't make a great show of waving papers around as you take the podium. Sometimes, if you are the first speaker, you can leave your notes on the podium before the audience arrives. Tape your notes down so that the person who introduces you doesn't accidentally walk away with them. Let him, or anyone who will be at the podium before you, know that you are leaving your notes there. Then, just to be safe, copy them and fold up your emergency copy to carry on your person, in your jacket or bag. Even if you are the fourth or fifth speaker, you may be able to leave your speech notes on a shelf of some of the fancier podiums.

Your legs tremble when you have to speak to a group.

Exercise them just before. Mix in some runner's stretching exercises. Once you're on the dais or at the podium, you can counter trembling by flexing your legs; alternately tense and relax them. Generally, you can cut down on the anxiety by cutting down on stimulants. Try natural tranquilizers like milk, B complex vitamins, and meditation.

God bless the podium. It's a convenient shield to hide behind. (For your first few speeches, your legs may tremble noticeably.) You can lean on it when you feel like collapsing. You can duck behind it when your audience starts hurling rotten fruit.

Whenever you are scheduled to speak, check out the speaker facilities in advance. There's almost always a podium or lectern somewhere. Even a music stand is better than nothing. Make sure it's going to be in place and dusted off before your appearance. Frequently, you will be able to see the exact setup you will be using. Don't pass up an opportunity to familiarize yourself with your set and props. Check out the mike stand. Is it easily adjusted? If the speaker before you is substantially shorter or taller than you, you will have to readjust the mike. Practice doing it quickly and efficiently without making lots of noise. If the sound engineer is around, talk to him about the acoustics of the place, the sensitivity of the mike you will be using, and the level he will pump out into the room. If you look interested, this is the person who may just take the little extra bit of effort to make your whimpering little squeak sound like the voice of Richard Burton.

The audience will search your face for the mood or character of your speech. They will appraise your bearing, grooming, and dress to ascertain your status. A stand-up comedian in a late-night club can walk up to the mike in jeans, sandals, and a tattered sweater with paint spots on it. You can't. You must dress conservatively for your audience, and one small notch above the audience average. Get your hair styled. Do your nails. Have your teeth cleaned. If you are very pale, get a slight tan or wear makeup.

Women, if you are speaking to a large audience, the body of which will be a good distance from you, you can (and should) go a bit heavier on your eye makeup, and a bit heavier and darker on your lips. Use lip liner for definition, and gloss for highlights. If you have rather faint, light eyebrows, help them a bit more with eyebrow pencil. Lean a shade darker with your foundation; bright spotlights will make you look even paler than you are. If your speech is going to be videotaped or filmed, and there will be tight close-ups, your stagelike makeup may look heavy-handed; you may have to split the difference. If possible, discuss it with the director or person in charge of the filming or videotaping. If possible, slip into the room or auditorium before the event and ask the stage manager, lighting director, or electrician to fire up the lights you will be appearing under. Stand at the podium and check your make-up with a small mirror. The colored gels commonly used in stage lights will probably enhance your skin tones, but they may make your blush look far too red, or your slate-blue eye shadow look totally black. No, they won't change the lights just for you. You have to fix your makeup.

A rule of thumb: Stage lights tend to add orangish-pink to warm up your skin tones; anything on you that's blue will tend to go darker. Dark blues will read as black. Yellows will read more orange or pink. Some light blues will pick up a lavender tint. Greens will look darker. Reds and pinks will look hotter. Whites will reflect the color of the gels in the stage lights, i.e., they will go "warm." So you can see that if you have a cold, and you were out drinking late last night, the red capillaries in your bloodshot eyeballs and the irritated redness of your nose will be inauspiciously amplified.

Men or women with black hair, beware the totally black background. You will look like you are only a face with no hair. If any pictures are taken, or videotape or film, that's how you'll look, too. Also, people in dark suits will read as only faces, shirts, and hands. Insist that some light be thrown on the background, to make for separation between it and the speaker. A lighter curtain or backdrop is another option. Anything with a color or pattern will provide a foil for speakers who have dark hair or are wearing dark clothing.

Men with terribly thin hair or no hair, if they have the power, should insist that the person in charge of the lights kill the top light for your speech. The top light will do a brilliant job of making your thinning hair look even thinner. It makes a bald head look like a hundred-watt bulb in the night, plus adds a brilliant hot spot to the crown of the head, stealing all the thunder from your flashing eyes. On the other hand, people with a full head of hair, especially women with a fuller style, will look fantastic under top lighting. The solution, of course, is a dimmer-board operator who brings up the top light for heads of hair and takes it down for bald and thin-haired people.

When you get to the podium, look out at the audience immediately. Scan them; assume a pleasant, confident expression; smile if your subject and audience warrant it. The instant you are behind the podium, take out your notes and, if they are folded, flatten them on the top of the podium.

If you must adjust the microphone, do it quickly and efficiently. Do not touch the mike itself but the stand or gooseneck that supports it. Try to restrict handling any part of the microphone equipment to a minimum. It all sounds funny to the audience. Do not blow into the microphone. Do not say "Testing, testing." Above all, do not flick the mike with your hand or finger. It sounds like an explosion to the audience. If you diddle around with the microphone and tap it and say things such as "Testing, one, two, three," it creates the impression that you are in some way responsible for the operation of the audio system. You aren't! If the system doesn't work or blows everyone out of the room with a sonic boom of feedback, or buzzes and hums, or sounds like you're talking from the bottom of a well, make sure everyone knows that it's not your fault. Look off to the wings or backstage or toward the projection booth and deliver some line that lays the responsibility where it belongs. "You said the strike wouldn't start till Wednesday, fellas." "Did someone tell the sound engineers to redeposit that check?" "You mean that really was the sound guy I pushed in the hotel pool last night?"

Give them about ten seconds to get the PA system working. Then you have to seize the bull by the horns. Try speaking without the PA system. Unless the auditorium is truly vast, you can make yourself heard. Tell the audience what you are doing. "You won't have any trouble hearing me, if I speak up, and you all stop breathing." Stand tall, take deeper breaths before you speak, tilt your face up and out into the audience, so that your chin is pointing to the feet of the people in the first row. Compress your lungs more and "throw" the speech into the far corners of the hall. Speak more slowly and very clearly. Do not trail away at the ends of words or sentences. There is no point in screaming or shouting. If your audience is so vast and the acoustics so bad that you have to shout to be heard, throw in the towel. Bow and leave the stage. This is rarely the case, however. Most auditoriums have fairly decent acoustics. Audiences can fall into a remarkable silence, enabling them to hear you better, and in doing so, they concentrate more on your words. Also, if the sound system does fail, it's a great opportunity for you to show your mettle by speaking unassisted by amplification. It is not the end of the world if the PA system fails. The world's greatest orators spoke without amplification for over two thousand years.

Your best stance behind the podium is with your feet comfortably apart and even; that is, one foot isn't in front of the other. Distribute your weight evenly on both feet. Do not lean forward, against the podium; you will look tired or lazy, and many podiums are top-heavy and terribly unstable—you will make a wonderful impression flung headlong into the first row. Do not stand so close to the podium that you will not be able to gesture comfortably with your arms. Ideally, you keep one hand on the podium, not lying on it like a dead eel, but holding the side edge in a relaxed manner. This gives you a sense of security and helps prevent you from swaying from side to side, which must be assiduously avoided. If you have a very strong tendency to sway or rock, place your feet farther apart, to provide a wider base, which will make it harder for you to do so. Not only does swaying and rocking look bad and reveal your nervousness, but it moves your mouth relative to the microphone, which responds by varying the volume of your voice.

Keeping the above in mind, relax now, and be as natural and comfortable as you can. You can loosen up your arm gestures in this environment; make broader facial expressions. Try not to clear your throat and cough before you speak. Warm up your voice by humming to yourself in the wings. The first three sentences are the hardest. All the rest will just come, and suddenly it's all over. So you rehearse the first three sentences with particular attention. These should be engraved in your mind.

Do not clutch the podium with both hands. And do not gesture exclusively with one arm. Switch-hit every few sentences; for special emphasis, use both arms to gesture. Do not look off into the wings. Do not stare at your notes too long. Look at one face at a time, for three to five seconds per face. Look into the audience as often and as long as you can. Don't be afraid to smile when appropriate. Go for big, relaxed smiles. Mona Lisa grins won't be seen by most of your live audience.

Many modern auditoriums have, or can get, video prompters. If you will be speaking at a sales convention, chances are a prompter will be installed as a matter of course. You must give your written speech to the producer or prompter operator well before the day of your speech; they'll tell you the deadline for the copy. Your speech is then transposed onto a roll that is advanced at your reading speed across the face of two video monitors concealed to the left and right of the podium. The copy is visible in two sheets of glass (no bigger than office stationery), which are held by a simple aluminum stand just below your eye level, about three to four feet from your face. These glass panes are almost invisible to the audience, as they have no frames. The copy is visible to the speaker, as the panes of glass, which are positioned at a forty-five-degree angle, reflect the copy from the TV monitors to the speaker. The audience sees none of this; their surface of the glass is pointed toward the dark ceiling. The prompter operator advances your copy as you read it and is able to alter speed instantly, or stop, if you do, for a parenthetical aside.

This system is extremely effective at creating the impression of a spontaneous talk. If you are faced with the prospect of having to use one of these systems, there are five things to think about:

1. They rarely malfunction, but have a copy of your speech in your pocket, anyway.
2. If you prefer to work from your notes, the prompter people will whine and complain. The operator doesn't understand your shorthand notes, so how can he advance the roll? You force him to pay attention. And what if he can't figure out where you are?
3. Remember to use both reflecting panes. In looking from one to the other, you create the effect of sweeping your eyes over the audience. Shift every couple of sentences.
4. Insist that the stage lights be set with the prompter's panes of glass in position flanking the lectern. The sheets of glass cut down on light passing through them, and the edges cast a hard-line shadow from a bright light. I saw a saleswoman-of-the-year speak for twenty minutes with a wiggling pencil-line mustache. She was shorter than all the other speakers, and the hard-edge shadow created by that pane of prompter glass and the key spotlight just happened to fall right between her upper lip and her nose. It was too late to move the light or the pane of glass, and the unfortunate saleswoman-of-the-year couldn't even see that anything was amiss. She had to suffer through twenty minutes of agony, wondering why some of her most telling remarks were met by snickers.
5. The prompter is a killer of the ingenuous, off-the-cuff speaker. It is a fine homogenizer of speakers; everyone will sort of have the same basic delivery.

If you are a spontaneous, turn-'em-on, motivational speaker, forgo the prompter and ask the producer of the meeting if you can have a wireless mike. Or, even better, a wireless *lavalier* mike, the small one that hangs around your neck, or pins to your clothes. It leaves both your hands free to gesture. Plus you can wander away from the podium, even into the audience. These are some of the blessings of our technological civilization.

Your principal goal in public speaking is to relax, be natural, and enjoy yourself. After all, this room full of people has seen fit to gather together and sit in quiet attention to hear your precious pearls of wisdom—you must be a special person. Shouldn't you enjoy being special? If you don't, what was the point of all your hard work? View your opportunity to address an audience as one of your rewards, something that comes with the territory of success. You might as well relax and enjoy it, because once you start toward that podium, the only way you can get out of it is to keel over dead. (When your throat closes up from tension, it may seem like a reasonable alternative.) You can be yourself, because it's you that earned the right to speak. You, not some professional orator or entertainer. Don't expect to get lots of laughs. You're not there to get laughs. If you want the audience to like you, relax, be yourself, and when you tell them something that amuses *you*, they'll laugh. When you get enthusiastic, they'll feel it, and they'll get caught up in your emotions. When you are—when you allow yourself to be—full of joy or faith or great expectations or intensity, your audience will follow you like a flock follows its shepherd.

If, on the other hand, you project fear, anxiety, or lack of conviction, or pose or play someone you are not, the audience will pick up on it in seconds. They won't like you, and they won't believe you. They will read your stage fright as the signals of guilt, fear of apprehension in a lie, or lack of sincere belief in what you are saying. If you are panicky and uncomfortable, your audience is uncomfortable. We all dislike people with a lack of courage. Perhaps the reflection of a less attractive flaw on the dark side of our own character makes us in the audience uncomfortable. (Everyone else in the audience would probably rather leap into a pool full of hungry crocodiles than get up and make your speech, but they all expect you to breeze through it calm, cool, and collected, plus be thrilled for the chance to address such an august assembly. Such is life.)

Anyone who makes speeches regularly has little or no problem with prespeech anxiety. Public speaking becomes routine, and the speaker may indeed find himself searching for ways to sustain or generate some level of excitement or energy so he won't seem flat or bored. Can you image such a thing? If you can, you have access to one of the ways to overcome prespeech butterflies. Imagine carefully, and in every detail, that you have given this speech dozens of times before. At night, before you go to sleep, "see" yourself going through the entire talk, point by point; replay questions from various audiences, if that is appropriate.

Another approach is to "get inside yourself." That is, from the moment you start for the podium, until you hear thundering applause, you don't worry about the audience at all. The audience is not there. This is just another rehearsal. You are the only one who is with you; you are speaking with yourself. (This approach works well where the audience is rendered invisible by bright stage lights.) You let the audience— if they happen to be there—eavesdrop on your internal dialogue.

A third technique is to assume the teacher role. You are the teacher, and the audience is your class. This is an environment that's very familiar to all of us, hence your role model is already established in your mind. If you employ this technique, you must be careful not to allow a patronizing tone to creep into your voice. Imagine that your class consists of grad-school students instead of sixth-graders.

One approach that will help you overcome the jitters is to focus on the fact that you have a secret—some choice piece of information or new idea or point of view—that everyone in the audience needs to know and will thank you for imparting to them.

Whatever technique you employ to deal with your fears, remember this: No one wants you to fail. Everyone wants your speech to be a rewarding, worthwhile investment of their time. If anything, your audience hopes you will do brilliantly. At the other end of the scale, what's the worst that can happen to you if your speech is less than inspiring? Will you be whipped, beaten, and thrown in the stockade? Stripped of your uniform and drummed out of the corps? Tarred and feathered and ridden out of town on a rail? No? So what is it you find so terrifying? Public humiliation and embarrassment? You know that you are not going to be humiliated; you know that your performance isn't going to be embarrassing. You have information the audience wants or needs to know. You are thoroughly prepared. You are comfortable with your material, you know it, and you feel strongly about it or believe in it. The audience wants you to pass that information on to them, clearly and in an organized, easy-to-understand fashion. You are well rehearsed, you've familiarized yourself with the room, lights, podium, and microphone. You don't have laryngitis or a contagious plague, and all your hair didn't fall out last night. Even if you stumble and fall flat on your face, you'll get right up again and win them over with a self-effacing ad-lib, such as "The man at Dale Carnegie said that would get a much bigger laugh." So what are you worried about?

The most effective nonverbal signals at the podium will spring from your attitude toward yourself. If you like yourself, it will show, and the audience will follow suit. You have an interesting, complex, unique personality—trust it. Let it soar. People will like your personality because, in the very act of revealing it to them, you establish your self-confidence, courage, openness, honesty, and trust. An audience will respond to that with warmth and empathy. Subterfuge will not work. Artifice will not work. Be yourself, trust yourself, and give them of yourself. The more relaxed, uncontrived, and outgoing you are, the greater your charisma. The less you try to consciously win or influence your audience, the more you are likely to succeed.

TRUE LIFE STORY: Making the Best of the Worst

I was scheduled to give a speech to a group of actors on my perspective concerning casting talent for TV commercials. It was a hotel complex. There were three conventions in the same complex. I was late. I burst into the room after the MC had made opening remarks. The woman at the door looked at me anxiously.

"Are you—"

"I'm speaking," I interrupted.

"Boy, you sure cut it close," she scolded, taking my coat. The MC was watching us. The woman signaled him that I was, indeed, I. He had the audience give me a round of applause, which helped get me to the podium, and I launched right into my talk. I spoke without notes. The theme was to scold the actors for having a bad attitude in auditions and to encourage them to be utterly positive and confident at all times, even though they had just been evicted and arrested for vagrancy.

I noticed my words were having a powerful effect on the audience. They were really squirming around in their seats. Their expressions included animosity, amazement, skepticism, and annoyance. Heads were turning. People were coughing and clearing their throats. I figured I had really hit a nerve. I forged ahead; I wasn't about to let their body language deter me from telling it like it was.

The MC was interrupting me, and just as I was hitting my stride. I was in the wrong room. This was a group of people who had all bought the same computer. I died. I turned red. Then white. Then blue. Very patriotic. I started to slink off the stage, the epitome of mortification.

"Hey," cried someone in the audience, "before you go, can you tell us how they make that white tornado?"

"Yeah, and how do they freeze the picture, but the one guy keeps moving and talking in that insurance commercial?"

I stayed for another half-hour, explaining traveling mattes and process cinematography. I got a standing ovation and three leads for new business.

Not bad for an utter catastrophe.

12

Conference-room Selling

Conference-room selling is somewhat more complicated than one-on-one selling. Usually, the reason you find yourself in a conference room is that you must present to more than one prospect. With multiple prospects, you run into the inevitable reaction of the beast called office politics. Each prospect comes armed with his corporate weapons and shields of power. Authority must be displayed. Underlings bent on promotion sharpen their teeth, flex their muscles, and challenge their immediate superiors or competitors; consultants recognize a good opportunity to make themselves look good; cost and efficiency people see you as the enemy; almost everyone in the room intends to use your presentation for their own purposes. It will help you to be conscious of these strong subplots as you make your presentation, to understand where intramural politics and ego-to-ego combat ends, and legitimate response to your proposal begins.

Arrive early and try to get into the conference room before anyone else does. Tell your contact that you have to set up a piece of AV equipment or you want to check the color on their videotape monitor or you have to collate and distribute printed materials—whatever. If you are the first one in the room, you can settle in and start to develop a sense of territorial command. Move the chairs. Straighten the pictures.

Play with the dimmer switch. Hide the ashtrays in the cabinet. If you really do have some piece of equipment to set up, now is the time to do it, not in front of your prospects.

Your hands start to tremble just before an important presentation.

Use them. Exercise them by squeezing something as hard as you can for five seconds and then relaxing them for ten. Repeat this until you have them under control.

The prospects will arrive in small clusters, or one at a time. Hover somewhere near the main door to the room, and introduce yourself to or greet each prospect as he arrives. Do not rush through these introductions unless people arrive in a bunch and you must. Try for a solid moment of two-way verbal and nonverbal contact and communication with each prospect. If you can leave each one with the impression that you really tuned in on his name and role (ask his area of responsibility; it is not incorrect form), you reduce what might have become an impersonal audience with a detached mass psyche into a gathering of separate individuals with far more empathy (see Chapter Eleven, "Winning Moves in Public Speaking"). Since you are already there, you have established some level of territorial imperative, plus the idea that it is "your" meeting. Since they arrive after you, there is always the implication that they are late.

You may not, however, be allowed to enter the room until your prospects are comfortably assembled and seated. You may be introduced, but no one may make any move to introduce members of the group. If they are fewer than five or six, or if you know a couple of them already, make it a point to introduce yourself to those you haven't met before. It's worth it to you to crack the solidarity of the potential audience effect. Also, when you start introducing yourself, you put a few people off-balance immediately; they feel guilty or remiss (or downright rude) for not making the introductions themselves.

If the conference table is very wide, or too wide to lean across, you may be able to move around behind the table to meet or greet prospects. If this is impossible, due to the narrowness of the room and the fact that it would be clumsy for everyone to push back their chairs and get up again, you will have to settle for reaching across the table to shake hands or simply nodding to each prospect as he is introduced or introduces himself. If you reach across the table, stand as close to it as possible with both thighs touching its edge, so you don't have to bend so much to shake a prospect's hand.

If the prospect group is too large (more than six or seven), and it looks impractical to go for individual introductions, you will probably be introduced to the group by someone on-stream at the company who knows you or your products/services, and who establishes the purpose of your visit. During this introduction, the other prospects will be looking from the person who introduced you, to you. Don't look down at the floor as if he were talking about someone else. Look right back at the prospects, meet their eyes, and hold long enough to show you're not intimidated. It's a good idea to help the person who introduced you with a verbal interjection if he misspeaks something or is short on information in some area. They'll appreciate your taking the pressure off them for a moment, and it takes the formality and stiffness out of your opening. It's no great shock when you start talking, because you've already talked.

If you want to seize and keep control of the meeting, don't sit down. The only time this is impractical is if there is to be some other subject of business that is to precede your presentation (which is unlikely—you are an outsider, and there isn't much they want to discuss in front of you). Try to remain standing through your entire appearance. The only good excuse for sitting is that your knees start to quake noticeably. Then again, standing and flexing leg muscles is still a better way to fight trembling than sitting, which provides virtually no physical release and may lead to uncontrollable leg jiggling.

The senior member or principal power-holder on the prospect team will normally sit at the far end of the table, away from the door, especially if this is any formal sort of presentation, or any decisions are to be made. Business procedure then dictates that the next man in rank sits to the boss's left, and so on around the table, to the weakest position at the key man's right (frequently a stenographer or record keeper). The position at the opposite end of the table, a power position in the domicile, is an undesirable seat at a conference table. Frequently, because of the limbo status of this position, it is bypassed, and no one sits there.

The limbo seat is an ideal position, therefore, from which to make your presentation. No one is offended because you took their place, everyone can see you and what you may show or demonstrate, and you can see all of them. If you have a film screen or video monitor, set it up at this end of the table, not behind the senior man's back.

If no one is sitting on the senior person's right, it is best for you to work from this position. Stand just behind the second seat away from the principal party, so he doesn't have to twist and crane his neck to see you. This puts you directly across from the most powerful players in the prospect group, who usually sort themselves in order of rank, the highest being closest to the man at the top of the table.

When the table is completely full, work behind the secondary players to the top man's right. They will have to wrench around in their seats or move them to see you easily. Better them than the important people to the top man's left.

Even though you may have succeeded in defanging the audience monster by breaking the components of the party into individuals, you are still expected to stage some kind of an official presentation, with the dogs and the pony. In other words, a prospect group that receives you in a conference room expects you to do a fairly comprehensive show-and-tell. The question-and-answer period will follow your presentation. The more complete and informative your presentation, the fewer tough questions will follow. So prepare your material and your performance much the same way you would for a speech to a larger audience (see Chapter Eleven, "Winning Moves in Public Speaking"). At the same time, you don't want to lose the immediacy and intimacy of a one-on-one presentation. In conference-room selling, you split the difference. Also, you will move from the performer to the approachable, human person. You perform the presentation, then you shift gears to respond to individual questions or comments.

When you are speaking, look at the prospects one after

the other. Read the audience. You can play to the less responsive individuals; you'll know who they are from their body signals and facial expressions. When you get a question or interruption from one of the prospects, address the beginning and end of your answer to the questioner. Use the middle of your response to enlist the understanding of the other prospects.

If you do not know who the real decision-maker is for what you are proposing at the outset of the meeting, you should by the end of it. It's not the one who makes a point of attacking you on every point (he's after the decision-maker's job). It's not any of the people who keep smiling pleasantly and have nothing substantial to say. It's almost always the person who pays you the closest attention, and whose questions or comments show they were listening carefully.

If you were an actor preparing to play the role of you making a presentation, you would not want to have to break your stride in mid-performance to search for a recalcitrant prop. All your props—AV aids, folders, brochures, charts, models, samples—must be organized, readily accessible, and well rehearsed. Imagine the skull scene from *Hamlet* if the actor were unable to find Yorick's skull. Or the dagger scene from *Macbeth* with no dagger.

It is smart to have your props and paraphernalia out on the table before you launch into your presentation. Or on a nearby sideboard or shelf. If there are reports or items you do not want to reveal until you reach a certain dramatic point in your presentation, make certain that these items can be produced in one easy, hassle-free move. Don't assume there's nothing complicated about taking a few reports out of a briefcase. If you are unrehearsed, the tension of the meeting may well cause you to accidentally pull your half-eaten tuna sandwich out onto the floor. You must rehearse all these moves beforehand, until they are functional, regardless of your anxiety.

Disregard the advice of programs that tell you to get your prospect "involved" by collating or distributing your reports or flyers. Important prospects do not want to demean themselves in front of subordinates with a menial chore. Neither do they want to be distracted from watching your presentation, reading your nonverbal signals. Don't think the clever solution is to engage the help of less-important members of the prospect team. They will not appreciate your calling attention to their low position on the corporate totem pole. Do your collations, distributions, and demonstrations yourself. If someone from the group pitches in, accept their help graciously and with no presumption.

When a member of the group attacks you on one point or another, with what you feel is unreasonable vehemence or unnecessary brilliance, remember that the performance is being staged for other members of the team, and don't take it personally. Your primary goal in this situation is not to display nonverbal signals that show your anger, frustration, or dismay. If an attack is being leveled at you for effect, you can deflate it substantially by not being affected. That is, if you don't show that you are affected, the attack is immediately exposed for what it is—a gratuitous assault intended only to score internal points. Answer and clarify, explain and qualify, "push" slowly toward your attacker and, as you do so, remain staunch and unshaken. You might even smile slightly at the conclusion of your reply, in a signal that lets everyone know that you are aware of the motivation for the attack.

Always maintain a firm level of control and an aura of internal strength and reliability. Stay "up, relaxed, and yes," no matter how long the meeting lasts. If the prospect team starts to get very informal, stay a few notches more conservative and in control. They may loosen their ties, remove their jackets, roll up their sleeves, and start passing beers all around. You don't put your feet up on furniture, you don't slump on the table, you don't loosen your tie and kick off your shoes. No matter how friendly you think you are with these characters, you are responsible for representing your firm in a business relationship that implies a complex web of obligations, expectations, and trust. They may not think you're a barrel of laughs, but they will tend to give you more business.

It's not bad form to move around a bit. You're on your feet—you can get a little exercise, and you attract the eye of the people when you move from position *A* to position *B*. If you are passing something out or demonstrating something with a working model, move around to various points at the perimeter of the table. In any case, it makes everyone uncomfortable if you freeze in one place like a wooden Indian. If you cause your prospects to move their eyes or bodies occasionally, it will produce greater alertness in them and thus increase their comprehension. Your moves should not be nervous or haphazard, of course. They should flow from your being at ease with these people. It is natural for someone at ease to move occasionally. And you must be at ease, because you move occasionally and naturally.

At the end of the meeting, the conference group will want to discuss your proposal among themselves. A senior member of the group will thank you, which is your signal to depart. Do not dawdle. Your attitude is that you are glad to be getting on your way because your time is valuable, and you have another presentation coming up very soon (you should, in fact). Do not shake hands in your leave-taking, except with those who offer to shake yours. Close the door behind you.

You are in the middle of a meeting, and your stomach starts rumbling.

Try regular meals. Don't chew gum; it just stimulates your hungry stomach to produce more digestive acids, which lead to more rumbling. Sit up; don't slump or twist your torso. Try changing your position. Talk louder. Move farther away.

TRUE LIFE STORY: How Prospects Like It When You Show You Can Function Under Stress

When I got out of the service in 1968, I didn't want to go back to work in advertising. The grandmother who had offered to put me through medical school had changed her mind, and my wife, who was pregnant, kept mumbling things about food, clothing, and shelter. So I started a film production company.

One thing led to another, and I soon found myself in a meeting with my first prospective client. It was a major communications company, and they were looking for a producer to make a short corporate-sales film. The budget was about $30,000, which was megamoney for a young veteran with $137 in the bank. They liked my letters and phone calls and the rough treatment I had sent them unsolicited. But they wanted to see "some of my work"; they wanted to see a film that would establish, beyond a doubt, my expertise, and give them an idea of what their film might look like.

I rented the showiest screening room in New York. Red plush chairs on swivels with individual ashtrays, thick carpets, extravagant curtains, and a projectionist who actually shaved. Three heavyweights from the major company came to the screening. I put them in the biggest, plushest seats of all and gave them a little zap of theatrical glamour by telling them the names of some of the prestigious producers and directors whose internationally celebrated butts had filled those very same seats.

I stood two rows in front of the three execs and explained that my cameraman was having some trouble getting into town in the snow, and since he had the only print of our latest film, we would have a few minutes to go over the treatment I had done for them.

We worked our way through the treatment, scene by scene. The executives got quite caught up in the creative process and in having me explain how I would go about achieving a particular effect or making some point in the story crystal-clear. They wanted something new and different, something entertaining.

Every ten minutes, more or less, the projectionist would ring through on the intercom and give me the progress report on the cameraman, whose calls were coming in on the projectionist's phone. He was stuck on a bridge. He was boxed in by a snowplow. (It was one of the heaviest snows of the decade.) His radiator was leaking. His heater was steaming up the inside of the windshield. His engine died about ten blocks from the screening room. Water condensation in the gas. He was running the rest of the way, but first he had to get someone to watch his car so it wouldn't be towed. The prospects

watched me closely as each one of these strokes of
bad news were announced. I showed no panic, no
despair, no crumbling confidence. I forged on ahead with
the development of the final treatment, with which
we were making a great deal of progress. After all, these
were the three men who would have to pass on the
project. And here they were, all together, working it out
as a team. It was one of the most productive meetings
I have ever had.

We were in the street shaking hands when the exhausted
cameraman finally showed up, the print in a can under
his arm. We all laughed. The executives, ever busy, had
various meetings to dash to. No, they didn't really
need to see the film, the senior man said. He was sure
I could deliver what they wanted. He liked my style.
He thought I had a good feeling for the kind of crisis
management they were accustomed to. He was looking
forward to the final script and a letter of agreement. And
suddenly they were gone.

The cameraman and I shook hands. We headed for
the nearest tavern for a drink.

"You should have seen the projectionist," I said. "He
was practically in tears for me!"

The cameraman, an old friend, shook his head in
stunned amazement.

"I don't believe you did it." He chuckled.

"Where were you calling from?" I asked.

"The coffee shop right in the lobby."

"How did you get your face so red when you came
running up?" I asked.

"I stuck it in a pile of snow and kept it there till it
went numb."

"Looked great," I said. "What's in the can?"

"Your latest work," he replied, and opened the
empty can.

"Look, you have to start somewhere," I offered.

"I'll drink to that," he replied.

We raised our glasses and toasted the future.

13————————————

Other Selling Situations

The techniques that work in offices, homes, on camera, in conference rooms, and in public speaking can, of course, be adapted for use in other environments and situations.

Consider, for example, selling over a table in a restaurant, at a convention, in a retail outlet or showroom, or at a trade show or fair. Obviously, selling is an activity that can be conducted anywhere with virtually every possible combination of players. Before we offer some specific ideas, we should make clear that the essentials, the keys and subtexts, the source of the basic moves, all remain constant in every situation. The salesperson who has the essentials will be able to generate winning moves naturally and spontaneously in any selling situation.

RESTAURANTS

If the restaurant doesn't have a doorman, hold the door open for your prospect. In any case, you enter behind him or her or them. If the place takes reservations, make sure you have one, and on the same call find out what forms of payment are acceptable. If you are selling, or hoping to, you are the host. Since paying is always a somewhat clumsy operation, try this: Tell the maître d' that you would like to have him run your card through in advance, and just to bring you the final sales slip for you to sign at the end of the meal. Upon your entrance, you give your card to the maître d' without the prospect noticing. Pay the tip in cash to eliminate the problem of having to do math and add up figures right in the middle of your best story.

When you enter, if you have coats, help your prospect get out of his or hers, and try to take all the chits for the coats so your prospect doesn't have to worry about digging out an elusive tip for the coat-check person. If there is some problem getting a decent table, or a delay, you may value the prospect enough to slip a five (or more) to the maître d'.

If you have an expensive briefcase (which you should), or it contains anything of value, take it with you to the table. The first time you don't will be the time they lose your briefcase. Put it at your feet, up against the legs of your chair.

Many prospects don't like to mix dining and dealing. Most Latins, for example, consider it a point of good taste to hold off discussing business until very late in a business lunch. One waits until the coffee is served. Conversely, I have participated in lunches in New York's garment center where nitty-gritty business was the focus of intense conversation before the menus arrived. Take your prospect's cue; wait for him to bring the subject up. In case he keeps avoiding it, you should broach it between the last course and coffee. Do *not* order dessert, especially if your prospect doesn't. Don't do a lot of hard sell at lunch, and never press for a written commitment. Prospects don't want to be seen "giving in" in public. They want to appear like the almost untouchable power-player. They want you to appear like a supplicant, pleading for a charitable moment of magnanimity. Use lunch for fact-finding and furnishing information. It's also a good place to enthuse about a new product or feature.

A restaurant is a wonderful place to lose a sale by exhibiting manners that place you substantially below your prospect in social amenities. Table manners for a simple business lunch are not terribly complex. The greatest faux pas are chewing with your mouth open, slurping, taking oversize bites, talking with your mouth full, and low-class use of your silverware. Middle-class Americans think it's de rigueur to put down the knife and switch the fork after cutting each piece. For a formal group, it is prescribed to put the knife down, but switching the fork is no longer a necessity. The important thing to learn, if you don't know how to do it, is how to hold your silverware. There is no surer way to signal your disadvantaged origins than holding your fork with your baby finger closest to the tines, or your knife with the fingertips across the top of the handle. It's not okay. It doesn't add to your charm as a mensch or real person.

Wait for everyone to be served before you start. Don't eat your plate clean. Don't sop up the last bits of sauce or gravy. Categorically, do not belch and say it's considered a compliment to the chef in China. Even if you do not know all the esoteric touches of table manners, you can create the impression you do by following this tip: *Eat as if you're not hungry.*

When the waiter asks for the cocktail order, do not order first. Stall until the prospect orders. If he orders mineral water or something nonalcoholic, don't you order a double Mai Tai. Generally, businesspeople who don't drink liquor at lunch have an elitist attitude toward people who do. You don't want your prospect looking down on you. Pass on the alcoholic beverage.

If your prospect doesn't smoke at the table, don't you light up. Never smoke a cigar in a public dining establishment. It will offend most people around you, especially nonsmokers. Why run the risk of provoking a feisty nonsmoker, such as an assertive pregnant woman, into telling you off and explaining to you how you are polluting her infant's blood and damaging its genes with your filthy, smelly habit? Nothing you can say or do will make you the winner in this situation.

Don't use your auditorium voice in a restaurant. Believe it or not, everyone in the world is not fascinated with you or your latest deal. Also, you never know when the person at the next table is from the competition. Practice a little discretion and modulate your voice. Especially when discussing your company, products, new developments, and pricing, move in closer and speak in a confidential tone. When you offer some special inducement or premium to your prospect, don't offer it to nine other diners at the same time. Remember the character in the E. F. Hutton commercials. The walls have ears.

You have taken a prospect to lunch and you go to pay with a card and they don't take cards, or with a check, and they don't take checks. Only cash, mister.

Don't start arguing with the waiter at the table. Tell the prospect you are going to take care of this. Get up and move away from the table toward the maître d'. Ask for the manager. Be blunt and brief, not apologetic. Clarify that you are on a business lunch, and the restaurant is jeopardizing your relationship with its unreasonable demands. Point out that a check is a viable legal instrument for disbursement of a legal debt. Since you don't want to create a scene (which you should do if you're not with a prospect), if the sniveling rat of a manager is still adamant, offer to leave your gold watch or credit cards (or something clearly worth more than the mediocre meal) with the manager until you return with the cash. And next time, make sure you always have enough cash for emergencies.

SALES CONVENTIONS

There are two kinds of people at sales conventions: conventioneers, and those selling to conventioneers. First, some ideas for conventioneers.

You are on display; you are selling yourself to your peers and superiors. Even if you are in Hawaii or Cancún, do not dress or act like a clown. Very few people look good in a fluorescent shirt and fruit-covered hat.

If you are in a sunny climate, go easy on the tanning. You cannot get a great tan in three days. You can get an agonizing burn, or melanoma.

If it is hard for you to run around introducing yourself or greeting everyone in sight, try pretending you are one of the hosts or committee heads. It's easier to be cordial and friendly when you feel it's part of your job, your role.

Wear your name tag on the *right* side of your jacket or

shirt. When you shake hands it's easier for people (especially nearsighted ones) to read your name. And wear the tag everywhere—even for golf or tennis. No, everyone doesn't know your name by the third day.

Wear a pleasant expression, but do not walk around with a mindless grin twenty-four hours a day.

Don't just shake someone's hand and walk off. Try to give at least three sentences to each person you meet or greet.

For meals with random seating, always try to start a table. As people arrive to join you, you introduce yourself (or greet them) one by one. You have a nice feeling of territorial imperative, and the other diners have a better chance of remembering you.

Attend all the meetings and sessions, especially those emceed by people above you in management. Look interested, take notes, participate, and ask questions, even though you're dying to get out on the course, the courts, or the water. If you're lucky, it'll rain when you have to be inside. Don't be pushy, but maintain a high profile. When a speaker asks for a volunteer, volunteer.

Get up half an hour before everyone else; you won't look quite so wiped out at breakfast. Do some exercises or go for a run. It makes you look and feel better all day.

Don't get bombed at night. Don't close the joints on the wrong side of town. Don't make a play for someone else's spouse, especially if that someone is your superior.

If you are selling at a convention, you may be one of the speakers or may be conducting a seminar (see appropriate chapters), but do not appear only for these exposures. Go to every meeting you can. Try to arrange to take meals with the group you are selling to. Dress a bit more formal than everyone else. If you bring along members of your staff, make sure they understand that they represent your company and products as much as you.

Never act patronizingly toward the conventioneers, even if you are picking them up off the floor from where they couldn't make it under the limbo pole.

Take running notes on everyone you meet. By running, I mean taking them in bits and pieces throughout the day.

Don't wait till the end of the day, trusting your memory to sort out all the names, titles, and stories.

Give business cards to anyone who will take one. Conversely, get as many cards as you can for follow-up later.

The only time you should be in your room is to sleep, dress, and use the bathroom. The rest of the time you should be visible: working, observing, or playing.

Don't pursue only the big accounts. They probably know you already, and they're under a constant barrage of ambitious reps, which tends to make them a bit skittish around salespeople (other than their own). You can win this character's high regard by not coming on like gangbusters, especially in this environment. Try creating a solid good impression with the people who control medium-size accounts.

If you want to give something to the conventioneers, try to find something that will exist after the meeting is over. A big barbecue with a steel band is fun while it's happening, but soon it is only a faint memory. Some tangible gift the conventioneer can take home and cherish or be proud of for years is a much wiser gift.

You are expected to run around and glad-hand just about everyone in sight, so don't feel reticent about mixing. Every personal contact puts you one degree closer to a prospect (presuming you don't run around alienating people). Don't drink too much, and if you do, disappear quickly. Gossip at a convention travels close to the speed of light, and the details of each story are amplified geometrically. Make certain you don't become grist for this mill.

RETAIL OUTLETS OR SHOWROOMS

One appreciates that there is a virtually infinite number of retail or showroom situations, ranging from the Mom-and-Pop candy store to a Rolls-Royce showroom. I can only offer some very general suggestions that may help improve the nonverbal presentation in many of them.

Evaluate the light. Sometimes the light that makes the products look good makes the salespeople (and everyone else) look bad. Diamonds, for example, look their best under an intense, cold blue-white light, which makes white people look absolutely cadaverous. Butchers use lights with a pink cast to showcase their goods. Meat lights are also wonderful people lights. The upscale novelty shops that sell cameras, video equipment, calculators, little porcelain figures, transistor radios, gadgets, and gizmos always seem compelled to light their windows and interiors with nine million watts of brutal, pulsating neon light. Each and every item is lit from all sides, but the poor salespeople look like gaunt lizards with sunken eye sockets.

If there is no reason to light the products in some way that is unappealing for the salespeople, it makes sense to light for the people. The best environment is not bright but pleasantly illuminated with warm light; that is, light tending to red rather than blue. Diffused, soft, or indirect light is always easier on the eyes than hard, direct lights.

Lighting your scene right will make working and shopping there a more pleasurable experience. The salespeople won't tire and become irritable so soon; they will look and feel better, and so will the customers.

The salesperson must work hard to remember that the customer does not care that you have been working on your feet like a slave for eight hours, that you were up half the night with a sick child, that your left foot died two hours ago, and that your ogre of a boss just gave you a severe dressing-down for no discernible reason. The customer expects you to be as cheerful and courteous as someone who just got a refund from the IRS. And respectful and patient to boot. And that, of course, is the image you must project. I understand that you can't be expected to sustain a uniformly high level of cheerful, courteous, respectful patience at all times, every day. But one tries one's best.

Don't paste on a perpetual, phony smile. It reads for what it is. Find an open, pleasant expression that you can carry easily all day, and flash your winning smile when you feel like smiling or being winsome.

Don't let a customer catch you sitting when he enters and see you jump up to intercept him. Customers don't like to be intercepted. They like to look around for a while, get the lay of the land. If they want help, they'll send an obvious array of nonverbal signals to invite your approach. It is always effective, however, to welcome the customer to your space. In this sequence, the salesperson, acting as a cross between a host and a guide, welcomes the customer to the store or showroom, tells them anything important or offers a basic set of directions, offers help, and then moves away to let the prospect browse around. Customers hate to be asked repeatedly if they "need any help." If they do, they'll let you know with verbal or nonverbal signaling or both.

Try not to let the customer catch you "tracking" him all over the store or department. No one likes to feel they are being watched. (Naturally, if you are selling small, valuable items, or things that tend to be shoplifted, customers will simply have to cope with being under surveillance.)

If you want to earn the customer's trust, do not indicate approval of every item he or she seems to like. It doesn't take long for the customer to figure out you are making no value judgments. The customer distrusts and dislikes you immediately and isn't likely to return. The salesperson is wise to show or express an honest reaction to an item for which the customer solicits an opinion. If a dress, tie, suit, color, fur, combination, idea, or accessory is uncomplimentary or gauche, be straightforward about it. You quickly establish trust, and the customer feels you are relating to them and dealing with them as individuals. Then, when you say, "It's fantastic," "Perfect," or "It's you," you have some credibility.

When you touch or handle merchandise in front of the customers, do it with some sense of regard and admiration. Do not throw things around like so much junk; it demeans the quality and worth of the goods in the customer's eyes. When you do hold something up for customers to look at, hold it up higher than you normally would. Virtually every item you pick up to show looks better held higher in the air. There is usually more light, there is less distracting confusion in the background, and the gesture is more dramatic and focuses attention on the object. Holding an object higher also tends to show that the salesperson holds it in high esteem. I mean *somewhat* higher than normal; don't go walking around like the Statue of Liberty.

Watch customers' eyes for clues to items they really covet

(see Chapter Seven, "Selling to the Emotions"). With clothes or jewelry, you know the customer loves the item if they keep checking their own face, along with the item, in the mirror. When the customer isn't quite satisfied or fond of the item, they keep looking at it and less at their own face. The reason for this paradox must be based in the customer checking to see if the item fits his or her ideal self-image.

Here are some of the moves employed by the winners in the automobile showroom.

When showing a family car to a couple or family, open all the doors and the trunk.

Always show the engine, even though the prospect doesn't know the difference between a diesel and a dithyramb. The logic is, you wouldn't show it if you weren't proud of it.

Get the prospect behind the wheel. This helps the prospect support his image of himself as owner of the car. If it's a limo, of course, you want him to sit in the back. Keep your hand on door handles when you close doors. It makes a solider sound when the door *ka-chunks* home.

For new cars that don't have any leather upholstery, get a piece of chamois or scrap leather, rub it around in a neutral shoe polish or conditioner, and toss it under the front seat, out of sight. It adds just a touch of something special to that new-car smell.

Touch, caress, stroke, and fondle the car as you describe its features. Try to cause the prospect(s) to touch, feel, and sit in the car as much as possible. Then again, if the car has a ho-hum interior but very nice lines, it makes sense to stand at the position from which the car looks the best and let the prospect come to you with questions.

Assiduously avoid the image of the archetypical used-car salesman. Don't wear zoot suits and pencil-line mustaches. Don't rub your hands together as you present. Don't talk fast. Don't wear a forced smile. And never change your first name to Honest.

TRADE SHOWS OR FAIRS

I'm talking about the trade shows where you set up an area, room, or booth to: 1) sell to a qualified market;

2) impress investors and stockholders; 3) recruit; 4) show off to the competition; or 5) get some exposure.

Yellow and orange catch the eye; blue and pastels are inviting. Fabrics and carpets are warm and inviting; steel and plastic and glass are colder and more intimidating. Round and beveled are inviting; hard edges and points are not.

Don't front your booth with an unbroken counter, like the Great Wall of China. It prevents access and contact between prospects and reps. Have as much counter as you need to hold flyers, displays, or take-aways. The rest of the booth-front should be open.

TV monitors and Super-8 machines are impersonal and disinterested; people are not. Put most of your money into the people who will be representing the company.

The personnel on duty should have a consistent style of dress. Uniforms may be appropriate. Grooming must be impeccable. While "on," people should be friendly, open, and warm. They should be having a good time, the hosts and hostesses of a successful party. And you should have at least one member of each sex present at all times. Some prospects find it easier to approach a woman; others are more comfortable talking with a man.

Ideally, you have two or three teams of salespeople, so they can change shifts every few hours. You can get tired and stale very fast at a show or fair. The sales reps must stand when they are on duty; it is easier for a passerby who is on foot to relate to a standing rep than to one who is sitting.

It helps for the salespeople to have name tags—*large* name tags—which include the company logo if the company is not identified in some other way on their person. It should be fairly obvious that the character and quality of the company will be reflected by the style, class, dress, and personality of its representatives.

Do not wait for people to take flyers or buttons or whatever you are giving away; hand them to them. Do not, however, wade into the crowd and act like a carnival barker. You will draw far larger crowds with some unique attraction, like a dancing boa constrictor, a talking geranium, or a transvestite buffalo.

Keep order forms, questionnaires, and pens out of sight.

People are skittish about having their names on lists or being hounded by salespeople. If you are trying to expand your list of leads at a show, you will have greater success if you offer some premium or chance at a prize in exchange for that name and address. Also have take-aways that give the prospect a chance to contact you later with a call or return card. Since a trade show is a fairly good market draw, consider a gift that is a bit on the extravagant side. Sales reps can hide such items on the side or under the counter, and dole them out to the likeliest prospects. It's better, in any case, to give away nothing at all than a cheap plastic key ring.

The salesperson at a trade show or fair must make a special effort to offer solid eye contact to the person he or she is speaking to. There are so many other things to look at, so many faces going by, that the temptation to look everywhere but in your prospect's eyes is very strong.

The saleswoman who is cautioned against broad smiles and heavy eye contact with a male prospect in his office is encouraged to smile and exercise solid eye contact at a trade show or fair. With prospects of the same sex, there is far more opportunity for "accidental" or innocuous body contact or touching, because of the boisterous, partylike atmosphere.

If your product can be demonstrated easily or miniaturized for demonstration, the show or fair is a wonderful place to perform such demonstrations. Anything the prospect or passerby can do or handle himself adds to the effectiveness of the demonstration.

Because of the excitement and energy that is generated by the trade show or fair, the salesperson will be more effective with more dramatic gestures and expressions. A louder voice is necessary to overcome the ambient din. One's level of energy when presenting or discussing must rise to the occasion. The quiet, confidential nature of a private office presentation is not "big" enough to survive in a trade show or fair.

At the end of an exchange lasting a minute or so, the salesperson may try, at the termination of the conversation, for a closing handshake.

14

The Smell of Success

In a typical one-on-one presentation, there are four kinds of scents being emitted and received to one degree or another:

- natural body scents
- covering, or enhancing, body scents
- natural ambient scents
- covering ambient scents.

All of the above can and do have an effect on your mood and your attitude toward the prospect. His office will have an ambient scent, which will be a blend of room and body scents and perhaps covering scents (room deodorizers). There is no question that this ambient scent will have some nonverbal effect on you. So nonverbal, in fact, that it is frequently impossible to capture in words. Also, we must recognize that different people have different levels of olfactory sensitivity, and different tolerances and responses to the same scent. Still, some generalizations for effective practice may be safely adhered to.

There is no excuse for offensive body odor or obnoxious breath. Europeans suggest that Americans are too paranoid about offensive body odor. It may be one of the reasons the Pilgrims left.

It is understood that anyone with a sales role must bathe regularly, change clothes regularly, and use whatever deodorants, antiperspirants, dental hygiene, mouthwash or sprays, and colognes or fragrances are necessary to ensure that no unpleasant odors are produced by a salesperson or detected by a prospect.

Men should go very light on the cologne. Categorically avoid floral or "sexy" scents. No musk oil, unless you're presenting to a doe in heat. The scents that work best on men are ones that suggest spice, apples, oranges or lemons, leather, waxed wood, pine, and the great outdoors.

Women can and should use a bit more fragrance than men. Avoid cheap perfume. No musk oil unless you're presenting to Donner and Blitzen. The scents that work best on women are florals, "fresh" scents, and evocative or slightly sexy scents. California fragrances, like strawberry or honey, are nice on younger women. A woman wears, of course, more perfume in the evening. Use it sparingly during the day. Avoid offbeat scents, like tea rose and scents inspired by incense. As a rule, the older you are, the richer (and more expensive) your perfume should be. Women under twenty-five should not wear the headier "old lady" perfumes.

Pheromones are organic chemical substances that act as sex lures. Their existence and use for pest control has been demonstrated with numerous species of insects, and pheromones have been used to facilitate and expedite breeding in livestock, especially pigs. The notion that pheromones in perfume will make for a strong but subliminal sex attraction in humans has not been proven in any respect. You might keep in mind that the pheromone in most commercially sold perfumes boasting the ingredient is made from processed pig's urine.

I have written earlier about the "smell of fear," and said that there is something other-dimensional about fear, something so untenable about the signals of its presence that we attempt to explain it by calling it a smell. I suspect that the lion's share of the signals that say "I am afraid" are visual, but that there is also a chemical shift in one's perspiration that may still be detected and deciphered in some ancient, dark corner of the brain. One tries one's best to fight the onset of fear, but should it start to take root, one can only hope that if it has a scent, it is covered by your perfume or after-shave.

15

Manners

Manners are the ground rules for civilized social behavior. The specific conventions may vary slightly with geography, and perhaps more radically with different cultural environments and class strata, but the basics still apply more or less universally. This is because good manners spring from a sense of courtesy, of putting yourself in the other person's shoes and making a conscious effort not to offend. There is no mystery about what makes manners good or bad. You must be sensitive and caring enough to recognize that a given act is likely to offend, inconvenience, or "turn off" others. Once you understand this, and decide it is to your benefit to have good manners, learning the rituals and conventions of the well-mannered person is greatly expedited.

Your good manners will almost always have the happy effect of causing those you come in contact with to be more courteous to you in response. If manners are practiced as a matter of course, with no great fanfare, they signal your good breeding and intimate things about your formative environment. They will signal how you expect to be treated. Another benefit of good manners is that they enable you to show respect for your prospect without seeming to project the affected obsequiousness of a petitioner with only a profit motive.

You enter a male prospect's office; his female secretary is also in the room. With whom do you shake hands first? Or do you shake hands with both people?

You shake the woman's hand first, then the man's. If the prospect is female and the secretary male, you still shake the woman's hand first, then the man's. If they are both male or both female, try to shake the prospect's hand first. Never eliminate one party from your handshake ritual.

Before we get into specifics, let's consider on whom we will use our good manners.

Everyone.

The well-mannered person does not turn deportment and courtesy on and off for the benefit of a selected audience. As good manners must become nothing less than a permanent dimension of your character, they must be inculcated to the point of being automatic. Therefore, if you were not innately gifted with good breeding or a natural sense of grace and charm, you ought to practice the good manners you consciously learn at every opportunity, thereby making them eventually second nature.

There will inevitably be times when you feel self-conscious about using your best manners or when you may feel compelled to tone them down somewhat to "fit" better with your prospects. Salesmen, for example, may rein in a bit on their courtly good manners when selling to a raucous crowd of men with hard hats and tattoos. Salesmen must exercise caution when dealing with female prospects who are radical feminists. They will bypass and reject any gentlemanly gesture or ritual that underlines sexual differentiations or implies any weakness or limitation of their gender. Southern gentlemen must be careful when selling in Yankee territory that their charm and gentility are not read as a tendency toward the effeminate of effete. And, of course, lower-class prospects may infer that a salesperson with upper-class manners is "puttin' on airs." Where men may adjust—slightly—the ardor with which they exercise their best manners, depending on their audience, a woman should always be a well-mannered person (once called a "lady").

You enter and accidentally catch the prospect necking with his or her secretary.

Continue to enter. Don't apologize or stutter or try to back out of the room. You might turn away for a moment to hang your coat, to give them a chance to recover. In essence, you enter and act as if absolutely everyone on earth necks with underlings. Don't smirk, snicker, leer, or wink. Bypass the incident and launch right into your opening. Introduce yourself to both parties with no innuendo or hint that anything embarrassing has happened.

The ground rules of proper manners for sales presentation, in no particular order, are:

Never spit; belch; exhibit flatulence; scratch personal parts; expose yourself; smoke a cigar in a tight space; sneeze or cough in someone's face; clean your ear with your pinky; arrive late; gossip; blow bits of food between your teeth; put your feet up on someone else's furniture; drop ashes on the floor; go to sleep; steal from the prospect; get dead-drunk; sell while even a little drunk; cast aspersions or ridicule the prospect's company, job, nationality, person, wife, clothes, politics, or religion.

Don't chew gum, tobacco, or betel nuts. Don't perform acts of personal hygiene, such as cleaning your nails with a paper clip. Don't apply makeup. Don't mispronounce the prospect's name. Don't yawn. Don't point. Don't touch or move anything belonging to the prospect. Don't raise your voice or use gestures that threaten the prospect. Don't bite your nails. Don't interrupt. Don't use foul language. Don't have offensive breath or body odor. Don't offend, period. Don't laugh with your mouth wide open. Don't laugh at your own jokes. If you are a woman, don't laugh.

· Do say "please" and "pardon me" and "may I" and "excuse me" and "I'm sorry" and "after you." Do be punctual. Pay attention. Open doors for others, or at least hold them open for those who follow you. Do try to be last in the elevator; hold back the bar in the door so others can get in without getting squished. Ladies ought to go first, except downstairs. Men, do offer your arm to women upon crossing the streets, riding the escalators, and getting out of the backs of taxicabs. Men, help women on and off with their coats. At a mixed table, men are supposed to talk mainly with the woman on their right, women with the man on their left (that works out nicely). Always eat like you're not hungry. But don't eat until everyone is served and the hostess or guest of honor has started. If you shake hands with a couple, you are supposed to shake the woman's hand first. (In any case, *never* shake the hand of only one member of a couple. Aside from being rude, it shows the person you neglect exactly how little regard you have for them.) Do remind mild acquaintances of your name when you meet them, immediately (they will appreciate this, as they probably drew a blank on your name, as you probably did with theirs). Do grab for restaurant and bar checks.

When in doubt, reflect on the wise words of Emerson, in his *Conduct of Life*: "There is always a best way of doing everything, if it be to boil an egg. Manners are the happy ways of doing things."

You are in mid-presentation and feel a sneeze coming on.

Sneeze. Away from the prospect. Into a tissue. Don't wait till the last minute. If you don't see a convenient wastebasket, put the used tissue in your own pocket or bag. Do not put it in the prospect's ashtray.

16

The Eyes

If we had to pick one part of the anatomy to read and send nonverbal signals (not sign language, body language), to the exclusion of all others, we would, without hesitation, choose the eyes. Not just the eyeballs, of course, but the lids and brows and area surrounding the eyes that act as a frame for these "windows of the soul."

The eyes have such expressive power, there aren't too many adjectives you can't use with them. One finds Spanish eyes, Bette Davis eyes, bedroom eyes; bright, dark, slow, cold, hot, unforgiving, defiant, longing, smart, ignorant, inquiring, sharp, happy, sad, attentive, misty, hard, soft, red, green (green-eyed, as in jealous), cross, blank, dagger, private, and evil eyes.

Until modern revelations of the physics of light and optics, it was commonly believed that the eyes transmitted rays that were capable not only of sight, but also of carrying emotions, will, and magical powers, both good and evil.

We still say, "She looked daggers at him"; "He shot her a look"; "If looks could kill..." And we are not completely persuaded by the scientists who say that there cannot be such a thing as *malocchio*, or the evil eye. The belief in the power of an admiring or jealous look to bring on a debilitating and sometimes fatal illness, especially in children, is very much alive today in a large segment of southern European cultures, particularly among Italians and Greeks. With perhaps no intentional malice whatsoever, the sender, or *jettatore*, of the *malocchio* casts a destructive spell over the innocent child, a spell that is customarily warded off by touching a religious charm or medallion, by immediately saying aloud or to oneself the word *benedicta* (Italian procedure), or miming spitting three times (the Greek remedy). If these first echelon defenses are not enough, and the child or person falls ill, an expert must be called in, usually a woman skilled in the mystical arts, and she must undertake a ritual of prayers, chants, and the use of water and oil to diagnose and exorcise the evil spell. Forms of *malocchio* have been found all over the world, even on remote islands in the Pacific.

It is standard procedure in the prizefighting ring to try to intimidate your opponent before the first punch is thrown, by nailing him with a "double whammy." Powerful figures have always been characterized by exceptional eyes. They tend to be either piercing and hypnotic (Genghis Khan, Attila the Hun, Napoleon, Rasputin) or empathetic, sincere, and charismatic (Jesus, Alexander the Great, Mahatma Gandhi, George Washington), but there is always a sense of indomitable will. And they all have one thing in common: They are all great salespeople.

Are we suggesting that you can't be a great salesperson—or powerful figure, for that matter—if you don't have sincere, steady, clear, honest, intelligent, friendly but indomitable, empathetic but powerful eyes? As a rule, yes.

Unfortunately, you can't run to the corner store and pick up a pair of hypnotic dazzlers. Except for tinted contacts, makeup, and operations that widen the lids or lift the flesh around the eyes, you're more or less stuck with the pair you've got. We can improve their appearance by a healthy, regular life-style. We can keep the whites clear by getting enough sleep. If we devote an evening to spirited dissipation, we can help bloodshot eyes the morning after with eyedrops.

If you are not a naturally powerful or charismatic personality, I suppose the hardest nonverbal characteristic for you to develop is powerful or charismatic eyes. For as our eyes provide wonderful windows for us to look out of, they also furnish windows for others to look into. The transparent personality, whose face "reads like a book," is revealing the most information through his eyes. Clearly you must first learn to discontinue transmitting all your emotions and reactions unedited through your eyes (see Chapter Four, "For Women Only").

Now, the next step is to become a more powerful or charismatic character. More easily said than done, you say? Your power comes from within; it's your personal quotient of willpower. You know that you have as much of it as you have ever needed. When you have really called it up, it rose to the occasion and helped you survive the crisis or overcome the obstacle. Well, you may ask, if I have so much willpower, how come I'm not King of the Mountain? (If you are King of the Mountain, you probably wouldn't ask that. Skip ahead to the next chapter.)

You know the answer. You knew the answer to that even before you asked the question: You took it easy. You started to get depressed. You had lots of rotten breaks. You have bad karma because your grandfather was a purse-snatcher. You're self-destructive. The Devil led you down the wrong path. You were born in the wrong age. The buggy whips you're selling aren't hot items anymore, and you're too old to retrain, etc., etc., etc. Choose any or all of the above. Your own litany of excuses why your willpower has dwindled may be far more original. There's a vicious cycle here: If your willpower wanes, you don't achieve your goals. If you don't achieve your goals, your willpower wanes. If that's what happened to you, or is happening now, *it will show in your eyes* more than anywhere else. You may be smart enough to watch your posture, dress, and grooming. Your moves and gesturing may be most reassuring. But your eyes will betray you if your mind is thinking "Help! I'm losing faith here. I can't do it anymore! I've lost the knack!"

Well, that was all yesterday. Today you set to work creating a new character for yourself. Your new character will not tolerate any of the excuses or self-limitations of the old one. Your new character believes in you because it knows your true potential (see Chapter Two, "Creating a Character"). Your new character has the courage to fight the temptations that may have been taking a bite out of your time, your income, or your mental or emotional stability—because you believe in it. You imbue it with the power it will need to overcome your obstacles (including you), and achieve your goals. Your new character is imperfect in some ways: It has no recollection of disappointments of the past, and it is deaf to negative attitudes, depression, and despondency in the present. It will not tolerate procrastination, self-persecution, or loss of faith. It enthusiastically embraces the possibilities of tomorrow.

What sort of eyes do you expect to find on this character? Powerful dazzlers, of course. And, as you start to experience the success wrought by your rekindled willpower, you will gradually develop or redevelop a self-assured warmth, or charisma.

You will have to teach your eyes how to transmit your new resolve, to reflect your deep reserve of willpower and courage. They will tend to cling to habitual patterns of behavior. You must find and rehearse eye moves and expressions that will clearly reflect the power and resolve you have generated within. And these moves and expressions must become automatic. Once you no longer have the mirror or videotape for reference and you are facing a live prospect, you will not be able to see exactly what signals your eyes are sending. Your rehearsals are therefore especially important.

Powerful eyes are not by any means eyes that do nothing but glare out indomitable power. Powerful eyes are also talented eyes. They can go from empathetic warmth to humor, enthusiasm, resolve, and stark power. Do not go into a meeting intent on staring down your prospect. Especially if you are a woman, you must be wary of unwarranted or overly intense, sustained eye contact. You use your strongest unwavering gaze only in the critical moments: to underline a promise; to guarantee or verify; to hold your ground during a prospect's attack; and during your response to an attack or charged question.

Eye-to-eye combat is so uncomfortable for most people that usually you only have to win the first crucial clinch. The prospect is not likely to try to stare you down again in this meeting. And even if he does, he is likely to lose, since you will have wrested the psychological edge from him. He knows you are not afraid of him. He will also begin to realize that you have the willpower to persist in trying to win him over.

Your eyes are among your principal instruments to

1. Underline and accentuate your verbal material.
2. Show concentration, especially in listening. (Your ears may hear, but they can show no sign of comprehension.)
3. Show enthusiasm, awe, wonder, surprise, and delight.
4. Evince fearlessness and courage.
5. Display agreement or disagreement.
6. Show understanding and empathy; or the withholding thereof.
7. Flirt, and also to draw the line with disclaimers.
8. Point or direct the prospect's attention somewhere.
9. Reassure; add sincerity to a promise; guarantee or verify.
10. Show deep willpower, strength under fire, and pertinacity.
11. Establish a sense of humor, personal warmth, and charisma.

Recalcitrant, indifferent, or hostile prospects are aware that their eyes are quite likely to give them away, so they will take great pains, especially in the beginning of the meeting, to hide them from you. They will use shields and masks created by the frames of glasses; long hair; their hands; their eyelids; their brows (by tilting the head forward); objects on the desk or table, such as lampshades and plants; and most effective of all—looking or turning away. Watch your prospect's blinking. Blinking is a visual editing-out of you and your presentation. When you see a flurry of blinks, or a long blink, that segment or point of your presentation was not well received.

When he is talking and he looks away, fixing his focus easily and casually on a middle range or on some neutral object on the wall, your prospect is thinking as he talks, and is also signaling that he doesn't want to be interrupted (not that you ever would). Even though there may be a long break between his sentences, he isn't finished yet. When he is finished and would like to hear your comment or response, he will punctuate by looking at you, even if it is nothing more than a glance. On the other hand, when he looks away while talking and his focus flits about nervously from one point to another, he is fabricating, fudging, or just plain lying.

As a rule, whenever you are employing the subtle "push" toward a prospect, you accompany it with a sincere, unbroken, powerful look. You will always go for peak dazzle and self-confidence in your eyes for the first six or seven seconds of the meeting, especially the handshake, and also upon your leave-taking—whether the prospect bought or not. Imagine that your parting handshake is the opening one of your next meeting with him. Never let him get the impression that he got the better of you or broke your spirit. Don't look down or to the side. Look him straight in the eye and let your eyes tell him you're not a quitter.

The background of your prospect may have something to do with how he handles eye signals. People from both coasts and major cities are less reticent with eye contact and the power stare. Male Southerners avoid heavy eye contact with male Yankees, unless they are Southerners of good breeding. Female prospects from upper-middle-class backgrounds will usually break heavy eye contact with salesmen, lest they be read as courting signals. Hispanics, especially if they are younger or female, will usually avoid eye contact rather carefully. The deeper they are steeped in Spanish rather than American culture, the more assiduously they will avert their eyes. As the Hispanic achieves stature, however, his or her gaze becomes bolder. American Blacks, especially those of less than upper-middle-class origin, have to work hard to offer unforced, comfortable eye contact to whites, especially whites with any status. Semitics, especially male Arabs, often use intense eye contact at close range, which frequently puts Westerners ill at ease. Generally, it is important for a salesman to be careful of the nature of intense or sustained eye contact with American male prospects. There is a tremendous sensitivity in heterosexual American men to anything that might be misread as an effeminate or gay signal. Keep your power stares clearly masculine in character by using them only in tight spots, by breaking them off at the right moment, and by eliminating any overtone or accompanying signal that may be misinterpreted, such as heavy lids, moistening the lips, batting the lashes, opening the mouth, or showing the tongue.

EXERCISES: Your Eyes

With a partner

As you present, have your partner react nonverbally to every claim you make with one of the following:

> skepticism
> indifference
> hostility
> flirting.

Use your eyes to support your response of, respectively:

> honesty, ingenuousness
> enthusiasm, energy
> courage, conviction
> polite turnoff.

Have your partner tell you immediately if your eyes are helping or hindering your message and what signals he or she feels your eyes are sending.

Practice the eye contact contest you used to do in grade school. Sustain mutual eye contact for as long as you can without looking away. Try it with or without blinking allowed. It's not important always to be the winner of this game; the point is to exercise holding eye contact and not being intimidated by someone with powerful eyes.

Alone

Write up a list of signals that you will want to be expert at sending and supporting with your eyes, such as:

> sincere
> honest
> enthusiastic
> friendly

amused
understanding
totally focused
fascinated
indomitable
determined
reassuring
approving

Pin the list up to a wall at a ninety-degree angle to a mirror. Pick a word on the list. Do *not* look in the mirror yet. Work up the expression you have chosen, especially concentrating on the areas around the eyes. When you think or feel that you have the exact expression you're after, turn and examine it immediately in the mirror. Only the first split second will give you a true picture of the expression you presented because the instant you see yourself, you start making adjustments, however minor, to the reflected expression. So concentrate on what you see in the very first second you see yourself. Experiment with variations of your eye, eyelid, and eyebrow position and degree. Always mount the expression or intended signal, and *then* look at it in the mirror. This is the only way you can feel from within the shape of the expression, and thereby learn to duplicate it reliably during a presentation where there will be no opportunity to see your work reflected (except in the face of your prospect, which may be too late).

Obviously, if you have a home video system, or a Polaroid camera, you can replace the mirror with a camera for these exercises when you get reasonably confident that you are sending the signals that you intend to send.

To help you maintain eye contact, or a confident look in the face of strong objections or scathing skepticism, try this:

Beg, borrow, buy, or rent a cassette recorder (audio) if you don't already have one. Write up a list of all the worst failings and shortcomings of your product, service, or idea. Familiarize yourself with the material. Assume the character of a hostile or skeptical prospect. Turn on the recorder. Start talking. Attack your product mercilessly. Grow in intensity or be horribly skeptical. Doubt every single product benefit. Explore verbally every avenue that the worst possible prospect could possibly devise. Really be hard on yourself. Now sit down in front of a mirror. Watch your eyes and expressions. Play the tape back from the beginning. Watch your eyes as the voice on the tape dumps all over you. When the voice finishes letting you have it, make your response to your own image in the mirror. Watch your eyes; you can train them to be utterly fearless, confident, and convincing. Don't worry about your verbal presentation at this point. Your nonverbals will determine whether or not the prospect was justified in his or her attack or skepticism. For variations, have someone else record the voice for you. Or try the exercise with a picture of someone intimidating or unfriendly taped to the mirror, and practice maintaining eye contact. With a minor shift in position, you can check your expression in the mirror just next to the picture. If you have a video camera, videotape your reactions while under fire from the recorded voice, and then play back the videotape immediately to see what signals you sent.

If you tend to have weak, wimpy eyes, there are a couple of things you can do to develop a more powerful gaze. For the sake of expediency, let's call it the Power Stare.

1. Work on not blinking.
2. Work on not blinking while sustaining eye contact.
3. Practice unblinking eye contact while under fire.

Certain bits of business add an extra dimension to the most intimidating Power Stare.

4. In the mirror, practice narrowing your lids a bit. It's not a squint, but more like the narrowing of

eyes you see in an animal just about to strike. Don't overdo it. It should be practically imperceptible.

5. When you move your gaze from one point to another (as in one face to another), try to do it without blinking. It's not easy. Everyone blinks to edit out the swish-pan associated with looking from one point to another. The farther apart the points, the longer and more certain the blink will be. It's completely unconscious; watch people's eyes, and you'll see how uniformly automatic such blinking is. When you pan from point A to B without blinking, it has an unnerving effect on anyone watching you, especially A and B.

   You assume some of the quality of a tracking beast of prey. (This might be an interesting area for a scientist to explore, whether animals on the hunt or moving in for the kill allow themselves the luxury of editorial blinks.) It is almost impossible to execute the unblinking swish-pan slowly. If you don't do it rather snappily, your eyes will try to focus on things on the way and will create a staggered panning movement. Practice a clean, smooth, rather rapid pan of the eyes.

6. I found a further refinement that adds a degree of threat to the unblinking pan. Move your eyes first from point A to point B, and follow with your head movement just behind the eye move. A repositioning of the shoulders or upper torso may support the head pan if it covers a wide enough angle. The movement of the head may start before the eyes have settled on their new focal point, but for short moves, say from one face to the next at a conference table, it is most effective to complete the shift of the eyes before following with the head. In any case, the head comes to rest when the face is squared to the object of the gaze.

7. Tipping the head forward slightly, so that the brow ridge starts to move protectively over the

eye area, adds to the aggressive character of the Power Stare.

Use the Power Stare only for effect and in clinches. Don't wait, however, until things have gone too far. The minute you feel someone is trying to intimidate you, whip out your Power Stare and defuse the attacker before he gains any momentum. If you only sell to pleasant prospects, you may never have need for such a technique, of course.

Animated, Expressive Eye Exercise

Many old-style salespeople seem to have protected themselves from the sales confrontation by developing eyes that are somewhat hidden, fogged-over, or dead, such as the glass eyes on teddy bears. You look in them for some access to the person inside, and there is nothing. They are two-dimensional mask eyes. Eyes that are so afraid of sending a mixed or ambiguous signal, or of showing fear, send *no* signal. It is true that such eyes are capable of hiding lots of negative signals. But it is also true that such eyes do not allow the salesperson to send positive signals, such as enthusiasm, sincerity, sensitivity to the prospect's needs, energy, and warmth. You want to "open" your eyes to people, to make them a two-way communications system. You can dare to do this because you have already bought what you are selling. Your emotional subtext is strong and functioning. Let people in, and then turn them on. Here is an exercise to help you bring your eyes to life, to "open" them for others to enter and share your point of view—with trust.

Put a mirror on top of your TV, or next to the seat from which you watch. As you watch various shows—dramas, comedies, sports, news—try to let your feelings flow and show through your eyes. Let it come naturally; don't fake it. Look at your eyes when you feel a peak of any emotion—joy, sadness, thrill, fear, anger. Let the feeling register in your eyes. Even crying is instructive, although this is usually counterproductive in a sales presentation.

Soon you will see the tremendous power your expressive eyes have, and you will start to sense from within the degree or scope you can use in your business life to help disarm a prospect, win him over, earn his trust, and turn him on.

17

Split-brain Psychology and How to Use It

In the early and mid-seventies, there was a spate of articles in scientific journals and general circulation magazines on exciting findings in split-brain psychology. Corroboration for the split-brain theory was found through research with brain-damaged patients; through brain-splitting surgery, in which the tissue connecting the two halves of the brain is cut; with dichotic listening, in which stimuli are presented to separate sides of the brain through the opposite ear (neural pathways cross, with each side of the brain controlling the movements and sensations of the opposite side of the body); and by feeding visual data to either the right or left field of view, then measuring the ability of opposite hemispheres to process the information.

In a May 1973 *Psychology Today* article, "Right and Left Thinking," Robert Ornstein, of the Langley Porter Neuropsychiatric Clinic, wrote, "Reason versus passion is one of its guises; mind versus intuition is another. The feminine, the sacred, the mysterious...have lined up against the masculine, the profane and the logical. Medicine argues with art, yin complements yang. In fable and folklore, religion and science, this dualism has recurred with stunning regularity."

In a 1977 interview, Marshall McLuhan said, "We have a

left-hemisphere establishment. Bureaucracy is all left-hemisphere.... The day when bureaucracy becomes right-hemisphere will be utopia."

In an effort to sprinkle some cooling water on the sizzling split-brain fad, Daniel Goleman, associate editor of *Psychology Today*, wrote in the October 1977 issue, "The right-brain metaphor expresses the need many people feel for a certain sensibility that has been lost in our technological age. In this sense, the qualities of the right brain are an image of Eden in a wasteland of consciousness; much of the theory's popularity must be traced to this source. But for the present, there is widespread confusion between the poetics of experience and the hard facts of brain function." In a similar effort to let some of the hot air out of the split-brain balloon, Howard Gardner of Harvard's School of Education wrote in the March-April 1978 issue of *Harvard Magazine*, "It is high time for investigators conversant with brain lateralization to announce that the unknowns in the field dwarf the little that is known, and the little more that is suspected."

We quote you such passages to call to your attention the fact that split-brain psychology is still technically in the embryonic stage. One appreciates that responsible scientists are required to weigh, to move methodically and meticulously, to verify and reverify each finding before carving anything in tablets and calling it "fact."

My first response to the initial public splash of split-brain psychology was to flash on two things: Picasso, and the seating positions at formal or business affairs.

Picasso could not have known about split-brain psychology prior to the sixties, when the first brain-splitting operations were performed on some victims of severe epilepsy, and subsequent examination supported theories of the split-brain division of responsibilities. How, then, is one to explain Picasso's habit of portraying the left and right eyes of his subjects as frequently having markedly distinct characteristics? In 1903, he painted *Celestina*, the one-eyed procuress of Fernando de Rojas's play, with a calculating, acquisitive right eye, and the left eye a blind gray. In 1906, in the faces and sketches for *Les Demoiselles d'Avignon*, we see a growing inclination toward the treatment of the eyes as reflecting different aspects of the personality. In many heads the left eye, which reflects the intuitive, subconscious right hemisphere, is blank. When the left eye is rendered, it is almost always softer and more heavily lidded. It is a more empathetic, understanding eye. The right eye, in contrast, tends to grow colder, more businesslike, less passionate. *Girl Before a Mirror*, 1932, shows a radically split face with the left side bright yellow and the left eye dark and heavily lidded. In *Dora Maar Seated*, 1937, the left eye is totally different from the right, and it is turned on its axis so that it appears to be looking back *at* the right eye. The right-left eye dichotomy grows stronger through the body of work with the character of each eye remaining surprisingly consistent. Did Picasso somehow intuit that the eyes reflected different, and perhaps opposing, sides of their possessor's personality and psyche?

Split-brain theory also causes one to reflect on the customs of social laterality, such as the classic position of honored guest (to the host's left) and the proverbial "right-hand man." The popular explanation for the host putting the guest on his left and his wife or right-hand man on his right is that, in ancient times, the guest was best placed in a position from which it was difficult for him to plunge a dagger into you. Your wife or most trusted lieutenant was seated on your right because, although this facilitated their stabbing you, the likelihood of their doing so was very small. That's the currently popular explanation. I have always found myself straining to suspend disbelief in an effort to accept this theory. I have always succeeded in the past because there didn't seem to be any other theories around. Before we propose one, let's look at a simplified list of the kinds of thinking the two sides of the brain are more or less responsible for in current split-brain psychology.

RIGHT HEMISPHERE	**LEFT HEMISPHERE**
emotional	logical
intuitive	verbal
passion, instinct	reason
inner voice	writing, speaking
unconscious	conscious
natural	affected
mysterious	rational
humming tunes	singing lyrics
sacred	profane
watching TV, movies	reading
the larger picture	the details
"hunches," "vibes"	logical conclusions
visual and spatial analysis	language skills

I suggest that medieval heads of households chose to put powerful guests to their left for the same reason that chairpersons sustain the tradition today: Your left field of view feeds into the right hemisphere of your brain, the side with the intuition, the animal instinct to detect evil intent or ill will in your powerful guest. Most of us feel more comfortable with someone we don't or can't really trust in our left field of view because it feeds images to the right side of the brain, which is the side best equipped to sense danger, recognize dissembling, or see through a false friend. It makes more sense than conjectural rigmarole about which side offers the best opportunities for dinnertime dagger-play.

Some researchers have found that prospects generally prefer to have salespeople sit to their left side rather than their right but offer no explanation whatsoever for why this is so. Split-brain psychology provides, I feel, a reasonable explanation: The prospect wants the salesperson where he can most comfortably read him on a visceral, intuitive level. Although there is no proof that this is so, there is good evidence to believe it is, and as with the proverbial chicken soup, it certainly wouldn't hurt you to know the theory and apply techniques based on it. As a general rule, then: If you have convinced yourself of what you are saying, to the point that your nonverbal signals will flow naturally and not contradict your verbal material, sit if possible on your prospect's left. If you have a fantastic verbal presentation, but your nonverbal signals are not entirely on-stream yet, try to stay more in your prospect's right field of view.

One must understand that the division of responsibilities alluded to above only applies with any consistency to right-handed people, and the regularity with which the rules apply have been calculated (depending on the scientist) at from rather modest to truly substantial percentages of the population. Still, a salesperson must make an effort to find and implement any edge he can to increase his efficiency. With these disclaimers expressed, let me take you a step further into a technique so new I may be the only person on earth using it.

If the responsibilities for the kinds of thought are essentially true, I reasoned, it might be possible to use the split-brain phenomenon as a lie detector. It is clearly helpful for anyone trying to sell something to someone else to know if the prospect is responding sincerely, from the heart, or is dishing up a mound of verbal obfuscation or simply lying. Fabrication and falsification are effected, verbal constructions, and are therefore the responsibility of the left hemisphere. A short, honest, impulsive answer, on the other hand, will be the province of the right hemisphere. I theorized that, when responding to a question, a prospect would tend to glance or look off into the field of view, or side, in which the corresponding part of the brain was forming the answer. In other words, when he gives a sincere answer, he looks to his left; during a calculated or false answer, he looks to his right.

The technique works best when the inducements to look either right or left are equal. If there is an interesting view out a window to the right, the prospect is likely to look that way regardless of which hemisphere of his brain is stimulated or engaged. A deeper field of view or brighter image will attract random stares and glances. Another person or persons in the room obviously will have a similar effect. For maximum effect, you and your prospect are in an environment in which there is no powerful visual distraction to one side or the other, you are one-on-one with the prospect, and he is positioned and postured in such a way that it is equally comfortable for him to look left or right. It is interesting to note that a speaker at a podium is presented with a symmetrical panorama; the lights are essentially equal on both sides, and the camera is usually central (neutral). A speaker in this environment is free to look easily to either side (or into the right or left prompter), and may reveal more than he intends by his choice of favoring one or the other as he presents verbal material. Watch next time you see a shifty-eyed politician being grilled at a press conference.

Let's look at some examples of how you can use a prospect's propensity to glance into the field of view of the hemisphere he is referencing for his response.

The prospect is enumerating reasons why he has not used your service or bought your product or whatever. (He is likely to be glancing or looking to his right.) You flatly ask, "If I were to correct, solve, and remove those problems, would you consider buying/using/giving?" If the prospect looks or glances to his left just before or during the first moments of his response, his answer is probably sincere. If he looks or glances to his right, he probably is just stalling, fencing with you verbally, lying, or he hasn't been frank about what's really bothering him.

The honest, impulsive responses that are generated by the right brain are, of necessity, short. This is because the left brain houses the language center. The minute an answer gets beyond three words, it will become the responsibility of the left brain to process the material and form cogent sentences. I think we all sense this, and that is why we usually hesitate a moment before presenting a first, unguarded, impulsive response. We learn to temper and qualify our instinctive, passionate, emotional response with the rational editing and review provided by left-brain processing. This is why, if you are moving to elicit an honest, visceral answer to a question, you try to frame the question so it can be answered with a very short response, such as "yes," "no," or "I do."

If you experiment with these techniques, and certainly you simply may observe your prospect's eye movements without doing any harm, you must appreciate that you are participating in your own research program in a very new field. If a prospect's eyes follow no pattern you can find, it is probably wise to discontinue trying to read anything into such signals. And, of course, there is always the possibility that he has a copy of this book in his top drawer and purposely glances to his left every time he lies to you.

18

One Character Profile: The Upper-middle-class Belonger

Let's make a wild but probably useful generalization and say that most of the important or powerful decision-makers (buyers) will be upper-middle-class, or at least like to think they are. If you are selling to this stratum of society, you ideally belong to it. If you belong to the prospect's class, he is more comfortable, more likely to like you. He will relax sooner, and communications thus will be facilitated. If you are of his class, you are of his "family," and those ancient clan loyalties will be stimulated at some level. The prospect may not go out of his way to help you, but he will certainly be more receptive to your presentation.

You communicate your membership in the upper-middle-class club not by printing a message on your shirt but through your nonverbal signals. Your vocabulary and diction are equally important, but consider that it is quite possible to have an extended vocabulary and university-level diction and still have the nonverbal signals of the lower or lower-middle classes. The reverse is rarely the case. In other words, upper-middle-class belongers sense that it is harder for a person of lower-class background to learn and imitate the nonverbal signals of their stripe than to learn, and use, their language. And, of course, they are right.

Anyone can learn Hamlet's words, but can he fill the role convincingly? Upper-middle-class belongers establish their membership with a complement of signals: posture, carriage, dress, grooming, movement, gesture, expression, and pitch and volume of voice. If you were not born and bred in the upper-middle-class, you must learn the signals by observation and make them your own through practice and use.

Keeping in mind that all the upper-middle-class signals are generated and governed by an upper-middle-class philosophy or attitude, let's look at some of the prominent characteristic mannerisms—posture, gesture, and expression—and infer what attitudes they communicate or suggest.

POSTURE AND CARRIAGE

Erect, relaxed shoulders; comfortably back, no slouch. Symmetrical, leaning ever so slightly forward. Carriage of the body flows from good posture; held high and light, a certain muscular tone seems to make carriage a small task. The walk is a purposeful but unrushed medium stride, with no exaggerated bounce, no loping, and no lateral swaying or tipping of the head or shoulders. Arms swing in a natural, relaxed manner. The key to upper-middle-class carriage is self-assuredness and pride.

DRESS

Conservative. Quiet colors. Well tailored, not too "European"-looking or too sporty. Brooks Brothers, Saks, Bloomingdale's, etc. Clean and wrinkle-free. Natural fibers mainly. See Chapter Four, "For Women Only" and Chapter Five, "For Men Only."

GROOMING

Meticulous, kept up, clean. No flamboyant hairstyles or odd beards, sideburns, or mustaches. Men must have clean, unbitten fingernails; a professional manicure is not necessary. Women must have clean, unbitten, shaped nails, with either clear or colored polish. No "new wave," iridescent, or two-tone colors.

MOVEMENT/GESTURES

The motor actions of the upper-middle-class man are confident, deliberate, poised, and relaxed. In the upper-middle-class woman, they are confident, controlled, graceful, and relaxed. The moves and gestures of both sexes are marked by a deep-seated self-assuredness. The upper-middle-class person gestures primarily from the elbows down. Elbows are kept close to the body. Generally, all movement and gesture is subtle, minimal, and used sparingly. Gesture only supports verbal communication, never supplants it.

The speed and scope of upper-middle-class movements and gestures suggest a relaxed mood bordering on complacency. The upper-middle-class salesperson must be careful not to project smug apathy. He must frequently add a pinch of enthusiasm to heighten his display of energy and sincerity.

The walk and large motor movements are executed with calm deliberateness and "flow." There is no lurching, head-wagging, or defensive elbow-out in the walk. The act of sitting is a choreographed move, not "taking a load off your feet."

EXPRESSION

Upper-middle-class people are relatively conservative users of facial expressions. They do not routinely use them to carry the thrust of their communications, as lower-middle-class people are inclined to do. A good case could be made that lower-middle-class people overuse facial expression for the same reason they employ exaggerated gesturing: a lack of facility with language or a lack of faith in their audience to correctly decode language.

Consequently, for the salesperson assuming an upper-middle-class role, it is advisable to limit facial expressions to a conservative few. Natural, clear, but conservative facial expressions can add another reinforcing channel to your multilevel mix of signals.

THE MASK

Another class indicator that is widely recognized, but quite difficult to define, is the "mask," or general look or expression one wears in public. Upper-middle-class people have nurtured a public countenance that may go unnoticed or appear neutral to members of lower classes but are membership signals as clear as a fraternity handshake to other upper-middle-class people.

The face is relaxed; muscles are not gnarled or pinched. There is no furrow between the brows from frowning because the upper-middle-class person rarely frowns (except around April 15). The eyes (actually the areas all around the eyes) evince an even, controlled temper, and are not "winced" with fear and flinching.

The mouth is carried evenly, closed when listening (not breathed through) in something very close to the beginning of a contented grin. Not a Cheshire-cat grin, not a mindless or mirthful grin, but a self-assured half-grin that comes from the certain conviction that you are in control of things, and everything is going to turn out just fine.

The upper-middle-class brow is held up and away from the eye, in a relaxed, "intelligent," natural arch. The upper-middle-class face achieves the effect of "brightness" or superior intellect by holding the inside tip of one or both brows slightly higher than it would be at rest. In other words, the inside (thickest) brow edge is held a fraction of an inch opposite where it would move were it expressing anger. The face can convey a sense of mild astonishment at the claims of the other party or parties if one brow assumes this slightly quizzical reverse arch, while the other frowns subtly (inside edge down). This last effect is disorienting to the recipient; he doesn't know which brow to trust.

The upper-middle-class person has ultimate recourse to a mask he is master of, the "stonewall." You saw a lot of it during Watergate. The idea is to show no emotion or guilt, even when fifty policemen catch you with a smoking gun. The upper-middle-class "stonewall" is like the top face on a totem pole. It is immobile, haughty, and untouchable. (It's disheartening to find one on a prospect.) It's very handy when you're playing poker or if you happen to get caught with a smoking gun. The "stonewall" is achieved by finding (in a mirror) a mask that is "closed" and transmits no signal, or transmits one and only one: grim stoniness. It is frequently useful to be able to mount this mask while you are trying to gather your senses to respond to an attack. Needless to say, it is very hard to sustain an effective "stonewall" for any substantial period of time without some telltale, involuntary signal slipping out or having some other system (posture, gesture, tone of voice) give you away. Consequently, the "stonewall" should be used only in emergencies, for desperately needed stall time. Used in excess, it is like pleading *nolo contendere;* you confess as much by saying nothing as you would by confessing straight out.

CHARISMA

Charisma is virtually impossible to define, and here we are trying to isolate upper-middle-class charisma. Let's start by agreeing that charisma is that ephemeral, extra dimension that makes you like or admire someone. Quickly. Charismatic people seem more charming, warmer, friendlier, more comfortable with themselves, more persuasive, larger than life, more confident. They carry power more gracefully.

Charisma may be thought of as being like one of those goals the Zen masters talk about: the harder you strive to attain it, the harder it is to attain. He who sets out to appear charismatic will surely appear contrived or possibly even ridiculous. You must instead allow your charisma to emanate naturally from within, like your aura.

What is it? How do you let it emanate from within if you can't quite put your finger on it? Simply said, your charisma is your personality unchained when you are at your best. Unchained, because it has to be spontaneous, ingenuous, natural. At your best, because the shades of personality that make you different are in full color. Your unique character expresses itself when it's in a positive frame of mind, on a high ("Up," "Relaxed," and "Yes" is appropriate here). This raises your charisma factor to a level where it is evident to others. It's your character when you are not afraid to let you be yourself—and that turns out to be a rather wonderful or interesting personality.

Since we have established that the upper-middle-class person is marked by restraint and conservatism, how do you generate the unfettered, spontaneous, natural something we call charisma without slipping out of character? Well, that's exactly what you do—you let yourself occasionally slip slightly out of character. You do it on purpose. You must first be completely comfortable with your character so that it is second nature to you. It is you. You establish it with your prospect or audience, and then you suddenly relax it and do or say something that doesn't quite fit in the normal parameters of the character. Put another way, every once in a while you let the prospect see a less formal, more human side of you. This always disarms and charms the other party, because they feel you are making a spontaneous gesture of friendship.

To have peak effectiveness, the charismatic moment ought to be unexpected. It is a short moment, perhaps just a beat, a flash of a gesture or expression that expands the character by poking past its preset margins. Several or many charismatic peaks are strung together to build a unique, interesting character. The moments that comprise the effect of charisma must not be overused or they lose their power. The charismatic gesture or expression is spontaneous and therefore uniquely you. If it works, people feel you have charisma; if it doesn't, they think you are idiosyncratic, uneven, or even weird. It is advisable to leave the development of charisma to the last stage in your growth to supersalesperson. Remember that charisma is essentially extra fringe; it is not an absolute prerequisite to effective salesmanship.

EXERCISE: Enhancing Your Charisma

Alone, in front of a mirror or videocamera, give your typical sales presentation with all the average moves and expressions you normally use. Now pretend you are talking to a friend, and talk about something that really turns you on. You will be immediately aware of a different energy level and looser, more compelling moves and expressions. Now try goosing up your ho-hum sales presentation with some of the energy and moves and expressions of the excited, turned-on you. Try different levels of energy until you find how much of the effervescent, glowing you you can add to your sales presentation. You will almost always find you have been stifling too much of your personality and enthusiasm in presentations and that it will improve your presentation and enhance your charisma by letting more of your natural energy out. Now try it on prospects.

The emotional/philosophical subtext of the upper-middle-class character is basically the one we describe at length in Chapter One, "The Secret of Winning Moves." The upper-middle-class salesman is "*Up*," "*Relaxed*," and "*Yes*." He is confident and self-assured. If you are upper-middle-class by birth and breeding, you will probably need a key that will stimulate your enthusiasm and energy in order to complement or offset your relaxed, comfortable, self-possessed personality. If you are a self-made upper-middler, a recent arrival, or still in the making, you will find most functional a key that will help you sustain the self-possessed, comfortable relaxation that is natural to the born-and-bred upper-middler.

The born-and-bred upper-middler believes that he belongs in the upper echelons. It is his right, a matter of course. He assumes that if he plays by the rules and applies himself with some diligence, he will prevail and succeed. Part of his attitude may spring from the equipment his family and upbringing provided him with: a superior education, good manners, a sense of taste and style. An insider's knowledge of the upper-middle mix of identification signals. The upper-middler is less rattled by pressure because he doesn't take it that seriously. His high level of security provides a strong well-spring for a nonverbal display that spells out self-confidence, control, and a winner's positive attitude.

One of the dangers of the upper-middle-class belonger is that he may move very closely to the afflictions of affectation, snobbery, and conceit. These traits may be acceptable in the company of other affected, conceited snobs, but they will not help you with a salt-of-the-earth-and-proud-of-it prospect. Never let your character lose sight of his humanity, his humor, his humility (the three *H*s, for convenient recall).

We chose to profile the upper-middle belonger because this character is functional in most territories, can sell to almost anyone, and can sell top-of-the-line and top-dollar items. Also, he is the one most familiar to us.

We have described the character's nonverbal characteristics and attitudes in some detail. The intention is not for you to take on a totally alien role and desert the "you" you already are. You are to find a character that is close to you, then develop and improve it. If you are already an upper-middle belonger, you may need only a few ideas from the above profile to add to a projection you already create. It is probably a safe generalization to say that you will profit from always aiming a bit higher—another rung up the class or status ladder—with the character you build for yourself to play. And ultimately, you will become the super-you that is already inside you.

You walk into the prospect's office and see a copy of this book lying on his desk.

Compliment him on his good taste and settle in for a tough one.

19———————

The Indispensable Link

Salesman. Saleswoman. Salesgirl. The words still invoke a sense of disparagement. Authors still tend to present the salesperson as a cardboard cut-out figure with no dignity or dimension beyond his or her narrow little pigeonhole. Will the salesperson ever outdistance the legacy of traveling salesman jokes? When mothers brag about their children, how likely are they to trumpet "salesperson" with doctor, lawyer, dentist, architect, accountant, engineer? A beginning teacher, a dental hygienist, a landscaper, butcher, baker, candlestick maker, all seem to have more stature than the much-maligned salesperson. People standing near you at a cocktail party overhear that you are a life-insurance salesperson, and they suddenly drift away to the bar. Tax attorneys are asked by their company to offer a new sheltered investment program to their accounts, and they revolt, unwilling to function as "salespeople."

In fact, there are no salesmen and saleswomen anymore. Now we have people "in sales." We have brokers and agents and representatives and middlemen and traders and dealers. And we have the specialists who would blanch and gag with horror if you mentioned them in the same breath with salespeople: the marketing people; advertising folk; spokespersons; demonstrators; public relations and publicity people;

consumer experts; missionaries; ambassadors; consultants; test marketers; premium specialists; and media people.

What is it about the salesperson, the person engaged in helping us decide to possess something, that adds, in the public view, a tinge of the pejorative to the very act of selling? One, it's undignified, and prospects can reject you; and two, caveat emptor.

It's undignified. It's no fun to have to ask someone for something. There is a loss of self-esteem implicit in the very act. There is the horrible possibility that the object of your petition will turn you down, reject you. Then you lose on two counts: you lose stature by asking; and self-esteem by failing to get what you were after. It's an uncomfortable position to be in, no matter how you look at it.

People tend to look down on the salesperson as someone who wasn't clever enough to avoid the need for assuming this uncomfortable position. The salesperson petitions for things; he prospects for likely customers, pursues them, and then runs the risk of rejection and failure. People dread salespeople because people don't want to be players in this uncomfortable scene. They don't want to be sold, and they don't want to have to suffer the discomfort of turning the salesperson down.

The role of salesperson is often viewed as a last resort, something you can do if all else fails. People with very meager skills or little business experience assume they can always sell something; how much training could it take? The assumption seems to be that with dirty work like that, your mere willingness to deign to do it ensures your prompt employment. (It is true that sales is one of the best areas to get on board with a company, but your willingness to stoop had better be mightily exceeded by your enthusiasm, determination, and persistence if you are to prevail.)

Caveat emptor: Let the buyer beware. The original warning is in Latin to remind us that buyers have been tricked, ripped off, cheated, buffaloed, hornswoggled, sold a bill of goods, taken to the cleaners, fleeced, flimflammed, fast-talked, conned, led down the garden path, hyped, and seduced since the original snake hustled the original apple in Eden.

People are taught to be wary of anyone selling them anything. It is practically axiomatic that a salesperson, even an honest one, is not going to bring up a product's hidden faults or shortcomings. One also learns, or intuits, that a clever salesperson *will* mention (and play down) obvious faults with the less than ingenuous goal of seeming to be completely open and ingenuous.

We are taught to gird up our loins and armor ourselves for close-order psychological combat when we detect the approach of the dreaded salesperson. Even salespeople are wary of salespeople. The problem is that no one wants to "be sold" anything. People like to buy, to own, to possess, to acquire, to add to their collection. But nobody likes to think that someone else influenced them or caused them to make the decision. Nobody wants to look or feel as if they were conned or manipulated by a salesperson.

Caveat emptor is unequivocal in its assumption that the salesperson is out to get the innocent buyer at any cost, and ethics be damned. We are taught that to enjoy a play we must exercise the "suspension of disbelief." And that to survive a confrontation with a salesperson we must disbelieve everything and require verification of every claim. The advance notice for the salesperson's performance is "Beware."

With all these strikes against him, the person "in sales," the person selling—whatever he calls himself—goes right on to become the single most important ingredient in the life or death of any business venture. All the resources, research and development, programming, cost control, engineering, management, market surveys, packaging, distribution—everything is for naught without sales.

Selling is the pudding in which the proof is found. Selling is the front-line no-euphemisms, sink-or-swim proving ground for every product, idea, service, platform, or new venture. Is it viable? Does it work? Do people love it or hate it? The only way to find out is to climb into the trenches and try to sell it.

All the company people who think salespeople are working for them are, in fact, working for the salespeople. Everything that precedes the actual sales presentation is support for that presentation. The idea to fill a need, the market research, research and development, design, packaging, advertising, quality control, public relations—all provide ammunition for that humble salesperson when he goes out to meet the enemy face-to-face. The salesperson is the last link in the chain, the last fireman in the bucket brigade—the one closest to the flames—but he is usually relegated to the lowest position on the corporate totem pole. Managements that plunge ahead with this benighted view are often in for an unpleasant shock. Eventually they lose their best salespeople and thus their market share, or they lose their companies.

One small manufacturing company I know hired a salesman. He was European and had some problems with English. The four other salespeople on staff felt sorry for him. But he got up earlier than they did, and quit later. He started picking up accounts. Lots of accounts. One day the head of the firm walked in and gave the little salesman stock totaling a five-percent interest in the company. The salesman was very thankful. This five percent, plus the stock he had been acquiring by proxy, plus his influence with major accounts, enabled him to take over the company.

I know a salesman who worked for a consulting firm that had been formed by three partners. The partners were all experts in their individual specialty, but none wanted to get his hands dirty selling. My friend brought in the business. The company started to prosper. He then brought in two major, and I mean major, accounts. In less than four years, the hired hand—the salesman—took the company from Mickey Mouse to Disney World. The three partners were very happy until the salesman walked in and made his offer. He wanted controlling stock and the presidency of the company; the partners could stay on as senior vice-presidents. Or he would take his accounts and start his own consulting firm. The partners had no choice. They hung around for less than a year, then one by one, they drifted away—and were promptly replaced. There are plenty of experts, you see, but a great salesperson is a precious commodity. Within five years, this particular salesman became embarrassingly wealthy.

It is curious that while "salesman" is considered a pedestrian métier, "salesmanship" is commonly understood to be a necessary talent for success in a multitude of upscale ventures and vocations. What sort of success do we anticipate for a lawyer with no salesmanship, or politicians, entrepreneurs, administrators, managers, or revolutionaries with no salesmanship? Indeed, you will find it hard to discover any human endeavor in which salesmanship will not, in some way, enhance and support that pursuit.

Now, in the age of disillusionment, of credibility gaps and fast-buck irresponsibility, of the erosion of ethics and the loss of faith, the person engaged in the act of selling must search for and find every means available to make himself believable and sincere. Every major company with a sales force, and every individual salesperson, invest time and money in improving sales effectiveness, and the best way to improve effectiveness is to improve credibility. And there's the rub: Nothing you *say* makes your words seem true. It's what you *don't* say. It's the nonverbal dimension that builds credibility.

Customer-orientation selling, "needs" selling, features-and-benefits, probe-support-benefit, cushion-bypass-choice, behavior modification. The thrust of these techniques is directed at organizing and improving the verbal element. But now we understand that more than half—maybe more than seventy-five percent—of the communication between salesperson and prospect is nonverbal!

Read the Kennedy-Nixon debates. Neither man blew the other out of the water with brilliant rhetoric. Now watch a TV kinescope of the same debate, and you will *see* how Kennedy, with consistently superior body language, blew Nixon out of the water. The Carter-Reagan debate offers the same example. Reagan's oratory is far from inspiring, but he somehow comes off better, more believable and confident, than Carter. On paper neither man has a clear advantage.

As an ex-actor, a professional involved in image management, Ronald Reagan knows what to do and not to do in a personal appearance. His pacing, eye contact, bearing, and controlled and confident gestures and expressions are reassuring and believable. His expression admits the sudden bursts of personal intimacy or humor that build charisma. It is less important, somehow, that he may not have a complete grasp of the details on a particular issue—you get the impression that he knows enough to understand the crux of the problem, that he has read between the lines, and that if he feels he doesn't have enough input, he'll make it a point to get more. In a word, Ronald Reagan knows how to sell himself. You may not agree with his ideas, but you appreciate his sincerity.

Salesmanship is the indispensable, extra dimension that can take you anywhere you want to go. We have seen it grow from a knack to a talent to an art, and now to a science. Effective salesmanship can make all the difference in the world to a company or an entire economy. And effective body language can make all the difference in the world in making the sale.

- Develop your supersalesperson character.
- Find and use the key that keeps your courage, confidence, and enthusiasm up.
- Buy before you sell.
- Learn the moves and make them your own.
- Practice, role-play, do the exercises.
- Slow down.
- Relax.
- Never retreat or give up.
- Listen.
- Watch.
- Be persistent. Be persistent. Be persistent.

You are the principal player in making things move.

You are the indispensable link.

You've got all the words; now team them up with your winning moves . . . and nothing can stop you!

READING THE PROSPECT

POSITIVE SIGNALS

Any one of the following can signal "yes" or "maybe":

- Straightening up his desk when you enter.
- Firm, warm handshake not terminated abruptly.
- Sits up, and sometimes forward, in his seat with interest, not belligerence. Leans slightly toward you.
- Arms uncrossed, "open," sometimes on desk.
- Relaxed hands, more "open," less fistlike, not flat on desk.
- Face and mouth open, not obstructed by hands. His body and face generally centered and keyed on you when you are speaking.
- Sits relatively still, swivels only to face or follow you.
- Relaxed facial muscles (especially the jaw); mouth may even be open slightly during listening.
- Legs crossed, casually open, or scissored apart at the knee.
- Legs crossed, ankle rests on opposite knee, the nearest hand rests on raised ankle.
- Any casual personal action, like tying a shoe, loosening a belt, or preening.
- Eyes open and relaxed, clear, and maintaining reciprocal contact. (However, in a male/female situation, beware of flirting.)

- Pupils large. If they start to narrow and not in response to bright light, you're turning him off.
- "Mirrors" positions and your expressions, gradually, as you win him over.
- Breathes normally.
- Smiles or laughs at something funny.
- Even, relaxed movements.
- Pats his hair or grooms in some way.
- Strokes his chin (a fairly common "maybe").
- Makes single or double, positive head-nods (more than three is effected nod-service).
- Moves reluctantly if he has to take a call.
- Takes off or unbuttons his jacket. Loosens his collar or tie.
- Takes off his glasses or looks over them to see you.
- Invites you away from his desk into an informal area. (Careful: The prospect might be trying to defuse the encounter by turning it into a social thing. Stick to business; you can be sociable later.)
- Touches you, i.e., a light touch, prod, or a slap on the back, arm, or shoulder. A hand guiding you or a nudge with an elbow. (Women, beware: You almost never touch a man. Be extremely wary of male prospects touching you. Touching can be his effort to disarm you and win your affection so you won't react so badly to his ultimately *not* buying. The worst touch is the patronizing one that is likely to be bestowed upon petite young saleswomen by older male prospects.)
- Assumes a more casual position.
- Moves something between you and him on the desk out of the way.
- Leans toward you promptly to receive things (papers, pens, samples).
- Shows you pictures or awards or anything from his personal life.
- Puts his feet up in something, although not in your face.
- Moistens his lips.
- Looks skyward when trying to remember something.
- Gets up and paces while thinking. (He's on the fence—push him over to your side.)

NEGATIVE SIGNALS

Any one or combination of the following can signal "no":

- Sits dead center, close behind his desk.
- Leans way back, clasps his hands, or crosses his arms.
- Sits belligerently upright or forward with palms down on the desk or his hands folded directly in front of him, a defensive bulwark.
- Sits squarely, feet flat, leans forward somewhat, shoulders slightly shrugged, and places both palms on his thighs; elbows are out and thumbs point at one another.
- Swivels away from you in his chair.
- Signals termination of a short, perfunctory handshake.
- Avoids eye contact.
- Closes his eyes in long, frequent blinks as you talk.
- Points his pen or fingers at you.
- Holds his fingers up to enumerate points of his responses, palms toward you.
- Uses his hands as masks and shields to hide his mouth and face.
- Hands closed, almost in fists.
- Forearms held up, a shield or obstacle between you.
- Feet flat on the floor, legs together, not crossed.
- Forehead furrows, eyebrows knit.
- Eyelids narrow, pupils pinpointed.
- Lips and mouth tight, set, and dry.
- Puts on his jacket. Tightens his tie. Buttons his jacket.
- Plays with or arranges things and papers on the desk or fidgets while you talk.
- Does a series of more than three head nods. (Such a series is usually forced. Call it "nod service.")
- Doesn't return your smile. Keeps a serious look at all times.
- Puts on his glasses for no reason.
- Supports his head with his hands.
- Uses his hair to hide his eyes. Women with longer hair tend to use this a lot; they can block most of their face with a wall of hair.
- Bites down hard, displaying taut jaw muscles.

- Keeps plucking imaginary lint off his clothes.
- Puts his hands behind his head, like a pillow.
- Quick, jerky moves.
- Bites his lips.
- Opens and closes desk drawers, as if looking for something.
- Lets you catch him looking at his watch or clock.
- Head or body tilted to the side, or way back.
- Hands scratching or touching parts of head or face.
- Keeps getting up.
- His tongue in his cheek.
- Deep, labored breathing.
- Turns his body generally to the side or away from you when you talk, straight at you when he's on the attack.
- Smiles when you haven't said anything funny. Beware of the prospect that smiles right from the beginning of the call; he's using it as a mask.
- Moves quickly to take all his calls.
- Obvious universals, such as negative head shakes or yawns, intentional or unintentional.
- Doesn't lean forward when you hand or show him something. Takes things slowly and reluctantly.
- Pushes up the middle of his forehead with his fingers (boredom, irritation).
- Puts his fingers to the side of his nose (doubt).
- Rubs his nose a lot (but doesn't have a cold).
- Lifts his hand or index finger a bit while listening. (He will disagree with that point.)
- Puts his finger to the space between his lip and nose. (If he's talking, he just exaggerated or lied; if he's listening, he is displeased.)
- Hunches, chin to chest. (You are invading personal space.)
- Drums his fingers, rocks in his chair, hunches, "blocks" with his shoulder, moves or turns away, and blinks overmuch or overlong. (A typical you-are-invading-personal-territory display.)

Additionally, if you're a member of the opposite sex:

- Stares too long into your eyes (flirts).
- Touches you unnecessarily.
- Gazes at parts of your body.
- Mirrors your posture and gestures immediately (synchronizes).

All these apparently positive signals are not, unfortunately, responses to your products or services, or even your salesmanship, and represent, in fact, an obstacle you must overcome.

SUGGESTED READING

Archer, Dane. *How to Expand Your S.I.Q.* (Social Intelligence Quotient). New York: M. Evans, 1980.

Beier, Ernst. *How We Control Others, How They Control Us.* New York: Stein & Day, 1975.

Birdwhistell, Ray L. *Kinesics and Content.* Philadelphia: University of Pennsylvania Press, 1970.

Cohen, Robert. *Acting Power.* Palo Alto: Mayfield Publishing Company, 1978.

Culligan, Matthew J. *Getting Back to the Basics of Selling.* New York: Crown, 1981.

Dunton, Loren. *How to Sell Women.* New York: McGraw Hill, 1965.

Fast, Julius. *Body Language.* New York: M. Evans, 1970.

————. *The Body Language of Sex, Power and Aggression.* New York: M. Evans, 1977.

Girard, Joe. *How to Sell Anything to Anybody.* New York: Simon & Schuster, 1977.

Goffman, Erving. *Strategic Interaction.* Philadelphia: University of Pennsylvania Press, 1980.

Hemingway, Patricia Drake. *The Well-Dressed Woman.* New York: David McKay Company, Inc., 1977.

Henning, Margaret and Jardim, Anne. *The Managerial Woman.* Garden City: Anchor Press, 1977.

Hopkins, Tom. *How to Master the Art of Selling*. New York: Warner Books, 1982.

Katz, Judith Milstein. *Why Don't You Listen to What I'm Not Saying*. New York: Anchor Press, 1981.

Kleinke, Chris L. *First Impressions, The Psychology of Encountering Others*. Englewood Cliffs: Prentice-Hall, 1975.

Korda, Michael. *Power! How to Get It, How to Use It*. New York: Random House, 1975.

————. *Success*. New York: Ballantine Books, 1978.

Lamb, Warren and Watson, Elizabeth. *Body Code*. London and Boston: Routledge & Kegan Paul, 1970.

Lee, Linda and Charleton, James. *The Hand Book, Interpreting Handshakes, Gestures, Power Signals and Sexual Signs*. Englewood Cliffs: Prentice-Hall, 1980.

McCaffrey, Mike, with Derloshon, Jerry. *Personal Marketing Strategies*. Englewood Cliffs: Prentice-Hall, 1983.

Molloy, John T. *The Woman's Dress for Success Book*. Chicago: Follet Publishing Company, 1977.

————. *Live for Success*. New York: William Morrow and Company, Inc., 1981.

Polhemus, Ted. *The Body Reader*. New York: Pantheon Books, 1978.

Preston, Paul and Nelson, Ralph. *Salesmanship, A Contemporary Approach*. Peston, VA: Peston Publishing Company, 1981.

Roth, Chas. B. and Alexander, Roy. *Secrets of Closing Sales*. Englewood Cliffs: Prentice-Hall, 1983.

Scheflen, Albert, with Scheflen, Alice. *Body Language and Social Order*. Englewood Cliffs: Prentice-Hall, 1972.

Schoen, Linda Allen. *The AMA Book of Skin and Hair Care*. New York and Philadelphia: J. B. Lippincott Company, 1976.

Shook, Robert L. *Ten Greatest Salespersons: What They Say About Selling*. New York: Harper & Row, 1978.

Stanislavski, Constantin. *An Actor Prepares*. New York: Theater Arts Books, 1981.

Williams, Marcille Gray. *The New Executive Woman*. Radnor, Pennsylvania: Chilton Book Company, 1977.

INDEX

A

Acting techniques, 2
  belief in self and, 14–15
  courage key and, 15–19
  creating a character, 25–27
  role playing by saleswomen, 116–117
Age, distance and territory and, 52–54
Age gaps between salesperson and prospect, 151–161
  Geezer Gap, 154–161
  Whippersnapper Gap, 151–154
Alcoholic beverages:
  and bad breath, 143
  ordering during restaurant sale, 228
  at sales conventions, 230
Allergies, 141–142
Anger, of prospect, 73
Anxiety, voice and, 107
Anxiety attacks, 68
Apology, alternatives to, 76

Attack by prospect, responses to, 76–79
Audience reaction, 214–215
  in conference-room selling, 220–221
  public speaking and, 203–205, 207
Audiovisual aids, 193–201
  care of, 200
  equipment for, 195–197
  exercise to prepare for working with, 201
  interruptions during presentation using, 198–199
  prescreening preparations, 195–198
  at trade shows or fairs, 235
  types of, 194
Aura:
  during presentation, 74–75
  emotional response and, 167–168
  home showing and, 175–177
Automobile sales, 235

ABOUT THE AUTHOR

KEN DELMAR, producer/director/writer, has been the head of his own film production company—and its sales director—since 1969. He grew up in New York and Los Angeles, attended Trinity School (NY), Middlebury College (BA '63), and Columbia University. He is a member of the Dramatists Guild, the Authors Guild, the Screen Actors Guild, the American Federation of TV and Radio Artists, and the Stamford Yacht Club. He is an avid wind-surfer, a runner, and a student of aikido.

In 1968, after two years in the armed forces, Ken Delmar returned to "the world" with a pregnant wife and one hundred and thirty-seven dollars. He used the money to start Delmar Productions in a leaky barn he shared with a family of possums and several swallows. Within five years, using many of the techniques you will find in *Winning Moves*, he had offices in the Time & Life Building in Rockefeller Center, a home of his own (with a beach a hundred yards away), a new Mercedes, a twenty-eight-foot sloop, and an income of six figures. He closed the New York company to write *Winning Moves*, and now lives with his wife and daughter in Stamford, Connecticut, where he is producing video films and programs on nonverbal selling.

Mr. Delmar's company, Salesignals, Inc., offers a complete sales training program based on the Winning Moves techniques, with video programs available in every format, as well as audio cassettes.

Salesignals, Inc., offers seminars, for which Mr. Delmar may be personally available. In addition, there are Winning Moves workshops, in which scenes typical in sales presentations are developed and polished, and Winning Moves workbooks that allow the salesperson to measure and reinforce progress.

For more information, call or write:

Salesignals, Inc.

42 Gurley Road

Stamford, CT 06902

Telephone: (203) 357-7075

Help Yourself and Your Career

___**HOW TO MAKE A HABIT OF SUCCESS**
by Bernard Haldane   *(K30-501, $3.50)*

The Haldane system is one of the most important success and self-improvement books recently published. Its self-identification process and Success Factor Analysis techniques have become integral to career planning programs in leading institutions such as Harvard and Columbia Universities and The Peace Corps. Change your career by using your personal interests and talents in a new way.

___**POSITIONING: THE BATTLE FOR YOUR MIND**
by Al Ries and Jack Trout   *(K30-800, $3.95)*

"Positioning" is the first body of thought to come to grips with the problems of communicating in an overcommunicated (too many companies, too many products, too many media, too much marketing noise) society.

   You will learn in detail some unique concepts that can help you master the media: climbing the product ladder; *cherchez le creneau* (look for the hole); repositioning the competition; avoiding the no-name trap; and avoiding the line-extension trap.

___**GETTING ORGANIZED**   *large format paperback*
by Stephanie Winston   *(J38-344, $8.95, U.S.A.)*
                                                (J38-345, $11.95, Canada)

Guidelines to organization covering everything from financial to meal planning, maximization of storage space, living space and reduction of time required to complete everyday tasks.

___**DRESS FOR SUCCESS**   *large format paperback*
by John T. Molloy   *(K38-263, $7.95, U.S.A.)*
                                                (K38-264, $8.95, Canada)

The number-one book to make you look like a million so you can *make* a million will: make it easier for many men to sell everything better: open doors to the executive suite to men for whom they are now closed; make the right wardrobe less expensive; give women a simple, sensible guide to buying men's clothing; and teach men how women like them to dress.

WARNER BOOKS
P.O. Box 690
New York, N.Y. 10019

Please send me the books I have checked. I enclose a check or money order (not cash), plus 50¢ per order and 50¢ per copy to cover postage and handling.*
(Allow 4 weeks for delivery.)

_____ Please send me your free mail order catalog. (If ordering only the
          catalog, include a large self-addressed, stamped envelope.)

Name _____

Address _____

City _____

State _____ Zip _____

*N.Y. State and California residents add applicable sales tax.   72

Make the Most of Yourself

___**HOW TO SELL ANYTHING TO ANYBODY**
by Joe Girard with   (K32-516, $3.95, U.S.A.)
Stanley H. Brown   (K32-517, $4.95, Canada)
Also available in large-format paperback
                                  (K38-232, $6.95, U.S.A.)
                                  (K38-233, $7.95, Canada)

Joe Girard has shown millions of men and women involved or
interested in selling exactly how they can adapt the same selling
techniques that lifted Girard to the top of his profession. He tells
you: how to develop a personal and very effective direct-mail
program; how to size up the customer's wants, needs and what he
can afford; how to get the customer to trust you and to recommend
other customers; how honesty can turn a "no" into a "yes"; how to
turn customer complaints into orders; and how to make a lifelong
customer from the very first sale.

___**HOW TO SELL YOURSELF**
by Joe Girard   (K38-367, $9.95, U.S.A.)
A large-format quality paperback   (K38-368, $13.50, Canada)
Includes: building self-confidence and courage; developing positive attitudes; learning to listen; managing your memory; exercis-
ing enthusiasm; selling yourself without selling out; the power of a
promise; the sensation of a smile; and the payoff of persistence.
With an introduction by Dr. Norman Vincent Peale, HOW TO SELL
YOURSELF is the tool to a better, happier, more successful life for
every reader.

WARNER BOOKS
P.O. Box 690
New York, N.Y. 10019

Please send me the books I have checked. I enclose a check or money order
(not cash), plus 50¢ per order and 50¢ per copy to cover postage and handling.*
(Allow 4 weeks for delivery.)

_____ Please send me your free mail order catalog. (If ordering only the
               catalog, include a large self-addressed, stamped envelope.)

Name _____

Address _____

City _____

State _____ Zip _____

*N.Y. State and California residents add applicable sales tax.   71

IMPORTANT BUSINESS FROM WARNER BOOKS

____**THE ART OF JAPANESE MANAGEMENT**
Applications for American Executives (K32-322, $4.95, U.S.A.)
by Richard Pascale and Anthony Athos (K32-323, $5.95, Canada)

After World War Two, Japan borrowed and then adapted US business methods. Today, in industry after industry, from radios to automobiles to microprocessing, the Japanese have become, or are rapidly becoming, more productive than Americans.

Japan is doing something right. The authors of this provocative book assert that the biggest part of that "something" is managerial, and they explore the tools available to our managers for closing the gap between Japan and America.

____**OFFICE POLITICS**
Seizing Power, Wielding Clout (K34-054, $4.50, U.S.A.)
by Marilyn Moats Kennedy (K34-055, $5.95, Canada)

Marilyn Moats Kennedy is the founder and director of Career Strategies, a unique workshop-style consulting firm teaching successful career planning and offering a mastery course in effective office politics. In this book she shows you how to get to the top—and how to use preventive politics to stay there, how to recruit mentors and your friends upstairs, and how to use them. Above all, you'll learn how to define your career goals, set them, and achieve them.

____**WORKING SMART**
How to Accomplish More In Half the Time (K32-999, $3.95, U.S.A.)
by Michael LeBoeuf (K34-012, $4.95, Canada)

In his lively, humorous style, Michael LeBoeuf will teach you how to set specific goals on a daily, intermediate, and lifetime basis and how to analyze and revise your present use of time accordingly.

____**INC. YOURSELF**
**How to Profit by Setting
Up Your Own Corporation**
by Judith H. McQuown (K38-127, $7.95)
Available in large-size quality paperback

In easy-to-understand terms, Judith H. McQuown, an expert in the field of money management, explains the dollars-and-cents advantages of incorporating yourself: getting "free" life and disability insurance; setting up your own tax-sheltered pension and profit-sharing plans; obtaining greater benefits than you get through the Keogh plan; generating legitimate "cashless" tax deductions; and incorporating without a lawyer.

WARNER BOOKS
P.O. Box 690
New York, N.Y. 10019

Please send me the books I have checked. I enclose a check or money order (not cash), plus 50¢ per order and 50¢ per copy to cover postage and handling.* (Allow 4 weeks for delivery.)

_____ Please send me your free mail order catalog. (If ordering only the catalog, include a large self-addressed, stamped envelope.)

Name _____

Address _____

City _____

State _____ Zip _____

*N.Y. State and California residents add applicable sales tax.   74

The Best of the Business from Warner Books

__IN SEARCH OF EXCELLENCE

Thomas J. Peters and   (K38-281, $9.95, U.S.A.)
Robert H. Waterman, Jr.   (K38-282, $11.95, Canada)

Highly acclaimed and highly optimistic about the future of American management, this essential book proves that American business is alive and well—and successful! Subtitled "Lessons from America's Best-Run Companies," it reveals the secrets of the art of successful American management, the eight fascinating basic principles that the authors found hard at work at Johnson & Johnson, Procter & Gamble, IBM, Hewlett-Packard, Delta Airlines, McDonald's, and other well-run firms. Here are the native American policies and attitudes that lead to growth and profits—policies and attitudes that thousands of business people all over the country are now trying for themselves!

__MEGATRENDS
Ten New Directions Transforming Our Lives
John Naisbitt   (I32-922, $4.95, U.S.A.)
                         (I32-923, $6.50, Canada)
Hardcover: (I51-251, $17.50 in U.S.A., $22.95 in Canada)

Once in a great while a book so accurately captures the essence of its time that it becomes the spokesman for that decade. In 1956 it was *The Organization Man.* In 1970 it was *Future Shock.* In the 1980's it will be *Megatrends,* the only "future" book whose predictions for tomorrow are based on a dynamic analysis of what America is today. As Naisbitt details America's shift from industrial production to providing services and information, you can project your career and business moves. As you learn where the new centers of activity are developing, you can decide where you should live. If you have political goals, John Naisbitt's analysis of governmental trends can help you target your energies. This is the challenge, the means, and the method to better our lives . . . a must for everyone who cares about the future.

WARNER BOOKS
P.O. Box 690
New York, N.Y. 10019

Please send me the books I have checked. I enclose a check or money order (not cash), plus 50¢ per order and 50¢ per copy to cover postage and handling.* (Allow 4 weeks for delivery.)

_____ Please send me your free mail order catalog. (If ordering only the catalog, include a large self-addressed, stamped envelope.)

Name _____

Address _____

City _____

State _____ Zip _____

*N.Y. State and California residents add applicable sales tax.   46

MORE BOOKS FOR YOUR MONEY

___**STOCK MARKET PRIMER**
by Claude N. Rosenberg, Jr. (K32-620, $4.95)
Lucidly written, Mr. Rosenberg shares with you the fundamental facts about investing: buying stocks and bonds, how the stock market works, spotting bull and bear markets, how to tell which industries have the greatest growth potential. Mr. Rosenberg takes the mystery out of the stock market and puts valuable, profit-making ideas at your disposal.

___**WHERE TO PUT YOUR MONEY 1985** (K38-201, $3.95, U.S.A.)
by Peter Passell (K38-202, $4.75, Canada)
Available in large-size quality paperback
Not long ago, the small investor had few choices—and he didn't make much money on his savings. He could open a passbook account at the bank, buy a government savings bond, or perhaps, get life insurance. Now the savings rules have changed, increasing both the opportunities and the risks. If you have time to read half a dozen newspapers and investment magazines every week you can sort out your optimum choices, but here's a simple, clear guide that will help you to zero in on what's best for you. Written by a former professor of economics at Columbia University, who is also a *New York Times* expert journalist and author of THE BEST, it is soundly based, comprehensive information.

___**PENNY STOCKS**
by Bruce G. Williams (K38-010, $7.95)
Available in large-size quality paperback
Penny Stocks are priced at less than five dollars (and many between ten cents and a dollar) and often make gains of between 300 and 1,000 percent in two years or less. With careful management and a little bit of luck, you can use them to build your financial future. PENNY STOCKS explains how it all works—and how you can be penny wise and pound rich!

___**HOW TO MAKE MONEY WITH YOUR HOME COMPUTER**
by Clement C. Richard (X32-567, $3.95, U.S.A.)
(X32-566, $4.95, Canada)
Let computer consultant Clement C. Richard show you how to make your home computer work for you! Whether you want to design and sell your own software or begin your own data processing service, this book is a treasure trove of ideas for money-making services and how to market them. On your own terms, you can save money, earn extra money, create a new career and generate new jobs—part-time, full-time, anytime!

WARNER BOOKS
P.O. Box 690
New York, N.Y. 10019

Please send me the books I have checked. I enclose a check or money order (not cash), plus 50¢ per order and 50¢ per copy to cover postage and handling.*
(Allow 4 weeks for delivery.)

_____ Please send me your free mail order catalog. (If ordering only the catalog, include a large self-addressed, stamped envelope.)

Name _____

Address _____

City _____

State _____ Zip _____

*N.Y. State and California residents add applicable sales tax. 96

By the year 2000, 2 out of 3 Americans could be illiterate.

It's true.

Today, 75 million adults… about one American in three, can't read adequately. And by the year 2000, U.S. News & World Report envisions an America with a literacy rate of only 30%.

Before that America comes to be, you can stop it… by joining the fight against illiteracy today.

Call the Coalition for Literacy at toll-free **1-800-228-8813** and volunteer.

Volunteer Against Illiteracy. The only degree you need is a degree of caring.

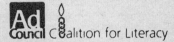

Ad Council Coalition for Literacy

Warner Books is proud to be an active supporter of the Coalition for Literacy.